Intergenerational Conflict and Authentic Youth Experience

This book explores how the youth experience, viscerally felt and deeply ingrained at a time of substantial physical, psychological and emotional changes, serves to authenticate that youth experience to the exclusion of that of ensuing youth generations.

Using Cohen's concept of moral panic to frame the intergenerational conflict, notions of generational exclusivity and authenticity are explored through Bourdieu's concept of habitus – how each generation privileges its own youth experience as the 'standard' by which other youth generations can be judged. Shared authenticated 'generational understandings' act as the benchmark by which ensuing youth generations can be assessed and found wanting. Intergenerational conflict has been brought into sharp focus by the emergence of the Millennial generation, digital natives, with their obsession with digital technology and particularly mobile phones.

The book will be of interest for the field of youth studies in general, particularly upper-level undergraduate youth studies courses and postgrads and social scientists. In addition, it will be of interest for scholars interested in the work of Pierre Bourdieu and Stanley Cohen and subject areas: intergenerational conflict, social change, popular culture, music, media and cultural studies, and social theory.

Barney Langford is a retired teacher and youth arts practitioner. He is the founding Artistic Director of 2 Til 5 Youth Theatre (now Tantrum Youth Arts), one of Australia's leading professional youth arts companies. He was for 15 years the Manager of the Loft Youth Arts and Cultural Centre. He lectured part time at University of Newcastle 1990–2003. He was awarded his doctorate in 2020 and his doctoral dissertation is the basis for this monograph. Barney's interests include youth arts, youth studies and psephology.

Youth, Young Adulthood and Society

The Youth, Young Adulthood and Society series approaches youth as a distinct area, bringing together social scientists from many disciplines to present cutting-edge research monographs and collections on young people in societies around the world today. The books present original, exciting research, with strongly theoretically and empirically grounded analysis, advancing the field of youth studies. Originally set up and edited by Andy Furlong, the series presents interdisciplinary and truly international, comparative research monographs.

Series Editors: **Tracy Shildrick**, *Newcastle University, UK*, **John Goodwin**, *University of Leicester, UK*, and **Henrietta O'Connor**, *University of Leicester, UK*

Digital Youth Subcultures
Performing 'Transgressive' Identities in Digital Social Spaces
Edited by Kate Hoskins, Carlo Genova and Nic Crowe

Neurodivergent Youthhoods
Adolescent Rites of Passage, Disability and the Teenage Epilepsy Clinic
Shelda-Jane Smith

Central American Young People Migration
Coloniality and Epistemologies of the South
Henry Parada, Veronica Escobar Olivo and Kevin Cruz

Intergenerational Conflict and Authentic Youth Experience
Adults Denigrating Young People
Barney Langford

For more information about this series, please visit www.routledge.com/Youth-Young-Adulthood-and-Society/book-series/YYAS

Intergenerational Conflict and Authentic Youth Experience
Adults Denigrating Young People

Barney Langford

LONDON AND NEW YORK

Designed Cover Image: © Getty Images

First published 2024
by Routledge
4 Park Square, Milton Park, Abingdon, Oxon OX14 4RN

and by Routledge
605 Third Avenue, New York, NY 10158

Routledge is an imprint of the Taylor & Francis Group, an informa business

© 2024 Barney Langford

The right of Barney Langford to be identified as author of this work has been
asserted in accordance with sections 77 and 78 of the Copyright, Designs and
Patents Act 1988.

All rights reserved. No part of this book may be reprinted or reproduced or utilised
in any form or by any electronic, mechanical, or other means, now known or
hereafter invented, including photocopying and recording, or in any information
storage or retrieval system, without permission in writing from the publishers.

Trademark notice: Product or corporate names may be trademarks or registered trademarks,
and are used only for identification and explanation without intent to infringe.

British Library Cataloguing-in-Publication Data
A catalogue record for this book is available from the British Library

ISBN: 978-1-032-54778-7 (hbk)
ISBN: 978-1-032-54779-4 (pbk)
ISBN: 978-1-003-42747-6 (ebk)

DOI: 10.4324/9781003427476

Typeset in Sabon
by Newgen Publishing UK

For all the thousands of young people for whom my engagement with their lives contributed in some small way to their 'becoming'.

Contents

List of Illustrations	*ix*
Preface	*xi*
List of Abbreviations	*xiii*

1 Introduction — 1
Habitus 4
Innocents Abroad 5
Moral Panics 6
Symbolic Violence 7

2 The Alchemy of Consecration — 17
Social World, Field and Doxa 18
Symbolic Capital, Misrecognition 21
Taste and Neo-Tribes 24
Generational Folk Devils and Moral Entrepreneurs 27
The Don Quixote Effect 30

3 Growing Up — 36
In-Betweenness, Adulthood and Grounded Aesthetics 36
Generations and Zeitgeist 38
Authenticity, Status and Memory 39
Walled Garden and Learning the Code 40
The Adult Voice 41
Introjection 45

4 Adulthood – The Final Destination — 51
Social Space 51
Lack of Respect 54
Self-Affirming Attributes of Authenticity 57
Helicoptering 60
Social and Temporal Distance 61
Stereotyping 68
My Dad Judges People – Living with Being Stereotyped 71

viii *Contents*

5 Memory, Certainty, Significance   78
Social In-Groups and Ownership 80
The Process of Embodiment and Investment 82
Expectations and Certainty at Risk 83
The Media: Agents of Moral Indignation 85
Identity: A Self-Reflexive Universe of References 90

6 Appropriate or Inappropriate? The Aesthetic Solera and
Habitus   98
The Psychologising of Miley Cyrus 100
A Sense of Entitlement 105
The Aesthetic Solera: Identity, Predisposition, Tendency,
  Propensity and Inclination 110
The Figure of the Profligate Millennial 113
Taste and Discernment: Hopes, Dreams and Adult
  Disappointment 116
Engagement with Cultural Products 118

7 Music – The Past in the Present   125
Nostalgia's Not What It Used to Be 128
You Can't Stop the Music 130
The Process of Latching – I Know What I Like 132
Embodied Awareness 134
Traditional versus Modern Music 136
Curation of the Soundtrack of Your Life 140
Authenticity Trolling 142

8 Feeding the Moral Panic – The Millennial Shorthand
Portrait   150
Generational Dislocation of the Social Structure – It's Got to
  Hurt Inside 152
Threatening the Future – Dealing with the Millennial Shorthand
  Portrait *154*
Sensationalism Attracts Attention 156
Moral Entrepreneurs of the Millennial Moral Panic 157
The Generations Defined Sociologically 163
Cabalism in Media Representations 163
Consensus and Hostility 166

9 Conclusion   175

Index   183

Illustrations

Figure

8.1 List of McCrindle clients   160

Table

8.1 Generations Sociologically Defined by Mark McCrindle
     (McCrindle Research)   161

Preface

Barney Langford

When he was 15 years old, my son, in one of his many assessments of his father's numerous foibles, remarked to me: 'You know what your problem is Dad? When it comes to music, you don't live in the now'.

Fourteen years later...

Just prior to the 2013 federal election, the ABC (Australian National Broadcaster) interviewed a researcher from the Australia Institute who talked in detail about research revealing a general lack of interest in politics by young people. The thrust of the interview was that young people were failing to be engaged by politics, and importantly, that this failure to engage posed a serious threat to our democracy. In short, if young people were not engaging with politics at this early age, then this did not bode well for the future of democracy in our country. After a lifetime of working with young people, and after a lifetime engagement with politics, I found this derision and under-estimation of young people to be a tipping point in my frustration at the way young people are perceived in society. Before I knew it, I was screaming at the radio: 'What about all the adults who are disengaged from politics? Where is the hysteria about that?'. Within weeks I had enrolled in the doc-toral research which has become the basis for this publication.

These anecdotes serve to exemplify many of the elements essential to the way young people are perceived within society, and the way that young people perceive adults. My son's succinct description of his father's musical tastes being fossilised in amber perfectly encapsulated the ossification of his father's musical soundtrack within the temporal confines of his youth and early adulthood. Similarly, that ten minutes of radio distilled all of the elements necessary for a moral panic about young people. Here were adults denigrating young people for lack of commitment, for failing to engage, and importantly, these failures were proposed to threaten the future of the nation unless young people could demonstrate that they too could accept their responsibilities as upright citizens.

I should declare from the outset that my status as a baby boomer puts me at more than arms-length from Millennials and Gen Z. Nevertheless, my lifetime's work has been with and for young people – as teacher, as youth

xii *Preface*

arts worker and youth arts administrator. My research for my doctorate was a culmination of that engagement. In my interactions with adults of my age while undertaking this research, there was a consistency of response from them to young people when the discussion turned to comparisons with ourselves and young people. This response was uniformly negative. Although these remarks were offhand and mostly said in half-jest, they nevertheless betrayed what appeared to me to be deeply held understandings that young people did not, could not measure up to the standard that 'we' set. They were, in Bourdieu's terms, *misrecognising* those young people. This failure to measure up was particularly applied to the music and other cultural forms of young people compared with 'ours'.

My doctoral research set out to determine if my suspicions would stand up to the academic rigour of postgraduate research. It began with a series of interviews and focus groups with a broad range of demographic participants aged from 16 years to 65+. This became the data which was the foundation for the research. For the duration of my doctoral research, I would be asked by friends and colleagues about my doctorate. I developed a self-mocking shorthand description. My thesis was about the moral panic that adults' generation display towards every ensuing youth generation. Further they're not as committed as we were; they're not as engaged as we were; and above all their music isn't as good as ours. To this description, there was almost uniform agreement. My self-mocking tone obviously failed to communicate the irony of my statement.

This research project has been a voyage of discovery for me. Sociology has opened a door to a new way of viewing the world. I could not have traversed this journey without the support, encouragement and advice of my two supervisors: Pam Nilan and Steve Threadgold who oversaw my doctorate. My eternal thanks go to you both for turning me into a sociologist.

To my wife Liz who has shared this journey, shared my frustrations, shared my disappointments, my elations, I thank you for your patience and your refusal to give me a hard time when I failed to do some job around the house or was distracted by something I was working on ('occupying the thesis bubble' as you put it). Thank you for being, as always, the objective ear and eye that pricks my pretensions and brings me back to reality, including editing out self-indulgences and longueurs.

To my son Michael, my daughter Jess and their partners Rosemary and Dave, thank you for supporting me. Michael your anecdote above reflects your and Jess's irreverence towards your father when growing up which has ensured that he has never taken himself too seriously as an adult. To Mirabel, Penny and Jack, our beautiful grandkids: whenever the mountain seemed too high, or the road too long, your existence and your laughter salved my bruised ego and reminded me of what's really important in life.

Finally, to the informants in interviews and focus groups: thank you for your candour and being so open with me. And in particular to 'Fred' who contributed so much to this research and who is no longer around to see this publication.

Abbreviations

FOMO   Fear of Missing Out
Gen Y   Generation Y

1 Introduction

The Youth of a Nation are the trustees of posterity.

(Benjamin Disraeli)[1]

Intergenerational conflict is an observable phenomenon. All of us have been young people. All of us have experienced parental/adult dissatisfaction/disapproval/anger. All of us as young people, fuelled by our own anger and frustration in response to that anger, have felt and expressed our resentment towards adults, have raged at the injustice and/or stormed off to our bedrooms. All of us have transitioned to adulthood. All of us, having made that transition, have experienced dissatisfaction/disapproval/anger with our children or with other young people. All of us as adults have given voice to that disapproval and anger. Those of us who are parents have 'arced up' over our children's response to our (what we believe to be) reasonable requests to them with regard to their attitudes and behaviour. Most of all, none of us (initially) set out as young people to irritate and enrage our parents and not live up to their expectations. As parents none of us set out to be inconsistent, arbitrary or unreasonable in our parenting of young people. Yet despite the best efforts of young people and parents, young people do irritate and enrage parents and fail to live up to adult expectations; adults are invariably inconsistent, arbitrary and unreasonable (and even if they are not, they are perceived to be so). Intergenerational conflict it would appear is an almost inevitable outcome of the process of young people growing up and metamorphosing into adults, and for many adults Disraeli's optimism about the future trustees of posterity may very well be described as 'heroic'.

Intergenerational conflict between young people and adults has been both an historical reality (see Horace and Gwynn, 1900; Hall, 1911; Cox and Shore, 2002) and a contemporary observable phenomenon as exemplified by the status of Millennials as possibly the most derided generation in history. This conflict occurs as young people enter into, and negotiate their journey from the relative certainties of childhood, dominated by the command and

DOI: 10.4324/9781003427476-1

2 Introduction

control guidance of their parents, to the autonomy of adulthood. In between is their teenagehood, their youth, characterised by uncertainty and unpredictability, by discoveries and learning, by exhilarations at new experiences and tasting of 'forbidden fruit'. It is a time of exploration, of testing limits, of challenging accepted understandings as their mind, body and emotional centre transform from child to adult. The onset of puberty transforms the architecture of their bodies into that of a young adult but their knowledge, skills and understandings remain rooted in childhood as their emotional and intellectual development struggles to keep pace with their physical development. The onset of puberty parallels Piaget's formal operations stage of development. This sees them develop the capacity to think in the abstract and to enter into the process of developing more concrete understandings of their identity as they contemplate their existence and their place in the world. And they develop the capacity to think about thinking, to undertake the task of self-reflection – of being able to see who they are, and where and how they fit in to the scheme of things.

The teenage years signal the advent of the loosening of the reins of adult control as adults come to terms with young people's burgeoning sense of independence. As adolescents typically seek more freedom from parental constraints, parents push back against this resistance to their authority (Deković, 1999; see also Grotevant and Cooper, 1986; Renk et al., 2005; Shearman and Dumlao, 2008). It is this ongoing concertina effect of young people breaking free and being pulled back into line, of adults loosening then tightening control which is at the heart of the transitioning to adulthood, and of the ensuing conflict between young people and the adults in control of their lives.

G. Stanley Hall was the first to promote a psychology of adolescence in 1904. Buhler (1935), Gesell (1956) and Erikson (1968) further advanced theories of adolescence. But the concept of youth reflects a broader understanding than adolescence. Over the past century the concept of youth has broadened to acknowledge growing interest and research into it (Hall and Jefferson, 1976; Furlong, 2013; Wyn and Cahill, 2015; Bennett, Cieslik and Miles, 2003; Furlong and Cartmel, 1997; Helve and Holm, 2016, among many others). This increased research focus has led over the past 50+ years to the emergence of Youth Studies as a major sub-genre of Sociology. This publication is sited firmly within that sub-genre.

Parent/child, adult/young conflict is part of the social and cultural landscape that young people practise within as they grow up. Their demands for greater freedom, and the desire of parents to curtail, or at least moderate, that freedom, inevitably lead to conflict. Wyn and Woodman (2006) argue that young people and the study of young people and their relationships with adults can better be understood if one frames the analysis within the ambit of 'generations'. Although the concept of distinct generations remains contentious (Pilcher, 1995), nevertheless, there is a compelling argument for

Introduction 3

basing the analysis of young people upon a generation's shared experience of the extant social, economic, cultural and political conditions unique to their timeframe of growing up; and that any previous or ensuing generations will necessarily experience different social, economic, cultural and political conditions (see Mannheim, 1952). A generational approach is more likely to account for notions of subjectivities and agency because of the changed circumstances within which those sharing a generational timeframe achieved adulthood:

> The adulthood that was available to the Baby Boomer generation was a historical artefact, a product of a particular combination of economic realities, social policies and industrial settlements that have long since ceased to exist.
>
> (Wyn and Woodman, 2006: 498)

Goodwin and O'Connor (2009) cite the concepts of *homo clausus* – 'a little world in himself' (Elias, 2000: 472) and *homo aperti* – the interdependent (open) person (Mennell, 1993: 193) to illustrate this. Viewing young people growing up as linked to, and interacting with, those around them as well as the 'wider world' reflects the framing of that experience as *homo aperti*. This permits young people to be seen and analysed from the perspective of interdependence, of shared experiences, where the individual and the social environment are inextricably linked (Mennell, 1993). The combination of nature, nurture and the interaction with the world around them combine to help form identity. It is the characteristics acquired as a *homo aperti* that make the teenage and young adult years so significant:

> It is the web of social relations in which individuals live during their most impressionable phase, that is childhood and youth, which imprints itself upon their unfolding personality in the form of the relationship between their controlling agencies, superego and ego and their libidinal impulses. The resulting balance ... determines how an individual person steers him or herself in his or her social relations with others.
>
> (Elias, 2000: 377)

Kelly and Kamp (2015) have described this process as the 'becoming' of youth. 'Becoming' perfectly encapsulates the transitory nature of youth. Young people 'are' and simultaneously are 'becoming'. One of the most frequently and repeatedly asked questions of every young person is 'What do you want to be when you grow up?'. From their perspective young people 'are'. They may envision 'becoming' an adult but they exist in the present. Their consciousness is in the present. It is sociologists and demographers and parents and teachers and adults in general who see them through the prism of 'becoming' – not yet fully formed.

4 *Introduction*

Habitus

How do we analyse these changes that take place between childhood and adulthood? How do we interrogate the intergenerational conflict both from the perspective of the young person and from that of the adult? And how do we maintain a consistency of nomenclature that can accommodate all of the changes which this publication seeks to analyse? In seeking to undertake this research I sought a theoretical base which would provide a research methodology which would enable the investigation of how and why conflict between young people and adults eventuates. Further, a theoretical base that would help to explain why young people, having themselves been the victims of adult denigration, then, upon becoming an adult, proceed to denigrate young people from ensuing generations.

Bourdieu's theory of habitus has been criticised for not being able to encompass what Chaney refers to as the 'widespread aestheticisation of life' (Chaney, 1996: 70), that cultural capital may be more widely acquired, and more widely spread, than Bourdieu's theory might allow. Similarly, Reay (2004) points to shortcomings in Bourdieu's analysis regarding women and for the Bourdieu's reliance on the nexus between economic and cultural capital. Rancière (1991; see Drury and Oster, 2004) questions Bourdieu's 'presumption' of inequality.

Despite these concerns Bourdieu's theory of habitus does provide that workable methodology (see King, 2000). Importantly, habitus, being able to reflect notions of identity, dispositions and predispositions, provides a vocabulary and a grammar with which to describe and analyse adult denigration of young people. Habitus is the central component of that grammar and vocabulary.

For Bourdieu 'habitus' comprises:

> Systems of durable, transposable dispositions, structured structures predisposed to function as structuring structures, that is, as principles of the generation and structuring of practices and representations.
>
> (Bourdieu, 1977: 72)

Dispositional understandings of habitus accrue from our earliest experiences. They deepen as we grow up, influenced by the family, the institutions with which we engage, and the cultural milieu in which we are nurtured, eventually becoming our 'feel for the game' (Bourdieu, 1993: 5) in the arenas where we struggle for recognition and reward. Habitus is not static, but subject to modification as a young person moves through influential social institutions towards adulthood.

Habitus exists within, is integrated with, and is a property of, social agents which can be individuals or groups or even institutions. For Bourdieu, habitus is both a 'structured and structuring structure' (Bourdieu, 1994: 170). The 'structured' nature of habitus is provided by past and

Introduction 5

present circumstances: family, education, interaction with peers and so on. The 'structuring' nature of habitus comes from its fashioning of present and future behaviour leading to predispositions which influence future behaviour. It is these 'predispositions', this propensity to behave in a particular way, which serves to reflect (to ourselves, and to others) one's identity. Behaviour (or practices) is the interaction between habitus and 'current circumstances' (Grenfell, 2008: 52). Each person's habitus informs their behaviour.

Innocents Abroad

Resistance to adult authority has its genesis in young people's predilection for risk-taking and 'hanging out'. Adult concerns do not confine themselves to issues of safety. They often fear that young people are 'up to no good', that their time could be put to better purpose, creating a suspicion that their time is being lost or wasted. Hanging out with friends is perceived as doing nothing, in contrast to constructive organised leisure activities. Adult perceptions of young people engaging in activities that are dangerous or morally dubious or just 'doing nothing' can serve to create for young people a sense of social exclusion (Byrne, 1999). This exclusion brings into sharp relief the two fundamentally opposed, and often simultaneously held, perceptions of young people by adults. On one hand, they are innocents abroad in need of protection inside the protected environment which parents create for them. Faulkner (2010) calls this protected environment the 'walled garden'. Encased in the walled garden on the one hand, while on the other hand, they are delinquents in the making: 'folk devils' (Cohen, 1972).

Parents are overwhelmingly held responsible for not only the development of children, but for their survival. Parental investment in their children's development brings with it an expectation of a return on that investment. Having nurtured a child from birth, protection of that child is a foremost consideration.

It is young people's recent emergence from childhood, the inextricable link to the vulnerabilities of childhood, and attendant adult 'understandings' of childhood innocence, that help to inform adult responses to young people's burgeoning demands for freedom from adult shackles. These (real and imagined) vulnerabilities affect and inform adult responses. This 'sanctification' (Faulkner, 2011: 324) of young people impacts upon and serves to determine adult attitudes towards young people. Navigating the transition from child to adult involves the interaction of life experiences and individual choices made contemporaneously with those experiences. This creates a process of what Evans (2007) refers to as 'structured individuation'. It is young peoples' leisure time that provides abundant opportunities for this structured individuation. But it is this unregulated leisure time which is, at the same time, a cause of apprehension for adults.

As young people move into their teen years, 'time away' allows opportunity to compose and evolve their sense of autonomy and identity. The

6 Introduction

advent of online technology has served to enhance these opportunities. It is this largely unorganised, unsupervised, 'free time' which serves to facilitate young peoples' engagement with cultural products, an engagement that serves to assist them make meanings. It is this process of making of meanings that Willis (1990) has dubbed 'grounded aesthetics'.

As children get older, parental and adult attitudes struggle to recognise the changed status of the young people. Rather than adjust to the changes apparent in their children as they grow into young people, parents/adults tend to 'demand a containment of childhood' (Faulkner, 2011: 332), reflected in attempts to maintain 'control' over their teenagers and protect them by prolonging their childhood. Conflict then ensues.

Moral Panics

The term 'moral panic' has assumed common usage. Cohen, in interrogating moral panics, sought to explain the relationship between at-large perceptions of deviancy and the process by which that deviancy is amplified by pre-existing perceptions and distrust of certain groups – a distrust fuelled by media amplification of the 'threats' from those groups. Over the past 50 years, the concept has been reviewed, interrogated and refined by both Cohen himself (1980, 1987, 2002, 2011) and others (Goode and Ben-Yehuda, 2006; Critcher, 2011; Cottee, 2002; David et al., 2011; Garland, 2008; Jenks, 2011) amongst a host of others.

Rohloff and Wright (2010: 404) explain moral panic as 'a particular type of overreaction to a perceived social problem'. Inherent in any moral panic is a perceived threat to society and the publicising of that threat via the media and outgrowth of public concern. Young people are often perceived as the perpetrators of moral panics, as 'folk devils'. Although they may not be exclusively the cause of the moral panic, young people function as the 'other' in a large number of examples, often focusing on various subcultures within the larger demographic of young people. It is a small step from there to a moral panic focussing on young people in general. This tendency to 'pathologise' young people as a whole (Brown, 2013; Baines, 1997; McDonald, 2005) is reflected in the kinds of denigration applied most recently to Millennials and their obsession with mobile phones and digital technology.

Cohen's exploration of moral panics identified 'Teddy Boys' as exemplars of the phenomenon. Since then any number of moral panics have emerged seemingly on a regular basis. 'Illegal immigrants' threatening the security of Britain, the US, Australia and much of Europe are current examples. In Australia, much of the focus of moral panics has been on the threat to societal equilibrium by the actions of the 'other'. And the 'other' is very often a young person.

Music and other youth cultural forms have also been the focus of moral panics (Clarke, 1982; Martin and Segrave, 1993; McRobbie and Thornton, 1995). Homan describes how moral panics serve to link the perception that popular music is 'articulated as low culture' (Homan, 2003: 12) which permits the challenging of dominant cultural forms. It is this challenging of the status quo that prompts governments, media and opinion leaders to categorise pop music as 'worthless', paralleling De Nora's distinction of traditional vs modern music (2000).

Notably, many moral panics involving young people actually betray the inherent contradiction in adult perceptions of young people being simultaneously portrayed as 'victims', 'innocents abroad'. The moral panic derives from the fear that young people will be casualties of malignant forces. This is particularly the case with moral panics about drugs (see Hier, 2002; Stratton, Howe and Battaglia, 2011).

Young women often have a dual role in moral panics, firstly as folk devils. Barron and Lacombe's account (Barron & Lacombe, 2005) of the phenomenon of the 'nasty girl' is based upon the presumption of increased violent young female behaviour. Young women also function as victims as with Henry Giroux's depiction of exploited innocence in his account of 'nymphet fantasies' (Giroux, 2006). Similarly, Lumby and Funnell (2011) and Munster (2009) have scrutinised the moral panics which accompanied artist Bill Henson's photographs of nude pre-teen females in Australia.[2]

Symbolic Violence

Young people's engagement with cultural products has been central to analysis of the way young people function within their cultural milieu. Grounded aesthetics places notions of consumption of cultural products as an active process of engagement in the making of meanings. This process of young people symbolically and actively interacting with consumer items runs contrary to previous analysis of interaction with consumer products which viewed that engagement via the Gramscian prism of passive exploitation:

> Creative and dynamic moments of a whole process of cultural life, of cultural birth and rebirth. To know the cultural world, our relationship to it, and ultimately to know us, it is necessary not merely to be in it but to change – however minutely – that cultural world. This is a condition of life – in relation to the social group or individual and its condition of life – of the ways in which the received natural and social world is made human to them *and made*, to however small a degree (even if finally symbolic), controllable by them.
>
> (Willis, 1990: 22, emphasis in original)

Young peoples' engagement with cultural products is a two-way interaction. It reflects the cognitive evolution associated with the onset of puberty characterised by hypothetical and deductive reasoning – the capacity to think and reason in the abstract, to problem-solve, and what Flavell (1976, 1979) refers to as *metacognition* – the capacity to think about thinking.

8   *Introduction*

Young people encounter and then embody the cultural products they engage with. But that encounter involves their newly acquired capacity for metacognition. Listening to a song for example is not merely an aural experience. It involves reflections about that listening engagement. It involves reflections on the lyrics and how the lyrics resonate with how they are attempting to come to terms with their place in the world. It involves reflecting upon the circumstances of the encounter – with whom? Where? Time of day, whether alcohol or other drugs were involved. The young person now has the capacity to view, and re-view, and review, these interactions as part of a process of reflecting self to self, what De Nora (2000) refers to as *introjection*. This process of grounded aesthetics and introjection is experienced individually. It is also experienced collectively with each individual being part of a generational zeitgeist (Hegel, 1979). The act of reflection, individually undertaken, is also reflected upon collectively via a shared experience of all media, via discussion and via shared understandings flowing from that shared experience of the zeitgeist. Young people collectively engage with, and in, the cultural spirit of the age.

If it is correct, as Robertson and Rutherford (1988) have asserted, that 'Every generation blames the one before', then I contend that the converse of this truism is that every generation is suspicious of, fearful for, and feels threatened by the ones that follow. Why does every generation feel threatened by generations that follow? Why does each generation view their own youth cultural experience as the gold standard, the objective benchmark against which the cultural experience of succeeding generations can be measured? I maintain that it is the circumstances associated with the engagement with cultural products that is key to the denigration of succeeding generations. It is the process of grounded aesthetics and the process of introjection which are at the heart of adult concerns about ensuing generations. There is generally less than ten years between young people's farewelling their childhood to the advent of their entry into full adulthood. But it is the unique circumstances of this period which serve to make special the experiences of their youth. Play and engagement with cultural products is a central characteristic of young people's transition to adulthood. Their gradually evolving sense of independence from adult supervision permits them to engage with cultural products free of adult control. This engagement, deeply felt and fondly remembered, serves to privilege those experiences. They take on a position of eminence privileging them as uniquely memorable, uniquely significant. Embodiment at a time of this intense emotional, physical and intellectual development endows those experiences with the mantle of *authenticity*, an authenticity understood, known, affirmed by the unyielding belief that no youth experience could possibly match their experience. It is this certainty that privileges that authenticity over the youth experience of ensuing youth generations – an authenticity that cannot be emulated. Young people bear this grafted-on overriding conviction of the unique authenticity of their youth experience with them into adulthood.

A simple truth that young people very quickly realise virtually from birth is that the power balance between adults and young people is not in any way equivalent. It is very much in favour of the adult. Young people when they enter into arenas controlled by, or even just occupied by adults, realise very quickly that their status is inferior to that of adults. In these relationships, adults rely for their superior status upon the respect accruing to the authority inherent in their adult persona. Authority demanding respect is the asset they embody, and the currency they demand in payment is deference (Goffman, 1956). Young people in the presence of adults defer to them as a matter of course. It is expected and is granted (often begrudgingly). Upon arrival at adulthood, having deferred to their elders throughout their teenage years, they then in turn have an expectation that they too will be deferred to. They now possess the authority of adults, and the expectation is that the tithe of deference should be paid by young people and accorded to them in due course.

Having arrived with expectations of deference, they find that it is (at best) grudgingly applied, or worse, their authority as adults is ignored. The deference fails to materialise. The most recent example of this ignoring is a Millennial or later generation, with their head stuck in a mobile phone, seemingly oblivious to those (especially adults) around them. Adult expectations remain unmet.

Newly arrived adults then find themselves being confronted by a further cause for grievance when young people from ensuing generations then presume to claim for themselves the legitimacy, the authenticity of their own youth cultural forms. That which they know with certainty is called into question by 'upstart' young people who can't possibly understand the legitimacy the adult claims for their youth experience. Bourdieu characterises the internalising of these concerns and grievances resulting in a pattern of denigration of young people as *misrecognition* (Bourdieu, 1984, 1986). 'Misrecognition' is what people do when they make unquestioned assumptions and judgements about others. Misrecognition embodies a set of active social processes that anchor taken-for-granted assumptions into the realm of social life. The response is often subtextual: irony, sarcasm and denigration – forms of *symbolic violence* towards the next generation of young people. So having themselves been misrecognised by adults when they were young people, they then, upon becoming adults, proceed to repeat the misrecognition that was applied to them. Becoming an adult seemingly operates to blot out, or at least transform memories of being misrecognised when young, thus permitting adults to repeat that same denigration of young people.

Misrecognition is the embodiment of symbolic violence, the incorporation of external forces and influences into the internal system of judgement. The synthesis of that incorporation is the expression of denigration and belittling of young people based upon the privileging of adults' own youth experiences which 'dominates [and] take[s] its own course in order to exercise that domination' (Bourdieu, 1977: 190). It is the language of adults which invariably gives expression to the symbolic violence of misrecognition as we shall see in coming chapters.

The short ten years or so between the onset of puberty and the entry into adulthood is dominated by the process of transition. Young people's emotional, intellectual and physical development during this period so completely transforms the individual that the newly emerged adult is quantifiably different to the child that began that process a decade before. But the process of transition is so fundamentally 'raw' in the experiencing of it, it indelibly 'scars' the adult which emerges. Adults see this process as 'becoming'. They see this process in all its developmentally exposed rawness. For the young person transitions occur in spite of them. Puberty and the transitioning to adulthood are simultaneously catalyst and driver; external to the process and deeply internalised; intellectually stimulating and emotionally wrought. And all this is happening in real time – there is no pause, no 'time out'. To paraphrase Dickens: the best and the worst of times. And the artefacts, the engagements that assist them to make sense of what is happening to them are the cultural products that act as balm, that serve to salve their curiosities and their hurt; that provide the absolute euphoria and the exhilaration of that engagement. And it is the exaltation they feel of sharing those engagements with friends, of the unique moments that no adult is present for, cannot possibly comprehend, that make these moments extra special. The sharing of the cultural experience of the age's zeitgeist unites them as no other experience can.

In the following chapters, I will explain how the process of transition to adulthood creates the exceptional circumstances that sees young people privilege their own youth cultural experiences and how that privileging in turn allows them to misrecognise the youth cultural experiences (and the young people themselves from ensuing generations.

In Chapter 2, I will set out the theoretical landscape which will permit the exploration of adult misrecognition of young people. It sets out the framework for understanding the processes involved based upon the work of Bourdieu and Cohen. It establishes the nomenclature of Bourdieu, and how that vocabulary can assist in explaining the process of 'becoming', reflected in the concepts of *social world*, *fields and doxa* and how that transition to adult is reflected in Bourdieu's conceit of the *alchemy of consecration* (1986: 250). It goes on to contextualise how Cohen's concepts of *folk devils* and *moral entrepreneurs* can be adapted to explain the deviance of a generation as a whole.

Chapter 3 investigates the process of growing up – how the 'in-betweenness of no longer being child, not yet adult, affects the way young people evolve their habitus. It examines the impact of the generational zeitgeist upon the sense of solidarity young people share with their generational cohort. It then explores the role that authenticity, status and memory play in the embodiment of the youth cultural experience in the habitus of the adult – how this embodied certainty is transformed into the capacity to speak with certainty

Introduction 11

about that embodied capital via Bourdieu's 'double language of disinterest'. The newly arrived adult does so in spite of the attempts by parents and adults to maintain the 'walled garden' of childhood. It is these attempts to constrain that contribute to the resentment felt by newly arrived adults.

Chapter 4 interrogates notions of adulthood: its unique role as the demographic classification by which every other demographic can be assessed and measured. It explores the field of power and the relationship between authenticity, authority and respect and the role that these play in the transitioning to adulthood. It then examines the role 'stereotyping' plays when adults misrecognise young people from following generations.

Chapter 5 focuses on the personal investment that young people make as part of their process of grounded aesthetics. Young people's personal investment reflects Bourdieu's concept of *libido sciendi* (1986: 82) – the embodied investment integrated into the individual's habitus as cultural capital. It is also reflected in the notion of shared specific generational experiences. Each of those generational shared experiences signifies the collective collegiality of the zeitgeist – their experiences! Their music! These shared generational experiences lead to the creation of social identity as members of what Hornsey (2008) refers to as a 'social in-group'. Each social in-group then evolves its own sense of a group prototype. Finally, Chapter 5 outlines how the advent of social media and the emergence of an 'online presence' has fundamentally changed not only the way young people engage with the social world, but also notions of identity curation.

Chapter 6 examines how notions of appropriateness and inappropriateness contribute to the misrecognising of the behaviour of young people. It finds form in the 'helicoptering' of parents and other adults protectively hovering over children and young people, motivated by their concept of an idealised child/young person. This is exemplified by the mythologising of Miley Cyrus 'tween' character 'Hannah Montana', venerated as the exemplar by which young people should be measured against. Cited by a group of the informants, Cyrus' Montana alter ego committed the cardinal sin of growing up and becoming her own person. The chapter goes on to examine how the ossification of the habitus contributes to the process of misrecognition. As we age, the amount of new material being embodied in our habitus decreases, and the older material which is deleted also decreases. To illustrate this, I have used the metaphor of the 'aesthetic solera'. As less newer material is added to the habitus, and less older material is deleted, so the habitus begins to ossify. The effect of this ossification is to, over time, create within the habitus predisposition, tendency, propensity and inclination. Predisposition, tendency, propensity and inclination manifest themselves through the concepts of 'taste' and 'discernment'. Taste and discernment are the means, the medium by which misrecognition evolves.

Chapter 7 examines the role that music plays in the evolution of habitus and in the way that memory consecrates those musical experiences to allow us to relive the past in the present. Music's centrality as a maker of meanings for young people is reflected in the way it contributes to what De Nora refers to as 'embodied awareness' – the nexus between the experience and the environment where the experience occurs. Music is the experience, but all of the associated environments – physical, human, mood – contribute to this awareness. And that embodied awareness lives on through our remembrances of the process of embodiment. Via the aesthetic solera, we create and embody the 'soundtrack of our life'. This soundtrack, now part of who we are, travels with us into our adulthood. And it is those memories, embodied and ennobled, privileged by the generational circumstances of their acquisition, which are the conduit for the re-imagining of those experiences in adulthood. It is this embodied awareness that creates a sense of entitlement, an entitlement to endorse elements of the soundtrack of our lives as authentic. This conferring of authenticity creates simultaneously the sense of entitlement to misrecognise musical acts that are pronounced and dismissed as not able to meet the authenticity test. This conferring of the label of inauthenticity is equally privileging. The band Nickelback and performer James Blunt are prime examples of this misrecognition.

Chapter 8 places misrecognition of young people within the wider context of institutionalised misrecognition of those young people. Generational misrecognition identifies the entirety of a generation as deserving of misrecognition. Millennial 'deviance' puts at risk the future of society – what Cohen refers to as the 'dislocation of the social structure' (2002: 47). The misrecognising of Millennials centres on their seeming obsession with mobile phones and technology. This obsession threatens the future. Millennials' 'difference' must be explained and 'managed'. As a result, a group of moral entrepreneurs have emerged to 'explain' Millennials to older adults. These are the 'futurists' and their focus on Millennials' difference represents Cohen's concept of *amplification* (2002). Only when adults 'understand' Millennials can the social structure regain its equilibrium. In doing so they play to, and exploit, the existing widespread misrecognition of Millennials among adults. The futurists play to these widespread understandings which Cohen references as *cabalism* (2002).

In the following chapters, I will address the conundrum at the centre of adult misrecognition of young people from ensuing generations. The conferring of authenticity by each generation upon their own youth experience entitles them to apply the judgement of deviance to following generations. This dislocation of the social structure caused by this deviance threatens the future. Adults respond by misrecognising the cultural forms, the behaviour and, by extension, the young people themselves of those ensuing generations. It is Bourdieu's theory of practice that permits analysis of how cultural capital, embodied as deeply felt experiences of the 'newness' of the totality of the youth experience, is internalised and converted into misrecognition of generations following.

Notes

1 Disraeli B., Colburn H., and Harrison and Co (London England). (1845). *Sybil or the two nations* ([First edition]). Henry Colburn Publisher Great Marlborough Street.
2 See www.abc.net.au/archives/80days/stories/2012/01/19/3415368.htm

Bibliography

Baines, M. (1997). Mad, Bad or Angry? Gender, Sexual Abuse and the Pathologising of Young Women's Behaviour. *Youth Studies Australia*, 16(1), 19–23.
Barron, C., and Lacombe, D. (2005). Moral Panic and the Nasty Girl. *The Canadian Review of Sociology and Anthropology*, 42(1), 51–69.
Bennett, A., Cieslik, M. and Miles, S. (2003). *Researching Youth*. New York: Palgrave Macmillan.
Bourdieu, P. (1977). *Outline of a Theory of Practice*, R. Nice (trans.). Cambridge: Cambridge University Press.
Bourdieu, P. (1984). *Distinction: A Social Critique of the Judgement of Taste*. London: Routledge & Kegan Paul.
Bourdieu, P. (1986). The Forms of Capital, in J. Richardson (Ed.), *Handbook of Theory and Research for the Sociology of Education*, pp. 241–258. New York: Greenwood.
Bourdieu, P. (1993). *Sociology in Question*. London; Thousand Oaks, CA: Sage.
Bourdieu, P. (1994). [1987]. *In Other Words: Essays towards a Reflexive Sociology*, M. Adamson (trans.). Cambridge: Polity.
Brown, D. M. (2013). Young People, Anti-social Behaviour and Public Space: The Role of Community Wardens in Policing the 'ASBO Generation'. *Urban Studies*, 50(3), 538–555.
Buhler, C. (1935). *From Birth to Maturity. An Outline of the Psychological Development of the Child*, E. W. Menaken (trans.). London: Keegan Paul.
Byrne, D. (1999). *Social Exclusion*. Buckingham: Open University Press.
Chaney, D. (1996). *Lifestyles*. London: Routledge.
Clarke, G. (1982). *Defending Ski Jumpers: A Critique of Theories of Youth Sub-Cultures*. Discussion Paper. Birmingham: University of Birmingham.
Cohen, S. (1972). *Folk Devils and Moral Panics*. Great Britain: MacGibbon and Kee.
Cohen, S. (1980). *Folk Devils and Moral Panics: The Creation of the Mods and Rockers* (New ed.). Oxford: M. Robertson.
Cohen, S. (1987). *Folk Devils and Moral Panics: The Creation of the Mods and Rockers* (New ed.). Oxford: Blackwell.
Cohen, S. (2002). *Folk Devils and Moral Panics: The Creation of the Mods and Rockers* (New ed.). London, New York: Routledge.
Cohen, S. (2011). Whose Side Were We On? The Undeclared Politics of Moral Panic Theory. *Crime Media Culture*, 7(3), 237–243.
Cottee, S. (2002). Folk Devils and Moral Panics: 'Left Idealism' Reconsidered. *Theoretical Criminology*, 6(4), 387–410.
Cox, P., and Shore, H. (2002). *Becoming Delinquent: British and European Youth, 1650–1950* (1st ed.). Routledge. https://doi.org/10.4324/9781315183497
Critcher, C. (2011). For a Political Economy of Moral Panics. *Crime Media Culture*, 7(3), 259–275.

David, M., Rohloff, A., Petley, J., and Hughes, J. (2011). The Idea of Moral Panic – Ten Dimensions of Dispute. *Crime Media Culture*, 7(3), 215–228.

Deković, M. (1999). Parent-adolescent Conflict: Possible Determinants and Consequences. *International Journal of Behavioral Development*, 23(4), 977–1000.

De Nora, T. (2000). *Music in Everyday Life*. Cambridge: Cambridge University Press.

Disraeli, B., Colburn, H., and Harrison and Co (London England). (1845). *Sybil or the Two Nations* (1st ed.). Great Marlborough Street: Henry Colburn Publisher.

Drury, J., and Oster, C. (2004). *The Philosopher and His Poor* (A. Parker, Ed.). Duke University Press. https://doi.org/10.2307/j.ctv1198z3b

Elias, N. (2000). *The Civilising Process*. London: Blackwell.

Erikson, E. H. (1968). *Identity: Youth and Crisis*. Oxford: Norton & Co.

Evans, K. (2007). Concepts of Bounded Agency in Education, Work, and the Personal Lives of Young Adults. *International Journal of Psychology*, 42(2), 85–93.

Faulkner, J. (2011). Innocents and Oracles: The Child as a Figure of Knowledge and Critique in the Middle-Class Philosophical Imagination. *Critical Horizons*, 12(3), 323–346.

Faulkner, J., and Monash University National Centre for Australian Studies. (2010). *The Importance of being Innocent: Why We Worry about Children*. Melbourne: Cambridge University Press.

FitzSimons, P. (2013, October 17). Why Oh Why Does Gen Y Not Get It? *Sydney Morning Herald*. Retrieved from www.smh.com.au/sport/why-oh-why-does-gen-y-not-get-it-20131016-2vn4u.html

Flavell, J. H. (1976). Metacognitive Aspects of Problem Solving, in L. B. Resnick (Ed.), *The Nature of Intelligence*, pp. 231–235. Hillsdale, NJ: Earlbaum.

Flavell, J. H. (1979). Metacognition and Cognitive Monitoring. A New Area of Cognitive-Development Inquiry. *American Psychologist*, 34(10), 906–911.

Furlong, A. (2013). *Youth Studies: An Introduction*. New York: Routledge.

Furlong, A., and F. Cartmel (1997). *Young People and Social Change: Individualization and Risk in Late Modernity*. Buckingham: Open University Press.

Garland, D. (2008). On the Concept of Moral Panic. *Crime, Media Culture*, 4(9), 9–30.

Gesell, A. (1956). *Youth: The Years from Ten to Sixteen*. New York: Harper.

Giroux, H. (2006). *America on the Edge*. New York: Palgrave Macmillan.

Goffman, E. (1956) *The Presentation of the Self in Everyday Life*. New York: Vintage Books.

Goode, E., and Ben-Yehuda, N. (2006). *Moral Panics: The Social Construction of Deviance*. Cambridge, MA: Blackwell.

Goodwin, J., and O'Connor, H. (2009/2017). Youth and Generation in the Midst of an Adult World, in A. Furlong (Ed.), *Handbook of Youth and Young Adulthood: New Perspectives and Agendas*, pp. 21–30. London: Routledge.

Green, J. (2008). *Bill Henson's Photographic Work Seized from Gallery by Police*. ABC. www.abc.net.au/archives/80days/stories/2012/01/19/3415368.htm?transcriptStoryID=3423905

Grenfell, M. (2008). *Pierre Bourdieu: Key Concepts*. Stocksfield, UK: Acumen.

Grotevant, H., and Cooper, C. (1986). Individuation in Family Relationships: A Perspective on Individual Differences in the Development of Identity and Role-taking. *Human Development*, 29, 82–100.

Hall, G. S. (1911). *Adolescence: Its Psychology and Its Relations to Physiology, Anthropology, Sociology, Sex, Crime, Religion and Education*. New York: D. Appleton and Co.

Hall, S., and Jefferson, T. (Eds.). (1976). *Resistance through Rituals: Youth Subcultures in Post-War Britain*. London: Hutchinson.
Hegel, G. W. F., Miller, A. V., Findlay, J. N., and Hoffmeister, J. (1979). *Phenomenology of Spirit*. Oxford: Clarendon Press.
Helve, H., and Holm, G. (Eds.). (2016). *Contemporary Youth Research: Local Expressions and Global Connections*, pp. 1–12. Abingdon; Oxon: Routledge.
Hier, S. (2002). Raves, Risks and the Ecstasy Panic: A Case Study of the Subversive Nature of Moral Regulation. *Canadian Journal of Sociology*, 27(1), 33–57.
Homan, S. (2003). *The Mayor's a Square: Live Music and Law and Order in Sydney*. Newtown: Local Consumption Publications.
Horace, and Gwynn, S. L. (1900). *The Odes of Horace. Book III*. London: Blackie
Hornsey, M. J. (2008). Social Identity Theory and Self-categorization Theory: A Historical Review. *Social and Personality Psychology Compass*, 2(1), 204–222.
Jenks, C. (2011). The Context of an Emergent and Enduring Concept. *Crime Media Culture*, 7(3), 229–236.
Kelly, P., and Kamp, A. (2015). *A Critical Youth Studies for the 21st Century*. Leiden: Brill.
King, A. (2000). Thinking with Bourdieu against Bourdieu: A 'practical' critique of the habitus. *Sociological Theory*, 18(3), 417–433.
Lumby, C., and Funnell, N. (2011). Between Heat and Light: The Opportunity in Moral Panics. *Crime, Media, Culture*, 7(3), 277–291.
Mannheim, K. (1952). The Problem of Generations, in P. Kecksmeti (Ed.), *Karl Mannheim: Essays*, pp. 276–322. London: Routledge.
Martin, L., and Segrave, K. (1993). *Anti-Rock: The Opposition to Rock'n'roll*. Hampden: Da Capo.
McDonald, J. (2005). Neo-liberalism and the Pathologising of Public Issues: The Displacement of Feminist Service Models in Domestic Violence Support Services. *Australian Social Work*, 58(3), 275–284.
McRobbie, A., and Thornton, S. (1995). Rethinking 'Moral Panic' for Multi Mediated Social Worlds. *The British Journal of Sociology*, 46(4), 559–574.
Mennell, S. (1993). *Norbert Elias: An Introduction*. London: Blackwell.
Munster, A. (2009). The Henson Photographs and the 'Network Condition'. *Continuum: Journal of Media and Cultural Studies*, 2–3(1), 3–12.
Pilcher, J. (1995). *Age and Generation in Modern Britain*. Oxford: Oxford University Press.
Rancière, J. (1991). *The Ignorant Schoolmaster: Five Lessons in Intellectual Emancipation*. Stanford: Stanford University Press.
Reay, D. (2004). Gendering Bourdieu's Concept of Capitals?: Emotional Capital, Women and Social Class, in L. Adkins and B. Skeggs (Eds.), *Feminism after Bourdieu*, pp. 57–74. London: Blackwell.
Renk, K., Liljequist, L., Simpson, J. E., and Phares, V. (2005). Gender and Age Differences in the Topics of Parent-Adolescent Conflict. *The Family Journal*, 13(2), 139–149.
Robertson, B., and Rutherford, M. (1988). The Living Years on Living Years. Retrieved from www.youtube.com/watch?v=5hr64MxYpgk
Rohloff, A., and Wright, S. (2010). Moral panic and Social Theory: Beyond the Heuristic. *Current Sociology*, 58(3), 403–419.
Shearman, S. M., and Dumlao, R. (2008). A Cross-Cultural Comparison of Family Communication Patterns and Conflict between Young Adults and Parents. *Journal of Family Communication*, 8(3), 186–211.

16 *Introduction*

Stratton K., Howe C., and Battaglia F. (1996). *Fetal Alcohol Syndrome: Diagnosis, Epidemiology, Prevention, and Treatment.* Washington, DC: National Academies Press.

The Australia Institute. (2013, July 9). Disinterested Youth Feel No Party Represents Them. [Media Release]. Retrieved from www.tai.org.au/sites/default/files/MR%20Disinterested%20youth%20feel%20no%20party%20represents%20them.pdf

Willis, P. (1990). *Common Culture: Symbolic Work at Play in the Everyday Cultures of the Young.* Milton Keynes: Open University Press.

Wyn, J. and Cahill, H. (Eds.) (2015). *Handbook of Children and Youth Studies.* Singapore: Springer.

Wyn, J., and Woodman, D. (2006). Generation, Youth and Social Change in Australia. *Journal of Youth Studies*, 9(5), 495–514.

2 The Alchemy of Consecration

> The past is a foreign country, they do things differently there.
> (L. P. Hartley, 1953)[1]

Attitudes and values embedded in the adult persona have been acquired over, and as a result of, the lived experience of each person. Adult attitudes towards young people do not manifest themselves fully formed but evolve over the course of a lifetime. The role that the youth experience plays in that evolution is central in establishing and formalising the resultant adult attitudes towards ensuing youth generations. Adult personas are umbilically linked to the youth persona that helped to generate them. Moral panics generated and experienced by adults towards youth generations following theirs rely upon that umbilical link in order to privilege the adult's youth experience over the youth experience of those following generations. Bourdieu's concept of *habitus* provides a theoretical tool that helps to explain how the youth persona metamorphoses into the adult persona. Habitus, Bourdieu's reconciliation of the subjective and the objective, of individual agency and context, formed the basis of his theory of practice. Each person's habitus is the totality of this 'socialised subjectivity' (Bourdieu and Wacquant, 1992: 126) of each individual's experience – what Grenfell refers to as history existing in the present (Grenfell, 2008: 52). But although history exists in the present, it does so as remembrances, frissons of exhilaration, moments of recollections of delights and participations and intimacies, and embarrassments. History may exist in the present but it does so fleetingly. L. P. Hartley's quip, 'they do things differently there', reminds us that it is the momentary memories that exist. They colour our present but the 'country' they inhabited is long gone, existing now as snippets, fragments, remnants, frozen in amber in our contemporaneous personas.

The teenage years are a major engine room for the development of the adult persona. Youth, the intermediary period between childhood and adult, is a constantly evolving melange of physical, social, psychological and emotional development associated with, and following the onset of puberty

DOI: 10.4324/9781003427476-2

as rites of passage (Van Gennep et al., 1961) are negotiated and passed through, and activities are increasingly undertaken alone, or with friends and acquaintances, rather than adults. The period of youth sees the development of the first serious [and not so serious] romantic relationships, as well as experimenting with sexual activity and alcohol and other drugs. Above all, it is a time of constant testing, experimentation and risk-taking (see Piaget, 1972; Zuckerman, 1979; Tonkin, 1987; Irwin and Millstein, 1986; Evans, 2007; Bessant, 2008) as they become increasingly aware of, and are learning to function within, their ever-growing independence – an independence characterised by hypothetical and deductive reasoning, the capacity to think and reason in the abstract, to problem-solve, and metacognition.

Newly emerging independence inevitably creates the conditions for intergenerational conflict between themselves and their parents, teachers and other adults who populate their social world. The capacity for metacognition about their place in the world provides a springboard for questioning adult constraints as those adults try to mediate and control this burgeoning independence and experimentation. It is the 'developmental' nature of this 'in-betweenness' between childhood and adulthood, in which young people evolve and develop their habitus.

Social World, Field and Doxa

Bourdieu's notion of habitus posits that we are predisposed towards acting in certain ways because of the accumulation of experiences, knowledge and understandings arrived at as a result of interaction with what he refers to as the *social world*, the 'coexistence of points of view ... structured and doubly informed by the structure of the space' (2000: 183). In the social world, the habitus reproduces aspects of that social world. A young person growing up in a particular social world will 'speak the same language' (Grenfell, 2008: 95) as those around them (see Willis, 1979). Not only do birth circumstances contribute to the economic future of a young person, but the *social* and *cultural capital* (Bourdieu, 1977, 1986) that they acquire and incorporate also does. *Symbolic capital* (Bourdieu, 1984) in the form of legitimacy, prestige and value, acquired through that interaction, informs and influences the way that individuals see themselves and, importantly, the way they see others. This is the basis for the way class functions to create a series of closed systems – what Grenfell refers to as a 'closure of "ranks" and minimal social mobility' (2008, 96). This *distinction* allows each individual to see themselves within the context of the social world they occupy and to discern how they are similar to, and different from, others within and without that social world. They know where they fit because where they fit is learned, ingrained as they find their sense of place. It is in the teenage years, during the formal operations stage of development, that the young person evolves a clearer sense of their place in the world – not only how they fit in, but who they are. It is during this period of their development that they gain a clearer understanding of their sense of 'self'. It is this more clearly defined, and continuously developing, sense of self that the young person carries with them as they transition to adulthood.

The social world is a relational space. Subordinate spaces within this social world Bourdieu identifies as *fields*, representing specific activity or interests and ranging across a variety of areas. Each field acts like a 'separate universe governed by its own laws' (Bourdieu, 2005: 7). These autonomous spaces of practice make up the social world. Each field is an arena with a structure of relative locations and geography. Each of us is an actor 'performing' within these fields according to the learned behaviour and within the constraints of the rules we have learnt that apply to these arenas. Each field has a 'common currency' (Grenfell, 2008: 223), ensuring that each reflects a hierarchy of authority maintained and bolstered by membership – by those who function within that field and by those who are excluded.

Fields in which children and young people function are more often than not dominated by or controlled by adults. These fields include education, sport and media, to name but a few. Their subordinate status in these fields serves to ensure they are aware that the currency they possess within these fields is devalued, in comparison with that of the adults also operating within these fields. The exchange rate is very much in favour of any adults operating in these fields. Homologies between fields ensure individuals and groups occupy more than one field and function across fields. As young people move through their teenage years, the breadth of fields within which they are able to operate increases. As they do so, the opportunities of functioning within fields frequented by friends, and increasingly outside the ambit of adults ('hanging out', recreational activities), expand. As participation in these fields expands, and as their burgeoning arena of operations extends increasingly beyond the family home and school, so does the sense of independence from adult supervision increase as they move ever closer to adulthood. Nevertheless, these expanded arenas that young people operate within continue to overlap with fields that adults also operate within. This leads to wider and more varied interaction and opportunities for increased conflict with adults. This conflict more often than not is occasioned by mutual derision and distrust as motives of the young people are questioned and limitations applied by adults are tested. The central element in these interactions is the society-level field that occupies a common social space, which individuals and groups all share – that of the 'field of power' (Bourdieu, 1996: 264–272). Embodied social and cultural capital, as with all fields, is converted by those operating in each particular field into currency in order to be able to 'play' in that specific field. What young people encounter in the field of power is adult symbolic capital in the guise of 'adult authority' (Laupa and Turiel, 1986; Baumrind, 1967, 1971, 1978). Adult authority authenticates the power of the adult to influence, to lead, to mandate and to make the rules. Young people, deficient in the capital of authority and prestige, are therefore impoverished in their capacity to 'play' in the field of power. When they play in fields where adult

20 The Alchemy of Consecration

authority is at a premium, they are compelled to play by the rules adults set for entry into each field. A central tenet of playing in adult-dominated fields is that the rules demand that the young people submit to the authority[2] adults have embodied.

Each field has its own 'fundamental law', its own *doxa* (1984) – the 'rules of the game' that oversee the 'playing' in each field. Each person playing in a field must understand the rules of the game which are acknowledged and unequivocal. If young people enter into a field dominated by adults they must quickly adapt to the doxa of that field. Learning the doxa of a field and playing to that doxa is the only choice open to young people. They must learn quickly or else be punished or excluded. Because in the field of power, the most uniformly consistent field that we all play in, young people learn from birth that the rules of the game place adults at the centre of power and young people at the periphery.

The mainstay of adult power, the embodied symbolic capital is *authority*. And the currency that links to that authority is deference. Adult authority is the symbolic capital that requires no test, no approval other than the number of annual circuits of the sun to achieve. Having lived for a mutually and legally agreed number of years[3] confers the authority of 'adulthood' upon the newly arrived adult. This completion of the metamorphosis of youth to adult comes with its own 'rites of passage', most of which involve being able to do legally what had been, prior to reaching the required age, illegal.

This newly conferred authority accruing to their adult status comes with the implicit understanding that the mantle of adulthood now allows them to play in the field of power with their status upgraded. This transformation is not instantaneous, but with the gradual realisation of their (now) adult authority comes the associated understanding that their enhanced authority has irreversibly strengthened their status with relation to young people of ensuing youth generations. As Roy Orbison might have put it, they are no longer 'working for the man', they have become 'the man' (Orbison, 1964).[4] Once conferred, any interaction between an adult and young people occurs with the unwritten but deeply understood consensus that the young people will defer to the adult's authority. Any transgression may result in adult sanction. In this way, becoming an adult is not only a stage in life; it impacts upon the deeply held understandings that comprise an individual's habitus. It transforms their concept of who they are. The doxa understood by them as children and young people that demanded, at the peril of exclusion (or worse), deferral to their elders, has been transformed by Bourdieu's *alchemy of consecration*. This melds the memories of the youth experience with the authority of adulthood to ordain the authenticity of that youth cultural experience. Upon arrival, the newly consecrated adult now finds themselves being deferred to (at least in principle) by younger people. Moreover, the young person prior to turning 18 begins to anticipate the act of consecration. Having been on the receiving end of adult derision, the symbolic capital of adulthood conferred by the *primordial consensus* (Bourdieu, 1993: 98) creates the expectation of the same deferral from those younger to their newly arrived at adult status.

Symbolic Capital, Misrecognition

Acquired doxa is consensually understood, emotionally, viscerally, as common sense. The rules of the game are understood not only at an individual level but at a class level. However I contend that in addition to these, they are simultaneously understood at a generational level. As each generation progresses from childhood through their teenage years to adulthood, they intuit the doxa that applies to them as a generation, thereby creating a shared sense of solidarity (Eyerman and Turner, 1998: 98/99) based upon their shared experience of their youth.

The socialisation process undergone from birth influences not only the evolution of our habitus but also the means by which individuals interact with others. It is both informed by the social world and, in turn, acts to inform our interaction with that public world. This interaction comes overlaid with the attitudes and values incorporated as part of acquired symbolic capital. The legitimacy, prestige and values inherent in this symbolic capital influence and inform the interaction with others. Each person's habitus incorporates a hierarchy of understandings that enable (or not) engagement with fields. Understanding the doxa for any field carries with it the element of certainty. For young people, that certainty lies in the awareness of the legitimacy not only of the rules binding them but also of the legitimacy of the experiences they encounter and embody as they move through their teenage years. It is the intensity of these almost exclusively first-time experiences of music and film and friends, of hanging out, and romance and the agony of unrequited love that sanctify their legitimacy. In fields like music or art, the authenticity of these experiences is assumed because the circumstances of the experience are special. They appear in real time, and in our memory, to be natural, familiar.

Upon arrival at adulthood that privilege of authenticity, the mantle of naturalness and familiarity, serves to enhance the status inextricably coupled with the experience. In adulthood, this then confers upon the adult a kind of collective 'wisdom', as if each adult is authorised to speak on behalf of the 'family' of adults. Cultural capital in the form of the privilege of adulthood, conferred by the authenticity of earlier youth experience, is instituted by a process Bourdieu refers to as *collective magic* (1986: 248). And this magic accrues automatically to each of us upon our maturity.

Authenticity accruing to adulthood is made more secure by the knowledge that the journey to adulthood has been sanctioned by the defining authentic youth experience – **their** youth experience. The youth experience of succeeding generations must be an inferior experience to their own. The rules of the game, the doxic understandings, reflect not only this differentiation of authenticity but the generational superiority of the embodied symbolic capital of the cultural product of their youth experience. The cloak of legitimacy sits comfortably on their shoulders. That authenticity is doxic. The decline in the quality when compared with their own does not warrant or even accept the need for comparison. That decline is understood, embodied and made manifest by the authenticity of the lived experience that provides the certainty of their own youth cultural transcendence.

This raises an interesting anomaly. Given that negative attitudes towards each youth generation are a rolling chronological phenomenon, it follows that each generation, upon reaching adulthood, has themselves been the victim of that denigration. So, the transformation from a young person to adult and the acquisition of negative attitudes towards ensuing youth generations occur despite their own youth experience of negativity. What appears to be at play is a kind of transformational amnesia. As we will see in later chapters, young people undertake this amnesic transformation seamlessly.

It is important to point out at this point the one aspect of adult interaction where the roles of the young person and adult appear to be reversed – where the legitimacy appears to rest with the young person rather than the adult. This reversal of legitimacy comes about because the young person's cultural capital (and expertise) is greater than the adult's. This is the field of technology. Young people in the last 25 years or so have shown themselves capable of adopting digital technologies, or more accurately of growing up with digital technology. Their parents and other adults have had to adapt to, and overlay digital technological learnings and comprehensions over the top of their analogue understanding. This is the one field where the rules of the game are not only better understood by young people, but much of the time adults rely upon young people to guide them through the digital maze. They are the ones with the authority while the adult often looks on helplessly. Bourdieu refers to this as being *socially out of play* (1993: 96). As 16-year-old informant Helen outlines, 'My grandma gets me to post everything on her Facebook ... because she doesn't know how to'.

The cultural capital accrued by young people's burgeoning technological capabilities confers an authority upon them superior to adults. But this in itself becomes the basis for further denigration because the authority conferred on young people by their technological expertise serves to highlight the technological inadequacies of older people, placing them at risk of being *Has Beens* (Wainwright III, 2003) (Bourdieu, 1993: 101).[5] And Has Beens lack authority. So rather than exemplifying the current youth generation's capacities, their technical expertise is yet another excuse for denigrating ensuing youth generations.

The misrecognition of following youth generations is linked to the adult's experience and perceptions of aging, and it finds expression in the denigration of the cultural forms, and particularly the music, of those ensuing generations. Blaikie, recognising a related phenomenon, reflected on the popularity of 60s rock icons still performing in the present day, quoting Mick

Jagger on the 'Peter Pan' effect of Baby Boomer fans wanting their idols to present exactly as they were in their youth.

> They want you to be like you were in 1969. They want to, because otherwise their youth goes with you.
> (Blaikie, 1999: 107)

It's as if the idols can present themselves as they were in their youth, then nostalgic audience members too can suspend the aging process and momentarily relive their own youth.[6]

For Bourdieu in *Distinction* (1984), arguably his most significant work, aesthetic judgements as an arena of cultural practice are imbued with misrecognition. *Taste*, the individual arbiter of likes and dislikes, determines the hierarchy of aesthetic judgements. Taste distinguishes by ordering according to a pre-set hierarchy of classification, and the process of classification itself shapes that process:

> Taste classifies, and it classifies the classifier. Social subjects, classified by their classifications, distinguish themselves by the distinctions they make, between the beautiful and the ugly, the distinguished and the vulgar, in which their position in the objective classifications is expressed or betrayed.
> (Bourdieu, 1984: 5–6)

Each classification made reflects the individual's acquired tastes and preferences, accumulated as part of the evolution of habitus. Each classification is made according to the accumulated doxa incorporated into habitus.

Any taste distinction brings with it a set of binary judgements denoting that hierarchy of classification: good/bad; authentic/inauthentic; legitimate/illegitimate; awesome/ordinary; cool/lame. Those making the distinction base their judgement upon their own understandings, their own acquired cultural tastes. Their acquired doxa serves to pre-determine their understandings of what is 'authentic' and 'cool'. The rules of the game they function within prescribe that those judgements are the only legitimate, the only authentic ones. Those who do not share their understandings, their classifications, must be inauthentic, uncool, illegitimate. They misrecognise those who don't share their hierarchy of tastes by applying elements of symbolic violence to them in the form of denigration, mockery and dismissal. This becomes clearer if we look at the role played by the incorporation of youth cultural forms into habitus and how those accumulated cultural forms and understandings then impact upon the classification of ensuing generations.

In order to fully understand this phenomenon, it is necessary to explore not only the role that youth cultural forms play in the development of a young person's identity but also how that identity and those forms continue to interact as the young person transitions to adulthood and beyond. And we need to acknowledge the apparent amnesia displayed by adults of their own denigrated youth experience when they proceed to participate in that same negative disparaging of, and fearfulness for, ensuing youth generations – why they develop an apparent empathy gap between themselves and the next generation(s) of young people.

Taste and Neo-Tribes

Bourdieu wrote about cultural capital as the accumulation of knowledge, behaviours and skills that someone can deploy to demonstrate cultural competence and social status (1986). The privileging of shared generational cultural experiences needs to be placed within the context of a wider framework of cultural discourse. Willis' *grounded aesthetics* (1990) places notions of consumption of cultural products as an active process of engagement in the making of meanings. De Nora (2000) with a specific emphasis on music has identified this process as *latching* (161). The processes of grounded aesthetics and latching reflect the shared engagement with cultural products by young people of each generation.

Engagement with youth cultural forms requires the expenditure of a great deal of time and effort on the part of the young person. Central to this engagement is a commitment to the rules of the game. Once this commitment is made, the young person can begin the process of personal investment in the youth cultural forms that they use to make meanings. This personal investment reflects Bourdieu's concept of *libido sciendi* (1986: 82). Translated as noble passion or lust for knowledge, young people's personal investment in these ongoing encounters with youth cultural forms is incorporated into the individual's habitus as cultural capital. Knowledge and understanding of music, for example, often goes beyond the music itself, to gaining expertise in the biography of the performer(s) and the various influences on the development of their music, to buying memorabilia associated with the performer(s), to attending concerts. That personal investment in the cultural products of choice symbolically acquired during their formative years reflects 'an expression of a certain way of being in the world' (Grenfell, 2008: 160). The certain way of being in the world is not uniform across one's life. Childhood and youth – as sites of experimentation and novelty – ensure that the commitment to the rules of the game, the *illusio* (Bourdieu, 1996: 231), is more deeply felt because of the transitional nature of adolescence, in particular, as cultural forms are encountered and embodied. The way that this cultural capital is acquired most strongly influences how it is incorporated. Cultural capital acquired in childhood and youth is 'marked by its earliest conditions of acquisition which, through the more or less visible marks they leave' (Bourdieu, 1986: 83).

Originally a Spanish term for affection, *aficionado*[7] has entered the lexicon to represent not just the notion of fandom but also to signal a level of expertise in the person's chosen subject. Implicit in any understanding of the term is the attendant authority conferred on the aficionado by the knowledge and expertise embodied in their persona. In a previous era, they may be an 'authority' on the music of the Beatles or the Rolling Stones, or on Surf music or the films of John Hughes. The symbolic aspect of these acquisitions, the authority gained, reflects the importance of those earliest aesthetic and knowledge acquisitions. This authority forms a deeply rooted underpinning for the status that embodied capital occupies when accessed and acquired during the formative years. Acquired cultural capital, symbolically embodied and privileged by the initial conditions of acquisition, does not, of itself, create the conditions for moral panic towards ensuing youth generations. What is required for that moral panic to emerge, resonate and manifest itself is the need for a shared experience of cultural experiences and texts by each generation. Each generation, as they reach adulthood, not only privileges their youth experience but embodies a conviction that theirs is a shared *generational* youth experience.

For Bourdieu, misrecognition can be applied by those in one class towards those in another, deliberately or not. Class awareness can be both conscious and unconscious and is fundamentally a relationship between members of a particular class and between members of one class and another:

> Social class is not defined by a property ... nor by a collection of properties ... nor even by a chain of properties but by the structure of relations between all the pertinent properties which gives its specific value to each of them and to the effects they exert on practices.
> (Bourdieu, 1984: 105)

The *specific value* applied to the relations between properties is how one might define taste. If 'taste classifies, and it classifies the classifier', then the specific value(s) that we apply to properties provides the hierarchical structure to permit that classification to be undertaken. And the specific value one applies to oneself will always be greater than that applied to others: someone else's taste can only be measured by comparison with ours. If I deem someone else's taste as inauthentic, I can only do so if my 'authentic taste' is the value by which I can assess and judge that inauthenticity. 'Taste' and 'specific value' form a basis for class distinction. What distinguishes one class from another are the specific mores inherent in each class. One has a sense of comfort within a class, and the cultural capital accrued and understood by each class determines how other members of the class and members of other classes are understood. Cultural capital confers understandings and 'truths' upon members; they understand the rules of the game, and importantly, those 'truths' confer qualitative judgements upon those not part of a class. And this conferring operates for each class to the point that those from a 'lower class' will eschew the trappings of 'upper class' cultural capital:

> What makes the petit-bourgeois relation to culture and its capacity to make 'middle-brow' whatever it touches . . . is not its 'nature' but the very

position of the petit bourgeois in social space, the social nature of the petit bourgeois. It is ... the fact that legitimate culture is not made for him [sic] (and is often made against him), so that he is not made for it; and that it ceases to be what it is as soon as he appropriates it.

(Bourdieu, 1984: 327)

Bourdieu applies the concept of 'taste' to notions of class. But the concept of 'taste', 'specific value' and particularly the 'sense of one's place' can also be applied to generational understandings and relations. This is not to deny 'class' as a distinguishing feature. Obviously, there are class differences within each generation. But each generation has shared their youth experiences within a specific timeframe – experiences that most, if not all, members of that generation share as part of the process of growing up within Mannheim's defined temporal structure. And it is these shared experiences that serve to traverse class barriers.

In many other ways, class remains a distinguishing feature of each person's habitus and the social world they inhabit. But it is their shared youth experience –whether it be radio playlists, or cult films, or video games, or fashion statements – and all the other manifestations of youth cultural forms, which draw otherwise disparate groups and individuals together. In the nomenclature of chaos theory, this drawing together of disparate entities is referred to as a 'strange attractor' (Ruelle and Takens, 1971). A common youth cultural experience acts as a generational strange attractor.

An analogy can be drawn between shared generational experiences and Mannheim's example of returned soldiers from a major war. Those soldiers will have been drawn from across class boundaries. Prior to enlistment, they may not have had a great deal in common when it comes to issues of class. But they will have shared the experience of war. Although each of their experiences will have been different in terms of theatres of war served in, and severity or otherwise of combat, nevertheless they each have a common experience which sets them apart from those who have not served. It is a point of contact and of differentiation which is specific in time. It is both formalised and informal as experiences are shared, commented upon and remembered. So it is with shared youth generational experiences. For Baby Boomers, the Beatles, Rolling Stones, Easy Rider, 'rock and roll' would be, among a host of other shared experiences, familiar and instantly recognisable. But each Baby Boomer would have varying degrees of knowledge, understandings and even expertise. Individual musical and other cultural preferences create a myriad of associations and group memberships. Nevertheless, the wider youth cultural expression, on radio, TV, magazines and in day-to-day conversations, binds the members of each generation together. For many Baby Boomers, for example, the Beatles and Rolling Stones were an either/or – one was a Beatles fan or a Rolling Stones fan, rarely both (and obviously many were neither). But it is inconceivable for a Beatles aficionado to be unaware of at least the radio playlist of the Rolling Stones and vice versa; and it is equally inconceivable that fans of neither would be unaware of each. This applies for each generation; films like *The Breakfast Club* and *Ferris Bueller's Day Off*, for example, might be examples from Gen X.

In the 1970s, the Centre for Contemporary Cultural Studies attempted to reflect individual and class concerns via the concept of 'subculture' (Hall and Jefferson, 1976; Hebdige, 1979, 2012). Researchers posited distinct demarcations between and among subcultures. However, in terms of the 'real world' that young people inhabit, subcultural descriptions are rigid in their application and difficult to analyse objectively. Bennett's concept of *neo-tribes* (1999) has emerged as an alternative to subcultural theory because, as Bennet points out, our lifestyle is 'a freely chosen game' (607). Bennett observed that young people's stylistic commitments are not rigid, not consistently orderly. Indeed they are volatile, unpredictable, representing constantly reshuffled and reshuffling cultural associations and linkages. They represent likes and dislikes, interests and loyalties. They rearrange and meld, break apart and re-align, as each new experience is incorporated and subsumed.

Each young person growing up is surrounded by a plethora of influences: media in all forms, interaction with other young people, shared educational experiences, hobbies, sports, varying arts practices, films seen, and concerts attended, and even their parents' musical playlists. They do not undertake their *libido sciendi* in a vacuum oblivious to other cultural pursuits undertaken by their peers and others of their generation. Each young person in a generation is, to varying degrees, aware of and part of the *zeitgeist* of the age, and those myriad experiences bind them together. This parallels Bourdieu's common style that links those within a social class. Common style, or at least common cultural reference points, are common not just to class but to a period where the habitus embodies what becomes, as they age, each person's 'personal style' (interests, investments, acquired cultural capital). And this personal style exists in concert with the style of a period. Members of a particular generation operate at several levels and are shaped and influenced by a number of factors reflected in their 'personal style'. They are also reflected in their social embodiment, represented by their membership of a particular class, gender, race and sexuality, as well as their particular generation corresponding to their youth. It is this shared generational experience which permits each generation to view the generational experience of subsequent generations as failing to live up to the standards that they set – and by not living up to their standards, to take on the role of *folk devils* (Cohen, 2002; see also Bauman, 2012).

Generational Folk Devils and Moral Entrepreneurs

Central to Cohen's theory of moral panic are the 'perpetrators', the folk devils – those 'visible reminders of what we should not be' (2). It is the 'that which should not be' aspect of young people which characterises them as folk devils. Their seeming inability to measure up to the standards adults set for them sets them apart and ensures that each new youth generation will take on the mantle (collectively) of folk devil. The stereotype of the folk devil is 'a suitable screen upon which society can project sentiments of guilt and ambivalence' (Garland, 2008: 11).

In the preface to the 3rd edition of his landmark book, Cohen (2002: viii–xii) identifies seven clusters of social identity that characterise moral panics: young working class violent males; school violence; drugs; child abuse; sex and violence; welfare cheats and asylum seekers. Six of these seven clusters directly involve young people in some way. Moral panics most often involve short-term 'crises' which gain attention and then fade, only to be followed by the next moral panic. They are transitory, erupting, flaring briefly, and then subsiding. Although short-term volatility is the template for most moral panics, as Goode and Ben-Yehudas point out, some moral panics can become *routinised* or *institutionalised* (Goode and Ben-Yehuda, 2006) and can continue over a period of time. In this way, adult misrecognition of ensuing youth generations has become institutionalised.

Implicit in the idea of moral panic is the discourse of fear: fear of a menace to public order as represented by the 'other', the outsider, what Altheide refers to as the 'non-member' (2009). Goode and Ben-Yehuda (2006) list five crucial elements essential to any moral panic: concern, hostility, consensus, disproportionality and volatility. Garland (2008:11) offers two more: the moral dimension of the social reaction to the menace; and that the identified deviance is symptomatic of a wider problem.

Generational folk devils rely for their status upon the elements of concern, consensus, disproportionality, and, importantly, that the deviance is symptomatic of a wider societal concern. Generally, folk devils are deemed to be subgroups within society at odds with societal norms (Teddy boys, punks, African gangs). These subcultural deviants exist outside the social world that the rest of the community function within and thus threaten the equilibrium of the wider community. Generational folk devils represent not just a subculture or neo-tribe but the entirety of a generation. The entire following generation, symptomatic of the age cohort as a whole, threatens the authenticity and the authority of current adult generations. But it is not just the behaviour *per se* that threatens. It is the reliance of succeeding generations upon a whole new set of grounded aesthetics, with which they have made meanings, which is the threat. Ensuing generations claiming to have engaged with cultural forms that purport to be the genuine article, the apogee of youth cultural forms, defies adult 'common sense', defies the primordial consensus. How can young people from following generations make this claim? How can young people not recognise the authenticity of the youth cultural forms from the adult's generation? This cannot be. Adults, observing the ensuing generation from the complacent convenience of the authority of adulthood, know with absolute certainty of the absolute authenticity of **their** cultural forms. These are cultural forms which they have embodied, and which they have used to make meanings in **their** lives. Adults arrive at the incontrovertible conclusion that the youth cultural experiences of ensuing generations cannot, and will not, measure up. It is common sense. 'Everyone knows that'![18]

The focus for this misrecognition of following generations and the *suitable screen* upon which to focus their misrecognition are the outward manifestations of that generation's aesthetic preferences. Misrecognising the musical and cultural preferences of previous generations serves to validate the aesthetic preferences of the adult. The 'taken for granted' (Bourdieu, 1989: 18) legitimacy of the adult's youth cultural experience is unquestioned. It is truth. To dissent from that truth demonstrates the deviance of the dissenters. The only response to the 'deviance' of the ensuing generations not recognising the authenticity of the adult's aesthetic judgements is misrecognition. And because this 'deviance' afflicts the entire generation, the entire generation is misrecognised. Measures taken to deal with this 'threat' need to be taken against the entire generation. In the focus groups and interviews for this book, adult misrecognition was particularly focussed on Millennials' inability to commit, their obsession with mobile phones and, their profligacy (Howe and Strauss, 191). I will explore this in detail in later chapters.

Misrecognition of ensuing youth generations is made more complex by the concerns of adults throughout history that young people are at a vulnerable stage of their lives and need protecting and insulating from the ravages of the wider world. These adult apprehensions increase commensurate with their awareness of young people's attendant predilection for experimentation and risk-taking. Often with a nod to their own tentative adolescent peccadilloes, parental and other adult anxiety is often palpable at the potential risk of harm from alcohol and other drugs, sexual experimentation and declining moral standards (Eckersley, 1988)[9].

So the generational folk devil is coexistent, indeed often cohabits, with the naive, vulnerable young person at risk. The generational folk devil is up to no good, seeking to tear down the edifice of the cultural values of their parents' generation, and simultaneously susceptible to harm caused by their vulnerabilities and their naivete while navigating the pitfalls of transitioning to adulthood. The young person both fails to measure up to the standards set by adults and simultaneously requires protection from the menace of the world that their parents and other adults control.

Since World War II, the rise of consumer culture and the role that youth cultural forms play as the engine room of popular culture has served to fuel ongoing moral panics about young people. Adult fear of and simultaneous denigration of young people occurs within the milieu of the wider cultural context. The emergence of the 'rock and roll generation' in the 1950s signalled the advent of these ongoing concerns. A range of critics have assumed the role of *moral entrepreneurs* (Becker, 1963). Moral entrepreneurs include media personalities, politicians and prominent 'citizens' who promote the danger presented by certain deviant elements in society to that society and who should be 'forced to do what's right' (Goode & Ben-Yehuda, 2006: 80). In Chapter 8, I will explore how a group of moral entrepreneurs that

I collectively label as 'futurists', prominent among whom is futurist Simon Sinek, have chosen to 'crusade' against the emergence of the Millennial generation. Of particular note in these crusades is the place that mobile phones hold as representative of the dilettantism of the Millennial generation. The mobile phone represents in one ubiquitous talisman: all that is awry with the Millennial generation. The mobile phone brings into sharp relief those twin adult concerns regarding Millennials: the decline in standards of youth cultural forms and their mastery of a device that they have taken to and manage as *digital natives* (Prensky, 2001, 2005, 2008). But it would appear that it has always been thus. Critic John Aldridge, writing in the 1970s, pulls no punches in his derision:

> In ordinary circumstances, when they are not operating as a Tartar horde, the great majority of the young seem to be creatures of remarkably flaccid personality. One senses in them a singular blandness, even temperamental nullity … . Clearly, the young are suffering from a massive dissociation of sensibility, a loss of relationship with the living realities of the world.
> (Aldridge, 1970: 63)

Clearly Aldridge is not prone to understatement. What is interesting about his criticism is that the generation he criticises is the 'boomer' generation, the generation that now sits in judgement of the superfluity and frivolous behaviour of Millennials in particular.

The Don Quixote Effect

The process of ageing increasingly creates a dislocation between an individual's habitus, the accumulated and integrated cultural capital acquired during one's youth, and their interaction with the social world. As a young person ages and matures into adulthood, the dissonance between their habitus and the social space(s) they inhabit can increase. Since their lived experience is anchored in 'coexistence of points of view' (Bourdieu, 2000: 183) with those around them, as they age, those shared points of view tend to diverge from those of ensuing generations.

Bourdieu explains 'Social space' as the arena of 'different and competing' (183) fields. As they age, adults move out of certain fields and into other fields as they accrue economic and other forms of capital. Each individual has, at various times in their life, a 'sense of one's place' (184), and this sense of place evolves with the ageing process. When young, an individual finds themselves in competition not only with their peers but also with their elders who hold positions of power denied to them. A sense of place evolves as they assume more and more power. They compete with, and eventually win against, their elders – in the process gaining increasing amounts of economic, social and cultural capital.

This has been the trajectory of Baby Boomers. As young people, they competed with their elders, yet over time they accrued the necessary capital to achieve their current status and authority. However, the ageing process carries with it the seeds of their own superseding, as those younger than them seek, as they themselves did, to dethrone their elders. This sequence of the hunter becoming the hunted is a continuous process and functions as each new generation moves from their teenagehood to adulthood, to middle age and old age.

Because the social space is a scene of competition, the process of conflict between generations is two-way. As Davis has pointed out in *Gangland* (1997), the Baby Boomer generation has vigorously resisted relinquishing power and status. The dynamic of this process sees adults 'hanging on' rather than actively pursuing new opportunities. The 'lag between opportunities and the dispositions to grasp them' (Bourdieu, 1977: 83) causes them to take an increasingly closed view of the world. Ageing adults fail to comprehend and take advantage of emerging potentials presented by field change as a result of the passage of time.

This is particularly the case in the field of popular culture. Popular culture changes and evolves but in most cases, Baby Boomers have failed to progress with it. Moreover, as fields change, a process of ossification of their habitus and doxa precludes them from grasping emerging options and recourses that arise and are presented to them. This failure to 'move with the times' places them increasingly at odds with ensuing generations who recognise, grasp and occupy new opportunities. These ensuing generations, in turn, become the evolving new 'engine' driving change. Like *Don Quixote* and *the knights errant* (Bourdieu, 2000: 160), the adult generation is effectively bypassed by aspects of popular culture. They find a disconnect between their 'remembered' past and the reality of the present as represented by an ever-evolving popular culture engaged with by their children and grandchildren – this is the 'Don Quixote' effect.

Negative responses to this process of dislocation of social space generate misrecognition of the cultural practice of younger generations and, by extension, their behaviour and customs. Like Billy Pilgrim in the novel *Slaughterhouse Five* (Vonnegut, 1969), adults become 'lost in time'. They live in the 'present' but the present is 'created' via the past, with understandings acquired and 'hard-wired' as part of their habitus. Bourdieu calls this the 'garment' (2000: 143) of their habitus and this garment in turn enshrouds them, permitting the development of a 'collective faith in the universal' (192): the perception that their doxa privileges their individual and collective understandings when compared to younger generations. The universal they place their faith in, the credo which is at the centre of their belief, is their certainty of the authenticity of their youth cultural experience. Chapter 3 examines the process of growing up and the in-between status of young people, and how the alchemy of consecration makes holy each young person's youth experience.

Notes

1 Hartley, L. P. (1953). *The Go-Between*. H. Hamilton.
2 This disparity of power and authority between young people and adults does not deny the extant disparity of power that exists between adults, differentiated by class, race, gender, sexuality and so on.
3 Eighteen years in most western countries.
4 Working for the Man. See Orbison, R. (1964). *More of Roy Orbison's Greatest Hits*. Washington D. C., Monument. Products.
5 Loudon Wainwright III extends this label to those who come under the category of 'never was': 'At least you've been a has-been; And not just a never-was'. Wainwright III, L. *The Home Stretch*. So Damn Happy. 16. Sanctuary 2003. www.lw3.com/album/so-damn-happy-live
6 John Strausbaughs (2001) categorisation of septuagenarian Mick Jagger performing as part of a world tour as 'colostomy rock' does place this phenomenon of aged rockers in perspective.
7 www.merriam-webster.com/dictionary/aficionado   www.bustle.com/articles/144396-where-did-the-word-fandom-come-from-behind-the-term-that-changed-the-internet-forever
8 While undertaking the research for this study, I would engage with colleagues and friends about my research. I developed a shorthand summary to, in a semi-mocking style, summarise my research: 'young people are not as engaged as us, they're not as committed as us; and above all, their music isn't as good as ours'. To a person, my Gen X and Boomer friends and colleagues would respond only half-jokingly: 'That's a given. Of course it's not'.
9 Australian Researcher, Richard Eckersley, has written extensively (and many might argue from the perspective of a moral crusader) of the need for adults to more carefully look to the moral guidance of young people by adults. See Eckersley, R. (2005). Well & Good: Morality, meaning and happiness, 2nd ed. Text, Melbourne; Eckersley, R. (ed) (1998). Measuring Progress: Is life getting better? CSIRO Publishing, Melbourne.

Bibliography

Aldridge, J. (1970). *In the Country of the Young*. New York: Harper Collins.
Altheide, D. (2009). Moral Panic: From Sociological Concept to Public Discourse. *Crime Media Culture*, 5(1), 79–99.
Bauman, Z. (2012). *On Education: Conversations with Ricardo Mazzeo*. Cambridge: Polity Press.
Baumrind, D. (1967). Child Care Practices Anteceding Three Patterns of Preschool Behavior. *Genetic Psychology Monographs*, 75, 43–88.
Baumrind, D. (1971). Current Patterns of Parental Authority. *Developmental Psychology*, 4,(1, Pt. 2), 1–103.
Baumrind, D. (1978). Parental Disciplinary Patterns and Social Competence in Children. *Youth & Society*, 9(3), 238–76.
Becker, H. (1963). *Outsiders: Studies in the Sociology of Deviance*. New York: Free Press.
Bennett, A. (1999). Subcultures or Neo-Tribes? Rethinking the Relationship between Youth, Style and Musical Taste. *Sociology*, 33(3), 599–617.

Bessant, J. (2008). Hard Wired for Risk: Neurological Science, 'the Adolescent Brain' and Developmental Theory. *Journal of Youth Studies*, 11(3), 347–360.

Blaikie, A. (1999). *Ageing and Popular Culture*. Cambridge, UK; New York: Cambridge University Press.

Bourdieu, P. (1977). *Outline of a Theory of Practice*, R. Nice (trans.). Cambridge: Cambridge University Press.

Bourdieu, P. (1984). *Distinction: A Social Critique of the Judgement of Taste*. London: Routledge & Kegan Paul.

Bourdieu, P. (1985). The Social Space and the Genesis of Groups. *Theory and Society*, 14(6), 723–744.

Bourdieu, P. (1986). The Forms of Capital, in J. Richardson (Ed.), *Handbook of Theory and Research for the Sociology of Education*, pp. 241–258. New York: Greenwood.

Bourdieu, P. (1988). *Homo Academicus*. Cambridge: Polity.

Bourdieu, P. (1989). Social Space and Symbolic Power. *Sociological Theory*, 7(1), 14–25.

Bourdieu, P. (1990a). *The Logic of Practice*, R. Nice (trans.). Cambridge: Polity.

Bourdieu, P. (1990b). *In Other Words: Essays towards a Reflexive Sociology*. Stanford: Stanford University Press.

Bourdieu, P. (1990c). The Scholastic Point of View. *Cultural Anthropology*, 5(4), 380–391.

Bourdieu, P. (1993). *Sociology in Question*. London; Thousand Oaks, CA: Sage.

Bourdieu P. (1996). *The Rules of Art: Genesis and Structure of the Literary Field*, S. Emmanuel (trans.). Oxford: Polity Press.

Bourdieu, P. (2000). *Pascalian Meditations*. Stanford: Stanford University Press.

Bourdieu, P. (2005). *The Social Structures of the Economy*. Cambridge: Polity.

Bourdieu, P. (2010). *Distinction: A Social Critique of the Judgement of Taste*. London: Taylor and Francis.

Bourdieu, P., Darbel, A., and Schnapper, D. (1990) [1966]. *The Love of Art: European Art Museums and Their Public*, C. Beattie and N. Merriman (trans.). Cambridge: Polity Press.

Bourdieu, P., and Wacquant, L. (1992). *An Invitation to Reflexive Sociology*. Chicago, IL: University of Chicago.

Chaney, D. (1996). *Lifestyles*. London: Routledge.

Cohen, S. (2002). *Folk Devils and Moral Panics: The Creation of the Mods and Rockers* (New ed.). London; New York: Routledge.

De Nora, T. (2000). *Music in Everyday Life*. Cambridge: Cambridge University Press.

Eckersley, R. (Ed.). (1998). *Measuring Progress: Is Life Getting Better?* CSIRO Publishing: Melbourne.

Eckersley, R. (2005). *Well & Good: Morality, Meaning and Happiness* (2nd ed.). Melbourne: Text Publishing.

Eckersley, R., and Australian Commission for the Future. (1988). *Casualties of Change, the Predicament of Youth in Australia: An Analysis of the Social and Psychological Problems Faced by Young People in Australia*. Canberra: Australian Government Service for Commission for the Future.

Evans, K. (2007). Concepts of Bounded Agency in Education, Work, and the Personal Lives of Young Adults. *International Journal of Psychology*, 42(2), 85–93.

Eyerman, R., and Turner, B. S. (1998). Outline of a Theory of Generations. *European Journal of Social Theory*, 1(1), 91–106.

Flavell, J. H. (1976). Metacognitive Aspects of Problem Solving, in L. B. Resnick (Ed.), *The Nature of Intelligence*, pp. 231–235. Hillsdale, NJ: Earlbaum.
Flavell, J. H. (1979). Metacognition and Cognitive Monitoring. A New Area of Cognitive-Development Inquiry. *American Psychologist*, 34(10), 906–911.
Garland, D. (2008). On the Concept of Moral Panic. *Crime, Media Culture*, 4(9), 9–30.
Gennep, A., Caffee, G. L., and Vizedom, M. B. (1961). *The Rites of Passage*. Chicago: University of Chicago Press.
Goode, E., and Ben-Yehuda, N. (2006). *Moral Panics: The Social Construction of Deviance*. Cambridge, MA: Blackwell.
Grenfell, M. (2008). *Pierre Bourdieu: Key Concepts*. Stocksfield, UK: Acumen.
Hall, S., and Jefferson, T. (Eds.). (1976). *Resistance through Rituals: Youth Subcultures in Post-War Britain*. London: Hutchinson.
Hartley, L. P. (1953). *The Go-Between*. London: H. Hamilton.
Hebdige, D. (1979). *Subculture, the Meaning of Style*. London: Methuen.
Hebdige, D. (2012). Contemporizing 'Subculture': 30 years to Life. *European Journal of Cultural Studies*, 15(3), 399–424.
Hegel, G. W. F., Miller, A. V., Findlay, J. N., and Hoffmeister, J. (1979). *Phenomenology of Spirit*. Oxford: Clarendon Press.
Irwin, C. E., Jr., and Millstein, S. G. (1986). Biopsychosocial Correlates of Risk-taking Behaviors during Adolescence. *Journal of Adolescent Health Care*, 7(6 suppl), 82S–96S.
Laupa, M., and Turiel, E. (1986). Children's Conceptions of Adult and Peer Authority. *Child Development*, 57(20), 405–412.
Mannheim, K. (1952). The Problem of Generations, in P. Kecksmeti (Ed.), *Karl Mannheim: Essays*, pp. 276–322. London: Routledge.
Orbison, R. (1964). *More of Roy Orbison's Greatest Hits*. Washington DC: Monument Products.
Piaget, J. (1972). Intellectual Evolution from Adolescence to Adulthood. *Human Development*, 15, 1–12.
Prensky, M. (2001). Digital Natives, Digital Immigrants Part 1. *On the Horizon*, 9(5), 1–6.
Prensky, M. (2005). Listen to the Natives. *Educational Leadership*, 63(4), 8–13.
Prensky, M. (2008). Digital Natives, Digital Immigrants Part 1. *British Journal of Educational Technology*, 39(5), 775–786.
Ruelle, D., and Takens, F. (1971). On the Nature of Turbulence. *Communications in Mathematical Physics*, 20(3), 167–192.
Straughsbaugh, J. (2001, 13 August). Unplug the oldies – for good. *The Guardian*. Retrieved from www.theguardian.com/theobserver/2001/aug/12/featuresreview.review
Tonkin, R. S. (1987). Adolescent risk-taking behavior. *Journal Adolescent Health Care*, 8(2), 213–220.
Vonnegut, K. (1969). *Slaughterhouse-Five*. New York: Bantam Doubleday Dell.
Wainwright III, L. *The Home Stretch*. So Damn Happy. 16. Sanctuary 2003. www.lw3.com/album/so-damn-happy-live

Willis, P. E. (1977). *Learning to Labour: How Working Class Kids get Working Class Jobs*. Farnborough: Saxon House.
Willis, P. E. (1990). *Common Culture: Symbolic Work at Play in the Everyday Cultures of the Young*. Milton Keynes: Open University Press.
Zuckerman, M. (1979). *Sensation Seeking: Beyond the Optimal Level of Arousal*. Hillsdale, NJ: Erlbaum.

3 Growing Up

Youth Is a Disease From Which We All Recover.

(Dorothy Fuldheim)[1]

In-Betweenness, Adulthood and Grounded Aesthetics

The notion of youth, artificially constructed as a demographic categorisation, exists in a kind of nether world. No longer child, not yet adult, its status is ambiguous, seemingly always betwixt and between, amorphous – existing with the burden of the carryover of many of the residual restrictions and constraints of childhood, yet not quite attaining the autonomy and privilege of adulthood. In any event, as Dorothy Fuldheim notes, our youth will pass and eventually adulthood will descend upon us all. Recovery however is a moot point.

The relationship between young people and adults has always been fraught. Young people it would appear have always been at loggerheads with their elders.[2] As the desire to slip the bonds of childhood (as they leave their childhood behind them), they come into increasing conflict with adult desires to constrain and restrict the burgeoning independence of young people in their care. As we have seen, young people have been very prominent in discourses of moral panic along with wider discourses, outlining fears and concerns with regard to young people. Adult concerns centre on fears for and of young people – at risk of 'harm' and needing to be protected; and whose deviance from 'normal' behaviour standards threatens to put the equilibrium of ordered society at risk. Discourses emerging from these fears focus on the belief on the part of the adults that they know better than the young people themselves. They know what is the behaviour most appropriate to young people. Internalising these concerns and fears results in a pattern of misrecognition built around sets of active social processes that anchor taken-for-granted assumptions into the realm of social life.

DOI: 10.4324/9781003427476-3

Each individual, as part of a life trajectory, passes through a youth stage in their transition to adulthood. Each has to negotiate a maze of individual and societal learning experiences, and engage with, and pass through, a series of formal and informal 'rites of passage' which exist as signposts on their journey to adulthood. Each individual arrives at adulthood with accumulated and embodied learnings and understandings from their youth stage. This journey has as its end-point becoming an adult. This is the destination, and while notions of 'finished' are contentious, nevertheless, the significance of the youth stage in terms of 'getting there' reflects the hallmark role of the adult 'destination' in the life of each person.

Young people represent the liminal age demographic in between childhood and adulthood. Furlong (2013) has labelled it as 'intermediary' status between child and adult. Difficult to define, Tyyska (2016) has fittingly described it as 'elastic', its malleability ranging across varying timeframes and life experiences. In any event, it has no existence beyond the demographic framing that we have applied to it. And its meaning is very much determined from where one sits. Young people's concept of their teenagehood will differ markedly from many adults' concept.

The contemporary category of youth emerged following the post-second-world-war boom and the growth of consumerist society. The newly constituted research area of Cultural Studies sought to explore this 'in-betweenness' of youth. In particular, it sought to analyse the manner in which that 'in-betweenness informs both the way that young people function during this period of their lives and the way that they are perceived by adults. As young people mature, conflict emerges from the competing interests of the adults and young people centred on the young people flexing their 'newly independent muscles' as parental controls are loosened. At the same time, young people are exercising their newly acquired capacity for metacognition. Increasing independence, growing engagement with their cultural products of choice, and the capacity to be able to see themselves and their place within the world are the ingredients tailor-made for engendering experimentation and risk-taking.

What distinguishes young people from other generations is the relationship they enjoy with the cultural forms which constitute a central part of their lives. From the 1950s onwards, youth cultural forms served to distinguish young people from their parents and other adults. Hall and Jefferson's foundation work centred on the analysis of the way that young people interacted with cultural forms linking the interaction with cultural forms with subcultural resistance to dominant ideologies. Since the 1960s, academic interest in young people has increased substantially, with *Youth Studies* establishing itself as a sub-genre of sociology.

Increasing levels of risk-taking and experimentation serve to heighten adult concerns regarding young people's safety. Legal transition points (age of consent, drivers licence, legal alcohol consumption, right to vote) and informal rites of passage (unfettered alcohol and other drug use, and sexual experimentation) act as landmarks to adulthood, often outside of the knowledge and/or control of adult carers. It is these unconstrained and often secretive informal rites of passage which generate adult concern leading to parental attempts at restraining this freedom. As young people push the boundaries, already relaxed constraints may be re-imposed as the young people and their parents/adults participate in what often seems like the daily variation on the: 'you can't', 'why not?' 'because I said so' back and forth 'tango' as part of the ongoing adult/young person standoff. Outbursts of chagrin erupt as young people storm off to their bedrooms, or to hanging out with friends on the phone or online because, from their perspective, parents/adults have yet again forbidden them from doing just a straightforward part of their daily life. Faulkner's identification of 'play' as a site of anxiety for adults exemplifies how young people's experimentation and engagement with cultural products feeds into adult anxieties about young people's increasing autonomy.

Play is a central characteristic of young people's progression to adulthood. 'Play' is the arena where they engage with cultural products that assist in making sense of their world. This engagement is made more potent by the combination of hormonal and intellectual development that accompanies the onset of puberty. With this engagement, young people are able to determine their likes and dislikes. This is the process of grounded aesthetics – deeply felt and fondly remembered which serves to privilege those experiences. Music and other cultural preferences, acquired and embodied, take on a position of eminence, a cachet of quality, of specialness. Those privileged experiences and the memory of them form the foundation for authenticating those privileged experiences as singularly legitimate, singularly without peer. It is the authentication of these experiences as the apogee of youth cultural expression, uniquely unable to be replicated, which then becomes the basis for misrecognising the cultural forms and the young people of ensuing generations.

Generations and *Zeitgeist*

The concept of a generation, artificially constructed, is fashioned around a demographic cohort who are born and grow up within a specific timeframe of shared experiences of social conditions and subjectivities. The informants for this publication across all age ranges were very conscious of the zeitgeist of their generation. Many of them would recount aspects of their youth involving shared experiences. There were frequent references to 'you' and 'we' as in 'you would rush home to catch Top of the Pops' (Melissa, 65). These shared collective understandings signalled that, although the teenage years can be fraught with disappointments, feelings of rejection, self-doubt and even self-loathing, they are also populated by shared moments of delight and wonder at the 'newness' of the experiences. These 'distinctive generational subjectivities' (Woodman and Wyn, 2015: 1403), acquired individually and collectively, are understood viscerally as the members of any generational cohort enter and live through an epoch at the same time. Each member of a generation gains a sense of 'shared solidarity' and a shared popular memory (Brabazon, 2005), which Bourdieu (2000: 95) translates as a 'force of custom'.

Engagement with the cultural forms of the zeitgeist occurs both singularly and collectively. This force of custom transforms collective experiences of struggles and historical and political events into what Schwartz (1996) refers to as a 'collective memory'. These memories are populated with identities, the leading 'characters and ideologists' (Eyerman and Turner, 2005: 97) of that generation. The embodied 'cultural dispositions' (dress, jargon, emblems) form the 'language' of each successive generation, contributing to the grammar of the generational language. This language is instantly recognisable and understood by the generational cohort. It forms the basis for countless conversations as experiences and anecdotes are shared. Preferences in dance, movies, TV shows, and the music of a generation are mulled over, examined, reviewed, marvelled at, and sometimes even fought over – communally in the playground, in bedrooms, on the phone and (latterly) online. Melissa's example of shared joy at watching Top of The Pops on television perfectly exemplifies this. In this way, the experiences of young people of a social generation are embodied both at an individual level and collectively as part of the generational cohort.

Authenticity, Status and Memory

Participant consciousness of the zeitgeist shared by each generation was apparent throughout the discourse for this publication. They were very aware of where and how they fit into their 'era'. For adult informants, they were aware of the symbolic capital that framed the authenticity of their youth experience which in turn feeds into their sense of higher status as a 'finished' adult human being. It does so because the embodied cultural capital of that youth experience is transmitted and transformed by the process of memory into their privileged status permitting them to deride and look down upon younger people. It is the authority of transitioning to adulthood which coalesces with the authenticity of their youth cultural experience, to confer upon them the status of adulthood. That authority comes with its own expectations, chief among which is *deference* (Goffman, 1961). The alchemy of consecration that accompanies the transition to adulthood reverses the relationship of deference. Having spent their childhood and youth deferring to adults, the newly arrived adult now finds themselves expecting, even demanding, to be deferred to by younger people. Teacher Pauline (49) laments the lack of respect and the failure of her students to show due deference to her as teacher: 'They just don't … I keep coming back to the word respect'. Her annoyance at that failure displays the process of generational misrecognition with which she engages. Deference, either the failure of young people to display it, or the unmet demand by adults that it be displayed towards them, is a touchstone characteristic of adult/youth intergenerational conflict.

This 'common sense' understanding of the legitimacy and authenticity of the adult informants' youth experience was repeated throughout the interviews and focus groups. Individually and collectively, the participants reflected upon their youth, and how the authenticity of those youth experiences serves to set them and their generational colleagues apart from generations that follow. These experiences exist as 'echoes' of their youth, captured in, given pride of place, and then reflected back to them as popular memory. As such, those memories 'live' within the present. As Brabazon proposes, the present is not, indeed cannot be, as interesting as the 'glorified past' (2005: 32) of their youth. The halcyon ideal of their youth cultural experience may or may not be true or may be exaggerated, or may be selective in its remembering. But the filter of popular memory vouchsafes the youth experience so that it does indeed become idealised. And the recollections via popular memory of that idealised youth serve to sanctify both the experience and, importantly, the memory of the experience.

Memory is an essential element in the process of adults misrecognising young people of ensuing generations. The alchemy of consecration, which has transformed those past experiences into memory, allows those memories to live in the present, influencing adult behaviour – whether it be embodied social and cultural capital, or the process of introjection and latching, or popular memory. The sanctity of those memories ensures that their legitimacy, their genuine authenticity, cannot be matched by the youth cultural experiences of ensuing generations. Theirs is the definitive youth experience. Claims to the contrary by succeeding youth generations are therefore patently false.

Walled Garden and Learning the Code

As part of the transition to adulthood, each youth generation must negotiate or (in many cases) break through the walled garden, which is the last vestige of their childhood that parents and adults impose upon them in order to keep them safe. The 16-year-old informants in this research illustrated very clearly this dilemma facing young people on the verge of adulthood. On the one hand, they know that parents and other adults are constantly 'anxious' about their safety and the (in many cases quite justified) fear that they will engage in risk-behaviour and experimentation with sex and illegal drugs. Simultaneously, they are aware of the adult-dominated fields in which they are forced to play, particularly family and education. When they venture into the social world of adults, they also engage in the field of power. For one group of 16-year-olds, the exemplar of this duality was the conflict inherent in adult attitudes towards Miley Cyrus – her sweet, innocent persona of the TV character Hannah Montana, and the raunch culture of her 'Wrecking Ball' music video in 2013 (see Levy, 2005; Zeisler, 2008;

Powell, 2015). The persona of Miley Cyrus allows us to see, in one distilled example, the misrecognition of young people by adults AND the walled garden of adult concerns for their children growing up. It is an illustration that encompassed the concerns of the 16-year-old informants, who were able to very clearly see through the inconsistencies and the hypocrisy of adult concerns for Cyrus' transformation: 'She's heaps grown up… wearing all the skimpy clothes' (Eliza, 16). For Eliza, what Cyrus has done is to 'become' her actual self. She has reclaimed (post Hannah Montana) what Kennedy refers to as her 'authentic self' (2014: 228). Hers is an authentic self derived from an 'attributed celebrity' (Rojek, 2001: 17–18), a celebrity that has been made noteworthy by the 'cultural intermediaries' (19) of the media. For Eliza and Gina, Hannah Montana was just acting. However, 'Heaps grown up' Miley is the genuine article. The Miley Cyrus exemplar is explored in detail in Chapter 6.

Whether it be the field of family or education (the two fields they occupy most often during the process of growing up), young people learn the codes they need to adopt in order to operate in the presence of adults. It is young people who need to make the adjustment, to incorporate into their habitus the capacity to be deferential and polite when in adult presence. If they don't, they know that sanctions will be imposed. The process of becoming an adult involves learning to play the game – to understand the relevant code. The cultural capital accruing to adulthood entitles one to enter into an 'ever-expanding in-group' (Tzanakis, 2011: 85) of adulthood which, in turn, increasingly entitles one to misrecognise those outside the in-group. For Gina and Eliza, the example of Hannah Montana/Miley Cyrus encapsulates how the behaviour codes of growing up work. As we shall see in later chapters, this lesson of how to 'behave' is all important.

The Adult Voice

The 'figures' (Threadgold, 2019) of young people very often incite negative responses among adults. This 'social abjection' (Tyler, 2013) derives from the accrued privileges of achieving adulthood which entitles the adult to sit in judgement of young people. The symbolic capital of knowledge, experience and sagacity acquired as part of the ageing process enables the adult to determine what does and does not function as 'notions of authenticity, coolness and distinction within subcultural fields' (Threadgold, 2015: 54). Adulthood confers the authority to sit in judgement with an apparent disinterested prerogative to do so – Bourdieu's 'double language of disinterest', and it is reflected in the common saying 'been there, done that'. It is the voice of experience. It is the voice of authority. It is the *Adult Voice*.

Upon arrival at adulthood, the achievement of maturity accrues to itself the authority and the capacity for discerning hierarchies of taste. Adults sitting in judgement of young people do so with the 'self-assurance' (Bourdieu, 2010: 85) residing in their newly conferred adult status. For the adult participants in this research, it was apparent that it was the double language of *generational* disinterest that they spoke with. This was most apparent when analysing their relationship with music. An individual's engagement with music serves to privilege not only the relationship but the circumstances under which the experience occurs. Introjection, grounded aesthetics and popular memory describe how this process functions. Secondary data explored in this research included examples of music selected from the youth experience of participants ranging across the age range of the participants, reflecting various musical eras and musical genres. Young people's increasing cognitive capacities combine with their burgeoning freedom to make special these interactions as embodied awareness.

The special place the youth musical experience occupies sanctions the privileging of that experience over the musical forms favoured by ensuing youth generations. This is the basis for much of the discourse encountered in the discussions with participants, which very much focussed on notions of 'decline' in quality of the music produced by and for ensuing generations. Notions of decline is explored in detail in Chapter 7, which examines specifically the role of music's hallowed status in the adult persona, a role which reflects each adult's youth as Brabazon's 'glorified past'. The shared generational latching echoes the musical zeitgeist of their generation uniting each generation as they pass through their youth to adulthood. This shared generational experience is the basis for the misrecognising of both the music of ensuing generations and those young people themselves. Misrecognition represents the 'intuitive' understanding of the superiority of their youth musical experiences over that of following generations. When adults encounter each other and the subject of music of ensuing generations arises, there is absolute consensus as to the superiority of the adult generation's musical tastes and experiences. And all that is required to justify this determination is the application of the double language of generational disinterest. It must be so because they've been there, done that. Theirs is the voice of experience – the Adult Voice. No further analysis is required.

Youth cultural forms are integral to a young person's sense of self. Willis cites the way young people engage actively in discussions about TV shows, or creatively arrange posters on their walls as examples of their engagement. Several participants referenced the arrangement of posters on the bedroom wall as a signature activity of their youth. Young people synthesise this engaged cultural experience as they progress from youth to adulthood, a synthesis intimately linked to the development of identity. Cultural forms are accessed, experimented with, retained, discarded, assumed and incorporated as part of an ongoing process of identity development. Bennett (2013) cites the critical role that music plays in the development of the young person, and how this in turn serves to shape the adult. This aesthetic engagement as a young person links a person's youth to their adult understanding. The participant responses in this research reflect a privileging of the youth aesthetic – that the cultural experiences of youth hold pride of place within the habitus. This is particularly the case as we have seen with Melissa above and Top Of The Pops. The members of her focus group echoed her nostalgia for their youth musical experiences. This privileging is particularly reflective of informant Pauline's experience where she reflected on the importance of lyrics and their meaning:

> That's how I was exposed to so many issues through music and the Cold War. It reminded me of the Sting song: 'I hope the Russians love their children too?' ... You know Midnight Oil ... Is there still that today? Is there still a lot of messaging, political and social comment through music?
> (Pauline, 49)

Music is a key driver for adults in their negative assessment of subsequent youth generations. Fred, 73 years old, referred to the later musical examples played as part of the secondary data as like 'Viking hordes' at the gate. His preference for the Beatles, Scott McKenzie and 'Les Mis' located not only his musical era but his musical preferences and, in particular, his repugnance at the music of younger generations – Viking hordes reflecting one of the more overt examples of symbolic violence.

Rock music since its inception has been an arena which has caused controversy and conflict between old and young. Martin and Segrave explored this conflict in detail, illuminating its metamorphosis as new and more subversive musical forms challenge and then are incorporated into the mainstream. Pattison (1987) pursued a similar theme but from the perspective of rock music within the romantic tradition. Davis (1997, 2010) has explored how Baby Boomers, having been on the receiving end in their adolescence, have clung on to power into their middle age and beyond. Tara Brabazon has drawn upon the concept of *popular memory* to amplify and explore these phenomena. Because our youthful experiences are lived at a higher intensity, later experiences often struggle to match them:

> That is the nature of popular memory: the present can never be as interesting, important or special as a glorified past.
> (2005: 32)

Although her focus is on Baby Boomers and Generation X, Brabazon's thesis applies to adulthood in general. She points to the role that memory plays in both the creation of the adult persona and the way the adult's ongoing and continued interaction with memory continues to make and re-make that adult's understanding of themselves. We do not proceed in an orderly fashion from childhood to old age. The process of aging is fraught, brittle, uneven in the intensity of experiences and in their duration. The journey is uncertain, fickle, subject to sudden and unseen changes and subject to intense highs and lows. It is this melange of experiences that coalesce into that which becomes our memories. And this coalescence is fraught with inaccuracies and misremembered experiences and events. But this integration of memories, right or wrong, accurate or inaccurate, starkly viewed in hindsight, or vaguely remembered frissons of experience and emotions, is also what we use to make meanings.

Music provides many of the signposts for popular memory around which remembered experiences swirl and mutate, as the intensity of youthful experiences is transformed, and as teenagehood evolves into adulthood. As Brabazon notes:

> While a song may be in the charts for weeks, it is located in the back catalogue for years and popular memory for decades.
> (2005: 75)

This is one of the fundamental aspects of the ageing process. As trite as this statement is, we do not age in a vacuum. Ours is an interconnected journey through life. Each new experience accumulates, melds with memories of previous experiences, and transforms into a kind of hybrid understanding: past and present combining and synthesising constantly, transforming memory reference points into newly understood 'reality'. Although memory reflects and channels the past, that past in all its remembered and misremembered glory exists in the present and carries with it all the ferocity and severity, the euphoria and pain, experienced as part of the journey through life. And it is the transition from childhood to adulthood, encountering the memories infused with the turmoil and upheavals, the elation and exhilaration of the teenage years that we embody and redeem on a daily basis from our saved internal 'metaphorical disc' (144) located in our back catalogue.

Essential to this understanding is that our youth does not cease at 18 years of age. It remains with us as part of a continuum. We are who we are as adults because of who we were as children and young people. And this process is not static but is constantly evolving as the adult 'child's' relationship with their teenage 'parent' mutates, with adulthood experiences impacting and affecting this relationship. This is what Brabazon means when she says that 'memory is not safe' (70) and it is an essential element for understanding adulthood. To fully understand what transpires as we transform from teenagers to adults, it is necessary to come to terms with the concept of loss: 'To study (post) youth necessitates an understanding of loss' (144).

Loss and grief have been subjects of academic interest for a number of years (Bonanno et al., 2002; Kübler-Ross, 1969). Although they posit different processes of grieving and loss, both Bonanno and Kubler-Ross acknowledge the need for individuals to undertake that process internally as each person deals with the trauma of loss. The post youth experience is marked by a sense of loss – of the vitality of youth and of the intensity of the youth experience. The sense of loss at the passing of that critical period is both understandable and palpable. New adult experiences are acquired, integrated and coalesced into the ever-developing persona of the adult. These newer memories are then synthesised with teenage memories – teenage memories made more complex by the sense of loss at the passing of that teenage experience.

That sense of loss is found in commentary about music, particularly that of commentators nurtured by the 'swinging sixties'. After all, youth cultures following on from the boomer experience were always going to be viewed and assessed by 'critics raised on Bob Dylan' (Brabazon, 2005: 123). As the beneficiaries of the post-war economic boom and the emergence of their own musical expression of rock and roll, the baby boomers became the 'rock and roll generation'. Not only can it be said that baby boomers propagated rock and roll, but it was also the generation that invented rock criticism. The Doyen of rock criticism *Rolling Stone* and complementary rock journals pioneered the advent of rock criticism and journalism (Hagan, 2017; Friedlander, 1996; Gillett, 1970). The credibility and legitimacy assigned to music of the Baby Boomers by critics from the same generation is a kind of self-perpetuating feedback loop. The music of the Baby Boomers was best. How do we know? Because Baby Boomer music critics have bestowed upon it the mantle of 'authentic'; endowed it with the imprimatur of the first of the youth generations to 'sow its oats', the first youth generation to 'seize the day', the first youth generation to rise up against their parents and question the status quo via the power of popular culture. And the mantle of authentic has been the gift of boomers to bestow upon the limited number of later 'serious acts' that in their authenticity echo the gravitas of boomer serious acts.[3] As Brabazon puts it:

> Affirming the credibility of Simple Minds, The Smiths and REM while dismissing the triviality of ABC, Scritti Politti and Rick Astley.
> (Brabazon, 2005: 69)

It is the sense of loss of credibility and demand for 'authenticity' which is at the heart of the moral panic experienced by adults as they view with disdain the music of generations following them. Because the generations that follow can never live up to the *a priori* genuineness of their own experience of music and popular culture 'back in the day'. The assumed authenticity of each generation's youth cultural experiences has become seamlessly embodied as 'common sense', what Bourdieu refers to as the 'conductorless orchestration' (Bourdieu, 1990: 59) that is part of the doxa of that generation. The 'rules of the game' ensure that any encounter with cultural products from ensuing youth generations will privilege adults' remembered youth cultural experience over that of ensuing youth generations.

Introjection

Popular music's metamorphosis into rock and roll in the 1950s signalled the arrival of young people as not only a serious market for all things popular culture but also of the way rock and roll and young people seemed indistinguishable from each other. Young people were rock and roll, and rock and roll was young people. The synergies between the two were unambiguous. Over a period of less than a decade what began as a fusion of jazz, boogie woogie, rhythm and blues and gospel (see Friedlander, 1996; Gillett, 1970; Hatch and Millward, 1987) transubstantiated into an entirely new genre – a genre which spoke to, of and about, the young people for whom it became a talisman, emblematic of their 'arrival' as a distinct and separate demographic entity.

As young people age and move into their teens, and as the parental and other adult reins are loosened, they find themselves gaining with each birthday more autonomy in their life choices – school subjects, friends, sporting engagements, social clubs and, importantly, their creative engagements with the arts. These engagements occur holistically, often spontaneously. As an activity is sampled, a musical style is heard and found interesting; a novel is read and the series behind the novel or other works by the author are searched out and explored; a film is seen and enjoyed and the director, or the star, or the filmic 'style' is then awaited for the next instalment. And all the while, these engagements are being discussed and argued about with friends in the playground, on the way to and from school and online. And alone in their bedroom, they are able to engage with their musical choices that find a conduit into their heart and their mind and their soul that mutate and transform their being by the sheer exhilaration of the experience. The totality of this embodiment process defies individual analysis. It is the ongoing and constant process of the creation and metamorphosis of the individual habitus.

The musical conduit into young peoples' hearts and minds and souls is via a process that Tia De Nora identifies as *self-programming* (2000: 49). It is part of the ongoing process of the way we order social existence. Self-programming is more than merely accumulation. It involves self-reflection around, and in response to, each new stimulus and each repeat hearing. And with each reflection comes greater understanding of themselves. With each engagement and reflection, the young person evolves and holds onto a greater understanding of self. This capacity to be able to proffer and perceive a coherent self-image De Nora describes as a process of *introjection* (62–63). The notion of self-concept is constantly being reinforced by the way memory functions to frame and re-frame that self-concept. Our concept of self is arrived at via our memories of who we were, and how the who we were has become part of the who we are now. And the driving force, the vehicle for this process, is memory. It is the memories of our engagement with cultural product, the process of latching and introjection that allows us to excavate past experiences and images in order to reflect ourselves to ourselves. Musical experiences from the past become like a series of continuous and evolving identity signposts as past melds with present into future. Echoing Willis, it is the identification with aesthetic commodities and products that serves to provide meanings. When combined with the memories of this engagement, this identification creates a nostalgia for moments in the individual's past. Informant Melissa (65) reflected this nostalgia for her own teenage past, a yearning for a past reflective of her own shared aesthetic ambience: 'We ended up with our own generation of musicians and we still love it. Because that's from your teenage years'.

There are two processes at work in the process of embodiment. There is the engagement itself and the emotional association intrinsically connected to and integrated with the circumstances of that engagement and the resultant embodiment. This is *latching*. Implicit in the process of latching is an identification with the music in an instinctual and reflex intimacy with the music's properties. When this process of latching involves the music of an entire generation, that identification, that association, represents a kind of communal latching, whereby members of a particular generation share a common 'understanding' and a shared experience of the music of their generation. And because of the unique circumstances of their engagement with that music in their teenage years, that music is made special, made authentic by that experience. This experience 'consecrates' the musical encounter, sanctifies it via the cauldron of the emotional turbulence of adolescence, as deeply meaningful and special. And this sanctification occurs increasingly to the exclusion of others experienced later in life. This sharing of the veneration of their youth musical latching ensures that young peoples' musical experience and the music of their generation collectively is viewed, understood and intrinsically embodied as 'superior' to the music of ensuing generations. This generationally shared *introjection* links members of a generation to each other by this temporal mutual experience.

Baby boomers, in particular, are predisposed to transporting their popular culture with them through their life's journey. It is the 'specialness' of this nostalgia that confirms the uniqueness of the boomer youth experience. As Brabazon puts it when discussing this Baby Boomer propensity for the uniqueness of their youth experience:

> A youth culture cannot compete with an imagined 'sixties' that does not exist except through nostalgia.
>
> (2005: 14)

It is as if there is what Anderson (1983) refers to as an 'imagined community' shared by members of each generation. This was also Mannheim's point. Each age cohort, although they do not necessarily share the same tastes in cultural forms, do share the same experience of living through the timeline of a youth experience located within a shared cultural milieu, within a broad field like popular music. And with that shared cultural milieu comes a shared sense of exclusivity, an exclusivity which cannot be matched by ensuing generations. Chapter 4 will investigate how adulthood informs and shapes our self-concept. Adulthood is the 'destination' that all of us journey towards but the transition is both self-affirming and fraught.

Notes

1 Fuldheim, Dorothy. (1974). *A Thousand Friends*. Garden City, NY: Doubleday.
2 Conflict between young people and their elders has been constant throughout history. Horace (65–68 BC) referred to a process of degradation with each new generation: Our sires' age was worse than our grandsires'. We, their sons, are more worthless than they; so in our turn we shall give the world a progeny yet more corrupt (Quintus Horatius Flaccus [Horace, 1900]).Thomas Barnes reflected adult concern in Puritan England for their sons and daughters: Youth were never more sawcie, yea never more savagely sawcie . . . the ancient are scorned, the honourable are contemned, the magistrate is not dreaded (Barnes, 1624). In the early 20th century G. Stanley Hall, a proponent of the relatively new academic study of psychology, also articulated concerns about the youth of the day: Never has youth been exposed to such dangers of both perversion and arrest as in our own land and day (Hall, 1904: xv–xvi).
3 One wonders how acts such as The Archies, Ohio Express, Tommy Roe and The 1910 Fruitgum Company fit within the pantheon of serious 60s rock and roll.

Bibliography

Advertising Age. (1993). Generation Y. *Advertising Age*, 64(36), 16.
Anderson, B. R. O. G. (1983). *Imagined Communities: Reflections on the Origin and Spread of Nationalism*. London: Verso.
Barnes, T. (1624). *The Wise-Man's Forecast against the Evill Time*. I. Dawson for Nathaniell Newbery: London.
Bennett, A. (2013). *Music, Style, and Aging: Growing Old Disgracefully?* Philadelphia, PA: Temple University Press.
Bonanno, G., et al. (2002). Resilience to Loss and Chronic Grief: A Prospective Study from Pre-loss to 18 months Post-loss. *Journal of Personality and Social Psychology*, 83, 1150–1164.
Boston, J., Wanna, J., Lipski, V., and Pritchard, J. (Eds.) (2014). *Managing Risks, Responding to Crises and Building Resilience*. Canberra: ANU Press.
Bourdieu, P. (1990). *The Logic of Practice*. Cambridge: Polity.
Bourdieu, P. (2000). *Pascalian Meditations*. Stanford: Stanford University Press.
Bourdieu, P. (2010). *Distinction: A Social Critique of the Judgement of Taste*. London: Taylor and Francis.
Brabazon, T. (2005). *From Revolution to Revelation: Generation X, Popular Memory and Cultural Studies*. Aldershot: Ashgate.
Cyrus, M. (2013). *Wrecking Ball*. YouTube. August 25. Retrieved from www.youtube.com/watch?v=My2FRPA3Gf8
Davis, M. (1997). *Gangland: Cultural Elites and the New Generationalism*. St Leonards: Allen & Unwin.
Davis, M. (2010). *Gangland: Cultural Elites and the New Generationalism* (3rd ed.). Melbourne: MUP.
De Nora, T. (2000). *Music in Everyday Life*. Cambridge: Cambridge University Press.
Du Bois-Raymond, M. (1998). 'I Don't Want to Commit Myself Yet': Young People's Life Concepts, *Journal of Youth Studies*, 1(1), 63–79.
Eyerman, R., and Turner, B. S. (1998). Outline of a Theory of Generations. *European Journal of Social Theory*, 1(1), 91–106.

Faulkner, J., and Monash University National Centre for Australian Studies. (2010). *The Importance of Being Innocent: Why We Worry about Children*. Melbourne: Cambridge University Press.

FitzSimons, P. (2013a, April, 29). Waterhouse's Submission is a Joke that's not Funny. *The Tasmanian Times*. Retrieved from www.tasmaniantimes.com.au/index.php/article/waterhouses-submission-is-a-joke-thats-not-funny

FitzSimons, P. (2013b, October 17). Why Oh Why Does Gen Y Not Get It? *Sydney Morning Herald*. Retrieved from www.smh.com.au/sport/why-oh-why-does-gen-y-not-get-it-20131016-2vn4u.html

Friedlander, P. (1996). *Rock and Roll: A Social History*. Boulder: Westview Press.

Fuldheim, D. (1974). *A Thousand Friends*. Garden City, NY: Doubleday.

Furlong, A. (2013). *Youth Studies: An Introduction*. New York: Routledge.

Gillett, C. (1970). *The Sound of the City: The Rise of Rock and Roll*. New York: Outerbridge & Dienstfrey, distributed by E.P. Dutton.

Goffman, E. (1956). *The Presentation of the Self in Everyday Life*. New York: Vintage Books.

Goffman, E. (1961). *Encounters: Two Studies in the Sociology of Interaction – Fun in Games and Role Distance*. Indianapolis, IN: Bobbs-Merrill.

Gosse, D. (2017, January 4). Transcript of Simon Sinek Millennials in the Workplace Interview. *Ochen*. Retrieved from https://ochen.com/transcript-of-simon-sineks-millennials-in-the-workplace-interview

Hagan, J. (October 24, 2017). *Sticky Fingers: The Life and Times of Jann Wenner and Rolling Stone Magazine*. Camberwell: Penguin Random House Australia.

Hall, G. S. (1904). *Adolescence*. Volume 1. New York: D. Appleton and Co.

Hatch, D., & Millward, S. (1987). *From Blues to Rock: An Analytical History of Pop Music*. Manchester University Press.

Horace, and Gwynn, S. L. (1900). *The Odes of Horace. Book III*. London: Blackie.

Kahn, H., and Wiener, A. (1967). *The Year 2000: A Framework for Speculation on the Next Thirty-three Years*. New York: MacMillan.

Katz, E., and Lazarsfeld, P. (1957). *Personal Influence*. New York: Free Press.

Kennedy, M. (2014). Hannah Montana and Miley Cyrus: 'Becoming' a Woman, 'Becoming' a Star, *Celebrity Studies*, 5(3), 225–241.

Kübler-Ross, E. (1969). *On Death and Dying*. New York: Scribner.

Levy, A. (2005). *Female Chauvinist Pigs: Women and the Rise of Raunch Culture*. New York: Free Press.

McCrindle, M. (2006). *Generations at work: Attracting, Recruiting, Retraining & Training Generation Y*. Retrieved from https://2qean3b1jjd1s87812ool5ji-wpengine.netdna-ssl.com/wp-content/uploads/2018/04/McCrindle-Research_New-Generations-At-Work-attracting-recruiting-retaining-training-generation-y.pdf

McCrindle, M. (2016, December 20). *The ABC of XYZ: The Generation Map*. Retrieved from http://mccrindle.com.au/resources/whitepapers/McCrindle-Research_ABC-03_The-Generation-Map_Mark-McCrindle.pdf

McCrindle, M. (2019). *McCrindle About*. Retrieved from http://mccrindle.com.au/about-Australias-social-researchers

Meng, L. (2009). Megatrends Driving Planning Education: How Do We Future-Proof Planners? *Australian Planner*, 46(1), 48–50.

Pattison, R. (1987). *The Triumph of Vulgarity: Rock Music in the Mirror of Romanticism*. New York: Oxford University Press.

Powell, A. (2015). Young Women, Raunch and the Politics of (Sexual) Choice: Is Australian Youth Culture Post-Feminist?, in S. Baker, B. Robards and B. Buttigieg (Eds.), *Youth Cultures and Subcultures: Australian Perspectives*, pp. 215–28. Surrey: Ashgate.

Rojek, C. (2001). *Celebrity*. London: Reaktion Books.

Salt, B. (2016a, October 15–16). Moralisers, We Need You. *The Weekend Australian Magazine*. Retrieved from www.theaustralian.com.au/life/weekend-a/ustralian-magazine/moralisers-we-need-you/news-story/6bdb24f77572be68330bd306c14ee8a3

Salt, B. (2016b, November 5–6). What's More Important, Living Within your Means or Taking Selfies from a Bali Swimming Pool? *The Weekend Australian Magazine*. Retrieved from www.theaustralian.com.au/life/weekend-australian-magazine/money-mortals-and-money-magicians/news-story/98775cfad5f6819d9d7b11363abf2679?utm_source=The%20Australian&utm_medium=email&utm_campaign=editorial

Salt, B. (n.d.). *Bernard Salt Profile*. Retrieved from www.bernard-salt.com.au/profile

Schwartz, B. (1996). Memory as a Cultural System: Abraham Lincoln in World War II. *American Sociological Review*, 61(5), 908–927.

Shaputis, K. (2004). *The Crowded Nest Syndrome: Surviving the Return of Adult Children*. Olympia, WA: Clutter Fairy Publishing.

Sinek, S. (2019). Our WHY To Inspire People to Do the Things that Inspire Them So That, Together, Each of Us Can Change Our World for the Better. Retrieved from https://simonsinek.com/about/?ref=footer

Threadgold, S. (2015). (Sub)Cultural Capital, DIY Careers and Transferability: Towards Maintaining 'Reproduction' when Using Bourdieu in Youth Culture, in S. Baker, B. Robards and B. Buttigieg (Eds.), *Youth Cultures and Subcultures: Australian Perspectives*, pp. 53–64. Burlington: Ashgate.

Threadgold, S. (2018). *Youth, Class and Everyday Struggles*. Routledge: London.

Threadgold, S. (2019). Figures of Youth: On the Very Object of Youth Studies. *Journal of Youth Studies*, 23 (6), 686–701.

Tyler, I. (2013). *Revolting Subjects: Social Abjection and Resistance in Neoliberal Britain*. London: Zed Books.

Tyyska, V. (2016). Conceptualizing and Theorizing Youth: Global Perspectives, in H. Helve and G. Holm (Eds.), *Contemporary Youth Research: Local Expressions and Global Connections*, pp. 1–12. Abingdon; Oxon: Routledge.

Tzanakis, M. (2011). Bourdieu's Social Reproduction Thesis and The Role of Cultural Capital in Educational Attainment: A Critical Review of Key Empirical Studies. *Educate*, 11(1), 76–90.

Woodman, D., and Wyn, J. (2015). Class, Gender and Generation Matter: Using the Concept of Social Generation to Study Inequality and Social Change. *Journal of Youth Studies*, 18(10), 1402–1410.

Wordsworth, W., and Coleridge, S. T. (2013). *Lyrical Ballads 1800*. Abingdon; Oxon: Routledge.

Zeisler, A. (2008). *Feminism and Pop Culture*. Berkeley, CA: Seal Press.

4 Adulthood
The Final Destination

> The boy is the father of the man.
>
> (William Wordsworth)[1]

Wordsworth's truism reflects the time-honoured and real-world understanding of previous generations of how our adult self is arrived at via the combined understandings and experiences of our early life. The quote reflects less gender-neutral times, but the intent can be applied universally to the way the adult persona is shaped by the childhood and youth experience of each individual.

Social Space

This chapter examines in detail how the process of misrecognition of following generations ensues as a natural consequence of the young person transitioning to adulthood. It uses the data of selected participants in focus groups and interviews to illustrate the complex processes that combine to contribute to adults denigrating young people. It signals that the misrecognition of young people is not straightforward, not linear in the way it manifests itself in the vilification of young people from ensuing generations.

Each of the participants in this section demonstrated in their background and in their contribution to the discussion that they were both understanding of and empathetic to the trials faced by young people as they negotiate their teenage years. They demonstrated no overt hostility towards young people, no sense of upfront aggression or animosity. Each indicated their own personal struggles in coping with the ordeals of their own adolescence and cited these experiences in explaining how they understood the issues faced by young people today. Above all, each displayed a level of reasonableness with regard to their relationship with their children and other young people they personally knew, and of the generalities of issues confronting young people today. These understandings reflected an acknowledgement that, from their perspective, being a young person today is more complex, more convoluted and tortuous than were their teenage years. Nevertheless, as the conversations progressed, the reasonableness in their stated positions was undermined by an underlying misrecognition. The subtextual understandings displayed in their statements served to undermine, if not subvert, the totality of their overall support for young people. From my position as researcher, this tended to support my suspicions prior to commencing this research that, although we mean well, our doxic positions embedded in our individual habitus are often at odds with our conscious stated stance.[2]

The important conclusion to be drawn from these observations is that despite the questionable motives of many adults and particularly moral entrepreneurs in highlighting the failings of young people, most adults appear to have an outwardly benign attitude and understanding of young people. Misrecognising young people is an observable phenomenon but it is not necessarily aggressively so across the board. For most adults, the misrecognising of young people functions at a subtextual level, ready to surface when the circumstances trigger its emergence.[3]

Demographic imperatives and differences interact with our experiences, and these differences drive the evolution of habitus and doxa as young people transition to adulthood and middle age and beyond. Paralleling this is the evolution of misrecognition as part of the ageing process. The shared experiences of a generational cohort provide a series of chronological signposts, demarcations which set them and their demographic contemporaries apart from previous and ensuing generations to create a force of custom. As each generation ages, the collective understandings of that generation live on in memory. Significant characters, public personalities, celebrities, TV, music and film luminaries, as well as historical and political events, and cultural trends are transformed into collective memory. These trends and political events as well as the leading characters of the age populate our memory and become what Eyerman and Turner (1998) identify as 'cultural dispositions' (93). These cultural dispositions range over a wide spectrum of the youth experience. They include fashion styles, dress, language, emblems, as well as dance styles, jargon, memes. It is these cultural dispositions which serve to form the 'language' of a generation. They punctuate the generational patois by accentuating and emphasising the semantic subtleties of the language of each generation. The language of Baby Boomers, for example, is punctuated by references to Bob Dylan, the Beatles, Che Guevara, Marshall McLuhan, surfing, films like *Easy Rider* and *The Graduate*, dance forms like The Twist and The Stomp, places like Carnaby Street and Motown, and festivals like Woodstock, and Isle of Wight and Glastonbury, and Nimbin.

These are what Woodman and Wyn (2015) annotate as 'distinctive generational subjectivities' (1403) and exist in concert with, and are not separate from, individual circumstances of race, gender or class. Individuals will experience their social generation at their own individual level, while race, gender and class will influence their shared social experiences. A social generation exists as a kind of collective 'shell', with individual experiences and understandings being overlaid by this generational 'shell'. There is no overt differentiation between the individual and the social generation experience. Any 'demarcation' is seamless and indeed is not recognised by each person. Incorporation of cultural influences and products melds new and old into the maturing habitus, producing doxa which, over time, tends towards ossification – the Don Quixote effect.

Upon arrival, the new adult begins the adjustment of their habitus to their new status. No longer a young person, gradually the doxa of the adult subsumes their now superseded young person's doxa. The rules of the game have changed, and their self-concept – their understanding of who they are and how they fit in – undertakes a transformation. The realisation sinks in that they no longer need to seek permission to do things that only months ago required parental or other adult permission. It is at this point that the demarcation between their former self as young person and their now self-concept as an adult becomes fully formed. No longer a young person, they now view young people through the prism of the adult eye.

George (30) is ten years on from that adult transition point. He is now able to assess young people ten years and more his junior from the perspective of his adult persona. He is so confident of his capacity to analyse young people from his assured position of adult that, as part of a discussion about young people curating an identity, he invoked the double language of disinterest to invent an imaginary 16-year-old to illustrate his point about young people and social media:

> I'm a 16-year-old, my friend Jess curates her entire image, only posts the good shit, only posts the beautiful photo out of the hundreds and only posts that … you get a skewed image of the great life Jess must have.

Already, George is sufficiently distanced from his youth stage to be able to see 'Jess' not from his perspective of a fellow young person, as he was ten years ago. He now can analyse and interpret with absolute conviction, sustained by the inevitability of his conclusions from his now vantage point – the loftily attained position of his 30 years. George at 30, his newly arrived-at adult status now firmly entrenched in his habitus, is now able to view his encounters with young people from ensuing generations with the capacity to *voir* – with the eye of an adult. And what he sees is very different to what he had seen ten years previously. The dissonance between the social world he inhabited as a young person is evident. His perspective has mutated as he has embodied his adult status into his habitus. Instead of 'fellow-travellers', young people now occupy a position separate and inferior to his own adult status. He now has assumed the capacity to analyse and assess from the perspective of adult objectivity.

Neil (35) is similar in his unquestioned analysis of young people: 'they think they know everything, but they don't'. Neil and George's incorporation of their adult status and sensibilities into their personas has imbued them with the newly acquired doxa of the field of power where adults are preeminent. For George and Neil, this has created a disconnect between the social world they now live in and the social world inhabited by young people who are now manifestly, brazenly, different to them. George and Neil can now speak with the Adult Voice.

Lack of Respect

Respect, 'the single most powerful ingredient in nourishing relationships' (Lawrence-Lightfoot, 2000: 13), carries great weight and power as both a word and concept. Implicit in any notion of respect is the understanding, on the part of both the subject and the object of that respect, that one must behave appropriately (Birch, 1993). The object of respect (adult) occupies a status superior to those ceding that respect (young person). The interplay between the two can be fluid with the balance of power between subject and object varying markedly according to individual and social and cultural factors depending on the field (employment, education etc.). In any event, the object of the respect, the adult, aware of the power structure at play, will come to expect that the respect accorded their position will naturally accrue to them personally (see Goffman, 1956, 1961; Dillon, 2007, 2015; Birch, 1993).

No individual can arrive at adulthood free of the burden imposed by parents, teachers and other adults, of the need for them to demonstrate, on a daily basis, their respect for them and indeed all adults. Similarly, notions of disrespect on the part of young people directed towards adults are equally discouraged and proscribed. Respect, and the deference that attends it, is the currency exchanged on a daily basis by young people in return for being allowed to play in fields overseen by adults. It is the measure by which adults ensure the buttressing of the authenticity, the legitimacy of the superiority of the cultural capital they have acquired and embodied, over the cultural capital and the status of young people.

Respect is the mostly unspoken, always present, reminder of the imbalance in the status of the subject and the object – the young person and the adult. For Michelle, Pauline and Matthew, focus group participants in the 35–55-year demographic, respect was the amorphous talisman – nebulous, unstructured, that was an ever-present undercurrent in their focus group. Each was the parent of teenage children. Each demonstrated in the focus group they participated in empathy for, and an understanding of, the difficulties faced by young people today. They all interacted with their children's friends.

As a teacher, Pauline demonstrated her understanding of the historical role of education and the historical disadvantage that young people have been placed in in terms of their interaction with adults. She understood the social and economic forces at work in the development of each young person, and that education is the key to trying to negate these forces which serve to disadvantage young people from certain areas:

It would be my goal... by the end of the term [to] have ... local kids, that's what I call them, ... being able to have a conversation without dropping an 'F' or a 'C' ... because that's ... how they speak at home... They don't see anything wrong with going 'Yeah, fuck Miss'.

(Pauline, 49)

Her empathy is clearly with young people, and she has a grasp of the complexities, both historically and presently, of the way that young people function within the community and of the issues attendant to young people growing up in disadvantaged communities.

Yet despite this understanding, and despite her awareness and articulation of the concept of 'cultural capital', Pauline apparently ignored, or at least discounted, that understanding of class and context by comparing young people today with her own youth experience. Her comparison centred on the notion of 'respect': 'They just don't ... I keep coming back to the word respect'. Pauline is aware that the field of school education, for much of its history, inextricably linked 'respect' with 'fear' of the teacher – that respect followed fear because the teacher was the source of classroom punishment, particularly corporal punishment. In Pauline's eyes, education has moved on from this, it no longer relies upon the nexus between respect and punishment and this is 'a good thing'. However, Pauline then reveals that this 'good thing' is not an absolute by adding the caveat 'I guess ... [because] they don't have the respect, you know, that they should'. This last line was half-whispered as if embarrassed by her realisation.

When a young person, Pauline would have been the recipient of the respect and disrespect message as part of her experience of growing up and would have experienced the sullen resentment and impatience felt by all of us at the seemingly endless 'respect lectures' which are part of the normative landscape of being a teenager. She knows this. She knows she has no right to demand respect from young people in her care because of who she is – that respect must be earned. Yet she laments the lack of respect by the young people in her care, for her, and her teacher colleagues, and by extension for adults in general. As an educated individual grounded in concepts like social justice and fairness, Pauline understands that fear should not be the basis of any credible education system 'which is a good thing too... but...'. As Giles Fraser has succinctly put it: 'Everything before the "but" is bullshit' (2003).

Elements of respect include 'attention, deference, judgment, acknowledgment, valuing, and behavior' (Dillon, 2015). Clearly Pauline expects her students to pay attention, to acknowledge and defer to her, to value her and demonstrate their respect via their behaviour. In Pauline's mind, her (unspoken) entitled authority over her charges is ignored by her students. In her eyes, they obviously do not demonstrate the respect she expects. Her authority should be both acknowledged and respected, particularly as she 'understands' them, recognises the disadvantage and the negativity that afflicts their daily lives. Pauline's resentment at not being respected exemplifies her misrecognising their behaviour. She understands the difficulties young people face in negotiating the transition from teenager to adult, particularly in the low socio-economic area she engages with. Yet her expectation, as an adult and teacher, is that the young person should treat her with respect as a right. In her mind, the symbolic capital that she has acquired as an adult and teacher entitles her to the respect of her students. That they do not defer to her appropriately manifests itself as resentment expressed as negative judgement, as the symbolic violence of misrecognition.

Pauline's engagement with young people ('It would be my goal... by the end of the term [to] have ... local kids, that's what I call them, ... being able to have a conversation without dropping an "F" or a "C"') recognises the effect that disadvantage has upon young people and she is committed to redressing that disadvantage via the education system. Yet despite this enlightened position, despite her empathy for her charges, despite a personal commitment to fairness and equity, from her perspective her position as teacher demands respect, demands deference – because she is a teacher, because she is an adult. That they don't defer to her threatens her position within, and command of, the classroom. When her students ignore that accrued symbolic capital by their lack of respect, her response is to misrecognise that reaction and respond with resentment.

Matthew is a media professional in his mid-50s. He has a teenage daughter. He too demonstrates a commitment to fairness and equity in his public persona. However, when asked of his opinion of young people, Matthew's concerns zero in on the issue of rights. For Matthew, young people knowing their rights is at the core of why there is a problem with young people today. He cites a colleague's experience as a teacher:

> [My friend is] a school teacher. ... And they would all know their rights and there would be lack of respect there. And they'd say 'well, you can't do that!'.
>
> (Matthew, 55)

The use of the phrase 'you can't do that' is preceded by the conditional word, 'well'. In using the phrase, Matthew is mimicking the young person saying it. There are two levels of subtext at work here. From the young person's perspective, the subtext implicit in the phrase is that not only do they know their rights, but they revel in that knowledge and 'weaponise' its use to challenge the authority of the teacher. Implicit in what Matthew is intimating here is that all would be good if young people either were not aware of their rights or kept 'mum' on that knowledge. He appears unaware of the contradiction inherent in his position – that his concern with young people knowing their rights, by inference, promotes the position that if they didn't know, then actions could be taken by teachers which might infringe those rights. If the young people are right and you cannot indeed do that, then the denigration he expresses implies contempt for young people's knowledge of their rights.

Inherent in Matthew's position is the assumption that, in a kind of halcyon past inspired by popular memory, young people (Matthew's teenage incarnation?) were not aware of their rights. And that this was a good thing.

Curiously, Matthew was aware of the historical parallels that apply to young people's experience and place in the social hierarchy – that it has always been thus:

> A lot of the parenting and, say, grandparenting would be very strict and you mustn't do these sort of things… But there's a lot more … understanding these days of adults with… teenage children. Maybe it's because they've … come through the … 60s… So, there's probably a lot more tolerance.

Matthew's acknowledgement of the historical nature of the plight of young people did not temper his judgement. Symbolic capital, acquired via understanding and empathy, allows him to acknowledge the authenticity of the history of parental/young person relations and to incorporate that acknowledgement into his memory. However, Matthew's doxa does not allow him to see the inherent contradiction in his position on young people being aware of their rights. His common-sense position seems to be: 'we didn't know about the rules and it didn't do us any harm so the problem with young people today is that they do know the rules'. Perhaps it seems unfair because his generation had to conform to the rules and knew less about their rights. This misrecognising of the perceived advantage that young people today have leads again to his resentment. Again, it needs to be emphasised that as a parent of a teenager, Matthew intimated in the focus group his empathy with young people and the challenges they face in transitioning to adulthood. Nevertheless, he ignores and/or overcomes this empathy in order to misrecognise young people based upon the entrenched symbolic capital accruing to his adult status.

Self-Affirming Attributes of Authenticity

As Sharon Zukin (2010) has acknowledged, authenticity is its own reward. To be authentic brings with it its own reinforcement. The rite of passage of becoming an adult serves to bestow the mantle of authenticity upon one. As part of the adult metamorphosis, authenticity is appropriated by the adult as symbolic capital, acquired and embodied as doxa in the alchemy of consecration. Once acquired and embodied, the mantle of authenticity acts as a self-perpetuating self-regulating enclosed system: I have authenticity therefore I am authentic. Why am I authentic? Because I have authenticity. This self-affirming attribute of authenticity requires no further authentication (no pun intended). The symbolic capital embodied during the teenage years is in turn shared with the generational cohort as generational memories, sanctified by the shared emotional experiences of the teenage journey as part of the generational *zeitgeist*. Consider the following from Michelle (44) and Pauline (49):

Michelle: I think they're all quite short tempered with us old fogies
Pauline: And we were too. I was. I remember that.
Michelle: Yeah, that period of my life.

Clearly, Michelle and Pauline understand the communication breakdown between young people and adults that occurs naturally as teenagehood is negotiated and passed through. Yet that experience of their youth, of themselves being 'short tempered with old fogies', is, if not forgotten, then discounted, abated with the onset of adulthood. The composite disposition – who we are at any one point in time – of adulthood is arrived at as a result of the sum total of our experiences. It is how we see ourselves. But how we see ourselves as an adult seemingly cannot accommodate the possibility that another, younger generation can possibly have experienced a youth as authentic as ours. In the few short months or years it takes to metamorphose from young person into adult, the travails of our (as young people) deferring to adults are seemingly expunged from our memory – or at least re-shaped.

Knowing oneself is problematic when one considers the vagaries of the most important component of who we know we are: memory – since 'memory is not safe'. Pauline's coherent image of who she is represents a synthesis of her experiences and her memory of those earlier experiences. Memory is a *talisman,* what Brabazon calls the 'quick, sharp jolt back to the past' (2005:141), that carries with it the notion of in-group. In this way, Pauline's concept of herself carries with it the sense of loss at her own teenagehood's passing:

> You know I used to think young people ruled the world when I was young and now that I'm older I realise no, that's not actually the case.

Pauline's sense of in-group here is palpable. The promise of youth, the sense of hope and promise and belief has been replaced by the disappointments and cynicism of adulthood. Pauline is living her past in the present, pining for a past that can never be fulfilled in the present, what Garner refers to as the 'not really now not any more' (1973). This reflects what Fisher, in discussing the concept of *hauntology,* refers to as the:

> … postmodern impasse, the disappearance of the present and the possibility of representing the present. But it also points to an alternative temporality, another way in which time can be out of joint, a mode of causality that is about influence and virtuality rather than gross material force.
>
> (2012: 22)

Pauline's present is aware of the 'failure' of succeeding generations to measure up to the 'standards' of political activity she engaged with. Yet her past engagement with politics via music, her nostalgia for that halcyon past 'when young people ruled the world', lives, breathes, exists, in her present. It not only informs her present, it is her virtual present: past into present into future.

Allied to this sense of in-group is the elevation of the notion of authenticity that accompanied the teenage experience. It is the authentic experience of her own youth that Pauline invokes in her comparison with the young people today. In her memory, the aesthetic and the political were intermixed, seamlessly highlighting the link between art and politics:

> You know Midnight Oil ... Is there still that today? Is there still a lot of messaging, political and social comment through music?

Clearly, for Pauline, something important has been lost. Her memory clearly embraces that in-group. But that sense of in-group does not encompass the frustration and the angst felt when she was misrecognised by adults when younger. In her view, the young people of today lack authenticity because 'what they're really interested in is very superficial, you know celebrity stuff'. Pauline's experience and, importantly, her memory of that experience ensures its privileged position as she makes her judgements.

What Pauline presents here is both self-affirming and self-revealing in its 'truth'. Validation of the authenticity of her own remembered experience appears to be arrived at via an elliptical process in which authenticity manifested itself to her in the form of the integrity and the complexity of both the individual youth cultural experience and the accumulated impact of each of those experiences upon her persona (Midnight Oil writing political messages).[4] In her view, the experiences of young people today are less authentic and are, by comparison, superficial. Her observation of young people's experience reveals to her the paucity of those experiences compared to her own ('celebrity stuff'). She knows this to be true because her memory of that experience, stimulated by her observation of the apparent lack of political popular music, validates the authenticity of that experience on each occasion ('exposed to so many issues'). Pauline has established, in her mind, her authentic youth experiences as the benchmark by which later generations of young people's experiences can be measured. Pauline is seemingly unaware of the many examples of 'political' music today, of which there are actually many examples ('Is there still a lot of messaging?').

It is the notion of authenticity which is central to adult interaction with young people of succeeding generations. The experiences of today's young people cannot, by definition, match the authenticity of our own. Symbolically, they are condemned forever to being mere pale imitations of those of their elders. And the cycle repeats. The Baby Boomer experience is deemed more authentic than Generation X which itself is deemed more authentic than Millennials, which will be in turn deemed more authentic than ensuing generations.

60 *Adulthood*

By comparison with her authentic experience, young people's experience today is perceived to lack the gravitas of hers. Her use of terms such as 'respect', 'political' and 'superficial' and her derogation of young people demonstrate this binary thinking. Pauline is now 'tilting at windmills', enrolled in the ranks of *Don Quixote* and *the knights errant*. Her remembered past attempting to define, yet simultaneously in conflict with the present, has instead been bypassed by the popular culture of the present. And these negative responses to this process of dislocation of social space generate misrecognition of the cultural practice of younger generations and, by extension, their behaviour and customs. Pauline now speaks with her Adult Voice.

Helicoptering

Adult concerns about young people encompass the seemingly contradictory positions of innocent abroad and folk devil. These concerns have led to the emergence of the phenomenon of 'helicopter parenting' (Padilla-Walker and Nelson, 2012; Somers and Settle, 2010). This phenomenon applies particularly to middle-class families creating a sense of entitlement in the children via 'concerted cultivation' (Lareau, 2003: 2). 'Helicoptering' manifests itself as parents seek to ensure the best possible experience for their children in order to best prepare them for work and social situations upon reaching adulthood. The acquired social and cultural capital which ensues from this process allows the young people to make 'the rules work in their favour' (Lareau, 2003: 7).

Anne (42) is the mother of mid-teen boys and worked as a professional in the human services area. She is very conscious of the dilemma facing parents as they attempt to steer a course between protection and guidance, and the need to let go the reins. Her attitudes towards young people reflected her understanding of the complexities of the way youth generations have functioned. For her, young people have always been on the receiving end of adult criticism and her empathy extends to young people today:

> Every generation goes through that change and ... thinks [they're] ... old and daggy, not realising that we've all been through it ourselves. ... My kids ... my husband bangs on about ... they always want to play computer games. But ... my parents banged on about how watching television makes your eyes go square and your brain rot ... And I'm sure a lot of my aunties [got] pregnant.

Anne's experience of Millennials in her workplace is positive: 'they were fantastic'. Her own children were treated with optimism: 'They've been treated like they're part of everything and spoken to like adults'.

Anne's measured position highlights the tension inherent in the parent/young person relationship. On the one hand, young people are increasingly seen as independent, as equal members of the family unit rather than subordinates. Yet this enhanced status is accompanied by ever-increasing supervision by parents.

This cultivation and encouragement of the young person's role in the family and in wider society is designed to prepare them for adulthood. It relies upon the young person being treated with greater respect and their thoughts and opinions being encouraged to the point where their capacity to participate and engage is on a par with their parents and other adults. Yet, paradoxically, that independence is accompanied by an increased adult 'presence' monitoring and overseeing their children's activities. Nicole (55) outlines the difference between her own experience and the way she treats her own children:

> I think we had it *harder* ... I was the eldest of five ... so I was left to fend for myself. I used to *walk* ... 20 minutes to the railway station to catch the train to school and walk ten minutes to high school... I still drop Alex off every morning, pick him up ... most days. I was in Year 7 catching the train into the city ... to see Jesus Christ Superstar... I just wouldn't have let my 13-year-old catch the train into Sydney city (Emphasis added).

Nicole's concerns reflect Faulkner's walled garden we construct for children. In Year 7, she caught the train to Jesus Christ Superstar, but 'I wouldn't ... let my 13 year old catch the train into the city'. Both Nicole and Anne's concerted cultivation serves to create the environment which encourages their children to challenge their authority. The walled garden they seek to impose contains the seeds of disenchantment with the outcomes of their own parenting.

Social and Temporal Distance

Misrecognition of young people is not static, not rigidly fixed. One doesn't suddenly arrive at adulthood and begin to immediately misrecognise young people with the intensity of a 70-year-old. The process is gradual as each newly arrived adult's habitus processes their changed status as we have seen with Neil and George above. The doxa associated with adulthood evolves as they adjust to their changed circumstances and status. The capacity to misrecognise young people intensifies as they progress to and through adulthood. It is this social and temporal distance from their teenage years which acts to determine how the process of misrecognising young people grows and becomes embodied.

The fluidity of misrecognition was apparent in the informants closest to Millennials' age group. Neil, Joanne and George were on the cusp of Millennial/Gen X in their early thirties. Throughout the focus group, all three informants demonstrated an understanding of how young people function within their social and cultural milieu. Importantly, they also demonstrated a capacity for self-reflection. They saw that their status as 'tail end' Gen Xers placed them within the context of their teenagehood and young adulthood ten years previously. Their position was simultaneously one of 'distance' from their recently departed-from youth and young-adulthood, combined with the recent almost visceral 'memory shadows' of that same recently departed youth.

When asked to assess Millennials, there was both understanding and empathy for the 'plight' of Millennial young people. Joanne: 'they get a bad rap because it's pretty easy to say: "Oh they don't work hard"' (Joanne, 32). But there was also a perceived difference, even though there is only a ten-year gap between themselves and Millennials:

> They're very different to us. They have different experiences because of technology, and the changes that that's brought to society.
>
> (Neil, 35)

Clearly, Neil's analysis encompasses the societal forces at work. He can clearly see that the young people he encounters represent *homo aperti* and the societal forces that have had an impact in the ten or so years since his own young adult status. His doxa has already begun to incorporate into his habitus the distance necessary to be able to undertake this analysis. Technological changes have, in his assessment, been profound in that timeframe. Myspace has made way for Facebook, then Twitter, Snapchat, Instagram and Tik Tok (see Van Dijck, 2013; Boyd and Ellison, 2007; Woodman and Bennett, 2015).

All of the informants in interviews and focus groups across all demographics were at pains to point out the role of technology being the hallmark feature of Millennial activity and group culture. It seems the link between technological changes and Millennials has evolved to the point where the two terms are interchangeable: Millennial = technological obsession; technological obsession = Millennial. This interchangeability results in blatant stereotyping like the following from Neil: 'they're a bit narcissistic, lots of selfies'.

Neil's reference to Millennials being 'narcissistic' prompted an immediate rebuke from the other two: 'Look I'm 30 and I'm narcissistic … Every generation's kids are a product of their own influences and time' (George, 30). Joanne added with a nod to Willis: 'Yeah I think that happens in every generation. We used to decorate our bedroom walls and do that kind of thing to show our friends this is who we are' (Joanne, 32).

There is a clear understanding on the part of George and Joanne that the phenomenon of selfies outlined by Neil is not in itself a reason to stereotype. Neil's response to the rebuke was to pull back as the conversation developed. During this exchange between Joanne and George, Neil was nodding and vocalised 'Yeah' three times, as if saying: 'Yes I see that now'. It is possible he was convinced by Joanne's argument that what he had termed 'narcissism' could be viewed as the more complex phenomenon that Joanne put forward, one of creative engagement. As George pointed out in response to the stereotype of the technology-fixated millennial:

> They're no different technically to any generation., but you're always going to get the rebellious ones. You're always going to get the disconnected ones. It's just society.
>
> (George, 30)

Joanne (32) then highlighted the commonalities of each generation as a mediating factor when analysing teenagers:

> In terms of the selfies and things I think they're just trying to express... . That's the image they want to put of themselves to the world ... and what we want to be seen as. But now it's like the Instagram profile is what they are showing.

George then introduced the concept of pace of change:

> I think they're, they're growing up faster. They know a lot (laughs under breath), they've access to a lot of information, and different opinions. And they know that [said with a sense of resignation].

It was apparent that the temporal proximity of their adulthood to their own youth meant that their own passage through teenagehood and beyond loomed large in their consciousness. Having reached their now early thirties, they can now view their own youth stage through the lens of adult maturity. Their habitus now incorporates their adult status and the associated doxa of 'mature adult'. And these newly acquired understandings provide new insights to allow them to view and analyse their life up until this point. The transition to their present position was not one of strictly outlined demarcations between teenager and adult. This transition reflects the continuous spectrum of ageing. But as each person passes through these various stages, their habitus and doxa accommodate these new experiences and understandings. Joanne for example is a new mother. She now incorporates the symbolic capital of motherhood into her habitus, and these new understandings will influence and determine her attitudes and values – and how she uses this acquired knowledge to create new meanings.

That process of self-reflection (in this case on the adjacency of his present life to his previous teenagehood) is encapsulated in George's observation on teenagers that he has observed:

> I just see them as teenagers. And as teenagers you're going to have a certain world viewpoint. And you're gonna be skewed towards that and you're gonna go, in your late twenties: 'What the fuck was I thinking?'.

'What the fuck was I thinking?' indeed! This is George's adult persona succinctly summarising the metamorphosis that has occurred over the past ten years of his life. 'What the fuck was I thinking?' – these six words exemplify the temporal distance between his 19-year-old self and now. This was George's experience of the transition from teenagehood to his twenties, to adulthood, and the binary experience of freedoms and constraints that have come with that transition. When pressed to elucidate, particularly regarding diversity and complexity of experience, George was again adamant:

> Of course, there's nuances. But they're all gonna, you know, make stupid decisions at some point and they're all gonna say stupid things, cause they're going through a very emotional point in time.

George pointed out that he knew lots of people who 'didn't make the same stupid mistakes that I did'. Joanne pointed out that her teenagehood also didn't include lots of stupid things: 'I didn't do a lot of risky stuff [laughs], that's just me'.

What this exchange exemplifies is the contradiction at the heart of any assessment of young people by adults. Neil seemed to fall into stereotyping teenagers as risky subjects by default. His stereotyping occurred at the beginning of the focus group in response to the first question. Because it was the first question in the focus group, Neil's responses were the most spontaneous. So 'narcissistic' and 'growing up faster' were standard adult responses that would not be out of place if uttered by the older Fred or Pauline or Matthew. But, as those stereotypes were challenged, first by George and then by Joanne, Neil backtracked. In both cases, that backtracking occurred as a result of identifying individuals who do not fit the stereotype. George cited the example of friends whose personas were at odds with the stereotype he had just outlined. This occurred before Joanne entered the discussion with her own self-reflection. Neil then contributed to the contradictions by referring to 'the ones I know [not being] typical'.

What is being expounded here is a fundamental aspect of misrecognition of young people as practised by adults. Neil's initial response to the first question was based upon stereotyping. When challenged and, equally importantly, when they considered young people they know or adults they know who have arrived at adulthood devoid of this stereotyping, their opinion was modified to a more accepting discourse – an ontological shift away from stereotyping.

So where does this stereotyping come from? In a later chapter, I will explore the role of media. But in response to questioning about the origins of their attitudes towards young people, George identified his own experience as the basis of attitude:

> Your own experience. Whether you enjoy that period of your life or not I think is a big thing. Whether you had a really, really hard time, growing up through teenage years, and see things from that perspective, I think skews how you look at people who are in that age range.

Joanne sought clarification 'as to whether you think they've got it easier than you?'. To which Neil responded: 'I don't think they have it easier'. George then responded: 'I don't think they have it easier at all. I don't want to go through that emotional turmoil'.

George's reflections point to his capacity to reflect upon, and analyse, how he got to where he is. That enables him to develop and maintain a process of *introjection*. George acknowledges that hard times as a teenager inform not only who you are but may shape how you view the teenagehood of those now passing through that stage of their life – a prism through which an adult is able to view and analyse the young people they encounter. George, Neil and Joanne are in the demographic closest to Millennials. Unlike older informants like Fred, Pauline and Matthew, there is still a kind of visceral memory of their teens. George perishes the thought of going through 'emotional' experiences again. However, it is important to note here that George may invoke his own memories of his youth as the basis for his now (at 30) understanding of young people. But we have already seen how he has authorised, solemnised this understanding via his already embodied double language of disinterest of an adult.

George, Joanne and eventually Neil, all demonstrated a sense of empathy for young people. They were able, to varying degrees, to put themselves in the shoes of younger people. As we have seen, older informants such as Pauline, Matthew and Michelle also demonstrated that capacity to see things from the perspective of others. Even Fred, at an intellectual level, was able to demonstrate his understanding. This capacity for empathy and compassion can be considered as *emotional capital*. That idea was developed by Nowotny (1981), and then expanded upon by Reay (2004) and others (Allatt, 1993; Illouz, 1997; Scheer, 2012; Zembylas, 2007). Although Bourdieu did not deal in any detail with the emotions, Reay in particular has taken Bourdieu's concept of capital and extended it to incorporate the acquisition of empathy and compassion as another form of capital which can be deployed.

Reay highlights Bourdieu's focus on the family, particularly the central role that mothers play in the family of 'maintaining relationships' (Bourdieu, 1998: 68). Reay points out the shortcomings in Bourdieu's analysis regarding women, stating that his analysis 'position[s] women as objects rather than subjects in their own right; as means rather than ends!' (2004: 60). This 'positioning' also serves to frame the concept of emotional capital within the ambit of other forms of symbolic capital and their capacity to be converted into economic capital. Reay questions the notion of a default economic conversion (69), arguing that emotional capital does not necessarily follow that causal pathway to potential profit, particularly with regard to the field of education:

> Unlike the other capitals, cultural, economic, social and symbolic, the concept of emotional capital disrupts neat links between profit, or what

Bourdieu calls increases in capital ... The same relationship does not automatically exist.

(69)

So, breaking the nexus between acquired capital and profit creates the possibility of a two-fold reading of the attitudes of adults towards young people.

Both George's and Neil's initial response to being questioned about their attitudes towards young people was a spontaneous one of misrecognition ('narcissistic', 'growing up faster'). As with Matthew, Pauline and Fred, the subtext was one of disapproval. Implicit in Neil's responses was that he and his generation weren't narcissistic, and they grew up at the correct pace. Neil framed his observation from a position of what felt like objectivity: 'They're a bit narcissistic, lots of selfies'. He can only make this observation from a position of one who believes his youth generation in its time was not narcissistic. This misrecognition occurs because the cultural capital he has acquired, both as a result of introjection and popular memory, serves to privilege Neil's knowledge and experience over that of young people today.

George similarly has made his observations from a position of presumed objectivity – the double language of disinterest. His comment, 'they're growing up faster', implies that there is a 'correct' pace at which young people should grow up. Unstated in this observation is the inference that it would be better if they grew up at a more leisurely pace, a pace more in tune with that which George perceives his age cohort grew up. Neil's and George's initial responses misrecognised young people early in the discussion. However, once challenged, their positions moderated and they demonstrated emotional capital. The process of critical discussion caused them to reflect on their attitudes. They moved to seeing young people and their behaviour and attitudes more accurately through the prism of their own youth experience.

Neil encapsulated this transformation process and the dynamics at work within it succinctly:

I see it's a pretty even split between the people I know: ... sympathy for people going through that period of life ... who are a bit more empathetic and go 'Oh God high school, oh Jesus HSC, life'... And disdain from people who are like: 'Little shits get out of my way'.

(Neil, 35)

Neil's use of the terms 'sympathy' and 'empathetic' demonstrated his understanding of the relationship between the capacity to empathise and the resultant capacity to apply those feelings of empathy. Neil's initial response ('They're narcissistic') indicated a certain lack of empathy. His more considered response served not only to identify how empathy serves to temper misrecognition, it simultaneously encapsulated the binary nature and the constant tension between the unmediated response of misrecognition, with the mediated analysis where and when empathy 'kicks in'. Neil's initial response reflects the social distance between himself and young people 'measured in time' (Bourdieu, 1985: 726). Neil's initial misrecognising of young people reflects the fact that his capacity for a 'disinterested' analysis of an adult has already been embodied. Unmediated and unchallenged, the understandings behind that initial response would have remained static, unchanged. The longer they remain unchallenged the more they will become embodied. However, when challenged by the responses of first George and then Joanne, the social distance between Neil's current status and his previous teenager status reduces. His memories of being a teenager are still relatively fresh. As Bourdieu notes:

> The social world is, to a large extent, what the agents make of it, at each moment; but they have no chance of un-making and re-making it except on the basis of realistic knowledge of what it is and what they can do with it from the position they occupy within it.
> (1985: 734)

Challenged by George and Joanne, Neil re-makes his social world in order to accommodate the newly arrived-at position. Importantly, had Neil been in a different social space where his stereotyping had not been challenged, had his misrecognition been concurred with by others present, then his stereotyping of young people as 'narcissistic' would have been reinforced in a kind of feedback loop of misrecognition.

As Reay has pointed out, the nexus between other forms of cultural capital and their capacity to be converted into economic capital does not necessarily apply to emotional capital since it generates social rather than economic value. Neil and George's process of self-reflection and the attendant feelings of empathy are based upon their capacity to see and respond to young people today through the prism of their own challenging youth experiences. Their initial response of misrecognition was tempered by empathy.

Joanne managed to encapsulate this in her description of the transition from teenager to adult:

> I think as you age, it, you know, certainly ageing affects it, but it's the experiences you have as you age. It's just the passage of time ... as you get older maybe it's just harder to relate to younger... We use social media ... so ... we can still see that minefield that they're working on... As you get older, that gap widens and perhaps it does become harder to understand.

The longer the gap between the young person and their adult persona, the more difficult it is to *unmake* the social world of the adult. Joanne has identified the 'gap' that continues to widen between her teenage years and her present. The social distance between herself and her youth (and by extension) with young people today has grown and will continue to grow as she ages. Neil extended this metaphor of a 'gap' to identify the accompanying notion of 'distance': 'It's distance... As the gap gets wider, being able to relate to experiences is harder'. As the 'gap' widens and 'distance' between teenager and current age grows larger, the capacity for empathy diminishes and the capacity to misrecognise and to speak with the Adult Voice is enhanced.

Stereotyping

Stereotypes are culturally shared and are generally accepted and understood beliefs about particular types of people and groups of people, creating expectations about the group's personality, preferences, appearance or ability. Stereotypes are ingrained beliefs by sections of the community about other sections of the community. These beliefs allow the members of one group to predict and comprehend the behaviours of members of another group (see McGarty et al., 2002; Tajfel, 1978; Tajfel and Turner, 1979; Tajfel et al., 1971; Fiske, Cuddy, Glick and Xu, 2002). A stereotype is predictable. What is perceived with a stereotype is a composite image that is consensually agreed upon by those doing the stereotyping. In recent years, Millennials have been the target of one of the most concerted cases of stereotyping in recent memory. The prevalent stereotype of a Millennial is of a phone-obsessed/media savvy dilettante lacking in commitment. It is this stereotype that sports journalist Peter FitzSimons' 2013 article rails against:

> Something is missing in the current generation when it comes to what is expected of them when accorded the sacred privilege of 'playing for Australia'.
> (FitzSimons, 2013)

Note that it is not just the current sporting cadre playing for Australia. It is the entire generation. Similarly, Simon Sinek in his 2016 interview with David Gosse tars the entire generation with the same brush:

> They were told they can have anything they want in life, just because they want it.
> (Gosse, 2017)

Young people and particularly Millennials are fair game for adult stereotyping (Macrae et al., 1996). Adults embed the stereotype of the phone-obsessed Millennial in their doxa and it is this stereotype which emerges as the brunt of adult misrecognition of Millennials. This pre-existing specific stereotype perfectly complements the already existing youth stereotype whose cultural forms fail to match the authenticity of the adult's lived experience. It is this stereotype that awaits, latent, lurking, ready to make an appearance at the mere mention of 'millennial'.

Informants Joe, Elaine and Sharon were in their early 20s. Joe, a media and multimedia professional; Elaine, a university student; and

Sharon, community sector worker, all participate in civic and community organisations and projects. They therefore might be termed 'youth leaders'. They have experience, complemented by skills and knowledge and understandings gained, resulting in enhanced confidence and a capacity to clearly articulate a position. The doxa acquired as 'youth leaders' has been incorporated into their habitus. It informed not only their day-to-day lived experience but also their capacity to analyse. All three were aware of the misrecognition applied to them by later generations: 'We all seem to be thugs' (Joe, 19). Their role as youth leaders meant they engaged often with older generations and particularly community leaders. As such, they were aware and had observed at close quarters the contradictions so often evident in many adults' response to young people. The contrasting views reflect the youth equivalent of Summers' binary Madonna/Whore syndrome (1975).[5]

On the one hand, the positive view of youth was identified and articulated. Elaine singled out politicians as especially liberal with their accolades:

> The politicians that we get involved with say that they're always so amazed by how engaged we are and how much we know.
>
> (Elaine, 21)

Secondly, Elaine identifies the generic stereotyping by adults:

> We get stereotyped by adults as being really ignorant, ... self-absorbed, on our phones all the time... not interested, ... not engaged.
>
> (Elaine, 21)

Unspoken but implicit in this conversation was that quite often the person giving the accolades and the one stereotyping were one and the same person. Sharon's response was more measured, reflecting again the complexity of adult responses and how misrecognition is not consistently applied:

> I think it depends on which adult you ask because my parents would say something very different to someone who doesn't know me at all... They've raised a decent young lady who can look after herself, is independent, can stand on her two feet.
>
> (Sharon, 23)

But when the adults don't know you, the response is very different. Sharon too has been the subject of misrecognition. For her, stereotyping young people was a standard reaction from adults who don't know you:

> I think people are more likely to make assumptions based on the stereotypes and what's out there.
>
> (Sharon, 23)

When Sharon interacts closely with adults in different settings such as her family, or at work, that personal interaction serves to break down the stereotyping that would normally be applied to her by adults she doesn't know. So instead of being a nondescript, anonymous 'Millennial', she is recognised as a loved member of the family or a valued work colleague. Stereotyping applied to young people (the other), in general, is mediated by proximity. And as we saw with George and Neil, being challenged about misrecognition often serves to mediate that denigration. The social world that Sharon occupies includes family and work. Her interactions are specific and involve varying degrees of familiarity, a familiarity which mitigates embodied feelings of misrecognition on the part of adults she interacts with.

To most adults not familiar with her or interacting closely with her, Sharon is indistinguishable from any other young person they may encounter. We recall Fred (73). His considered response to young people encompassed a reflexive acknowledgement of the traditional animosity between adults and young people. He was able to recognise that in the (admittedly limited) fields in which he interacts with young people (family, children of work colleagues), the social proximity of those young people 'humanises' them. They become individuals to be interacted with. Yet as Fred admits, his perception of the wider youth demographic, informed in the main by the media, views a substantial proportion of them as ice-addicted, phone obsessed, socially isolated, uncaring Millennials. This habitual misrecognition of young people is 'taken for granted' when they are at a social distance.

Individuals function within the social space, and each individual develops not only a sense of 'one's place' but also a sense of the place of 'others'. Those understandings seem natural, comfortable – a matter of 'common sense'. Sharon understands the social spaces she functions within. Her habitus is not only a 'system of schemes of production of practices [but also functions as] a system of perception and appreciation of practices' (Bourdieu, 1989: 22). She knows how to behave and interact – at work, in her youth leadership role, with her family – because she understands the doxa, the rules of the game. When she functions outside the social spaces she feels comfortable within, her sense of place is altered by her knowledge of the sense of place of others. She knows and understands the misrecognition applied to her:

> They'll go to those generalisations because that's what they know about young people outside of their own personal experiences.
>
> (Sharon, 23)

'What they know about young people outside of their own personal experiences' is almost certainly based on stereotype. Sharon's self-awareness and her awareness of others combine to allow her to analyse and classify others. Yet, echoing Bourdieu, for her, nothing classifies somebody more than the way he or she classifies others. Categorising others creates a kind of feedback loop which constantly reinforces our prejudices, whether they be positive or negative. More often than not, the result is an example of stereotyping.

My Dad Judges People – Living with Being Stereotyped

What of young people who have not yet progressed to adulthood, who are in the twilight of their youth stage? At 16 years of age, informants Iris, Eliza and Gina were literally Millennial cusp babies, born in 1999. Like Elaine, Joe and Sharon, they were very conscious of generic adult attitudes towards them. Eliza's initial comment to the first question about how they were perceived by adults, 'We're annoying', was met with laughter and vociferous agreement by Iris and Gina. When asked how they know this to be true, their replies reflected the misrecognition directed at them by adults. They knew the perception was that they did not, or even would not, appreciate how well off they are: 'We're a lot different towards … when… they were kids… . we're not grateful towards what we have' (Iris, 16). It was apparent from the exchange that followed that they often encountered stereotyping. The experience of denigration and sarcasm, on the part of their parents and other adults, was evident. They clearly identified both the regularity of this kind of misrecognition and their impatience with the regularity and hyperbole of these characterisations based on their age. Eliza, mimicking one of her parents, said, 'Oh when I was your age I walked to school and three kilometres and didn't have any shoes'. The comparative phrase, 'when I was your age', was a frequently thrown barb.

Interestingly, given that they were born around the millennium, they did not identify as Millennials and, in fact, saw themselves as distinct from Millennials. Their indeterminate location within the 'pop demographic' classification brings into sharp focus their understanding of where they 'fit in'. This sense of self relates very much to what they can and cannot do:

> We're … referred to as the internet generation … We're all starting to get that little bit older [slight expression of irony] … going out and… . doing all the different things… Whereas Millennial, you know have already gone through that.
>
> (Eliza, 16)

Eliza implies here the 'walled garden' that she and Iris and Gina currently occupy because of their age. At 16, legally they are still children, under the care of their parents, and their rights are limited. But their self-awareness recognises that this is all about to change, that they will soon no longer be children and the 'walled garden' will cease to exist: 'It's coming' (Iris, 16). When it does, they will be subjected to the wider denigration applied to Millennials:

> By the time we get to year 12 or after … it'll be like… . all the same stuff … that Millennials had: It'll be like all the drinking stuff, and the drugs.
>
> (Eliza, 16)

The subtext of this conversation was that such judgements will be 'par for the course'. This is what young people go through. Their childhood and early teenagehood has seen characterised by adult misrecognition. They know that when they reach their late teens and are legally independent, they will become eligible for all the characterisations associated with young adults ('drinking stuff, and the drugs'). Moreover, because of their (from the perspective of adults) 'obsession' with technology, they are more likely to suffer worse misrecognition: 'I reckon we might be treated worse ... because we have experienced more with change' (Iris, 16).[6]

The demarcation that Gina, Eliza and Iris see between themselves and Millennials not only informs their analysis of the characteristics of Millennial, but how that broader Millennial categorisation informs their own analysis of where and how they fit into the scheme of things. The interaction of 'social structure and individual agency' (Grenfell, 2008: 50) is apparent in their understanding of their place within the wider social structure. Their awareness of themselves as categorically 'different' to Millennials influences their understanding of how they fit in:

> It's only just starting to happen because we're all starting to get that little bit older... Our generation is ... classed as the 'technology generation' [said with accompanying mimed quotation marks]. That's ... what ... we've all grown up with.
>
> (Eliza, 16)

Eliza has a clear understanding of broader societal influences at work. This understanding provides her with the capacity to see how older generations view her and her generational compatriots.

Gina, Eliza and Iris all worked at casual rates after school and on weekends in the hospitality industry. Each had direct experience of adult misrecognition in their interaction with customers and patrons where they worked:

> Sometimes they're just... . Rude... I had no ... dollar ... or 50 cent coins so I had to give it all in 10 cents and ... I said ... are you all right with me giving ... all in 10 cents? And she said that's fine. But when I went to go make her food she was like [taking on the persona] 'oh that girl gave me all ten cent coins that's so rude'.
>
> (Gina, 16)

Iris's experience was similar:

> I've seen them being served by ... employees ... a couple of years older than me ... in their 20s and I'm 16 right now and the way that they treat ... the 20-year olds compared to me is just so much more civilised ... with so much more respect.
>
> (Iris, 16)

Eliza is in no doubt as to the process at work in adults stereotyping and denigrating her on the basis of age:

From the first time that they see ... how you're presented and how you act towards them and your body language and ... how you stand and ... how you speak... . If you were out with your friends and laughing and ... being a little bit loud ... and 'oh those kids, they're so disruptive'... But if you're out with your parents at a restaurant ... obviously you're going to be nice and sitting down and not being too loud and they're like 'oh look at that lovely girl over there with her parents'.

(Eliza, 16)

While the hospitality industry openly exposes all workers to elevated levels of judgement, Eliza and the others are aware that context (physical and social) are important determinants in how adults respond to them. That context determines which 'persona' each young person (or group of young people) brings to each situation (here, the binary terms are 'disruptive' and 'lovely girl').

Fashion is an important component of young people's concept of self and a strong determinant of the perception of young people. The reflection of self to self very much includes the kind of 'fashion statements' each young person projects via their choice of clothing. It reflects an individual's habitus. But in the process of interaction with others, it posits their understanding of the doxa which reflects both their self-concept and how that self-concept interacts with others. Iris articulates this process in reference to her dad passing comment on young women he might see when out with her:

My dad judges people... Oh look at that lady, she's hardly wearing any shorts... . He doesn't know anything about them.

(Iris, 16)

This adult categorising of young people reflects not only Iris's sense of the unfairness of the stereotyping, it also highlights differing perceptions and understandings: 'She's wearing a nice dress ...but an older person might think ... it's tighter to her body [said with sarcasm]' (Gina, 16). When wearing a tight dress or ' "baddy" clothes, someone will always judge you ... and you could never get this right' (Iris, 16).[7]

At 16 years of age, the walled garden is still part of their experience. Tattoos, for example, were non-negotiable physical accoutrements as far as their parents are concerned. Getting a tattoo would result in dire consequences. Her father's response when the subject is raised: They're 'disgusting... [I will] make you get rid of them' (Gina, 16). Or worse, Iris knows that if she gets a tattoo, 'I have to move out of home' (Iris, 16).

This discussion brought into sharp relief the fundamental contradiction at the heart of the misrecognition of young people by adults. As we have seen with older informants, adults often demonstrate intellectual understanding of the difficulties faced by young people negotiating their transition from teenager to adult. They demonstrate varying degrees of empathy with young people they know and associate with, sometimes as a result of their recollecting their own transition experiences. They espouse their belief in their hopes and aspirations for young people and their fundamental belief in the 'goodness' of young people. Young people display many good qualities. Yet, despite this, misrecognition still ensues. Each of the parent adults in interviews and focus groups expressed their hopes for their children, outlined their parenting strategies for ensuring their children were well-prepared for adulthood. Yet each, to varying degrees, expressed dissatisfaction with young people. They seemed unable to extend their intellectual understandings and feelings of empathy so that the young people they associate with are viewed as equals. Iris encapsulated the contradiction of the adult/young person relationship at the heart of that habitual misrecognition:

> They teach us to be our own individual self but when it comes to hair colours and piercings, and tattoos, we can't show them, ... can't be individual with them. We can't be how we actually are.
>
> (Eliza, 16)

Iris, Eliza and Gina can't be how they 'actually are', because 'how they are' brings them into conflict with their parents' or other adults' imagined reality of who they should be. How they are puts them at risk of being stereotyped, and worse – made to change or move out of home.[8]

Misrecognition of young people reflects the social and temporal distance currently occupied by adults towards their remembered experiences of youth. The privileging of idealised memory is reflected in adults applying to their own youth an authenticity of experience that cannot be matched by that of ensuing generations. Each new generation accrues symbolic capital with which to challenge the preceding adult generation. On the other hand, each generation arrives at their adult status having been the victim of denigration at the hands of previous adult generations. As each generation reaches adulthood, they maintain the practice of stereotyping, misrecognising those younger than themselves.

The following chapter will examine the role that memory plays in the development of the adult habitus and the way that adult habitus acquires and embodies the certainty to authenticate their youth cultural experience.

Notes

1 'The child is the father of the man' (in Wordsworth, W. and Coleridge, S. T. (2013). *Lyrical Ballads 1800*. Abingdon, Oxon: Routledge) is the origin of this epithet from less gender-neutral times.
2 I need to point out here that I too am guilty of my own unstated doxic positions being at odds with my stated position with regard to my attitudes towards young people. Several times during the conversations, and in the writing of this material, I found myself checked by the realisation that I too was unconsciously misrecognising young people.

3 Young adults (18–25 years) are more likely to be negatively rated than those of older groups. See Trzesniewski, K. H., and Donnellan, M. B. (2014). "Young People These Days ... ": Evidence for Negative Perceptions of Emerging Adults. *Emerging Adulthood*, 2(3), 211–226.
4 This nostalgia for a time when the idealism and the hopes and aspirations of the 60s counter-culture is perfectly encapsulated in the song REMEMBER WHEN THE MUSIC by Harry Chapin. Chapin, H. (1977). *Dance Band on the Titanic*. Elecktra.
5 Articulated as *Damned Whores and God's Police* by Anne Summers in her landmark Australian book.
6 Given the responses generally from adult informants, this is a very perceptive observation.
7 Unspoken but apparent in these sequences is that the criticisms of skimpy clothing significantly were made by the fathers of the girls. No such criticism of boys' clothing was referenced by any of the participants in any of the informant sessions. Clearly, female young people have an added dimension to the *walled gardens* they need to escape the bonds of.
8 Obviously, this was hyperbole on the part of Iris in seeking to emphasise her father's vehemence.

Bibliography

Allatt, P. (1993). Becoming Privileged: The Role of Family Processes, in I. Bates and Riseborough, G. (Eds.), *Youth and Inequality*, pp. 139–159. Buckingham: Open University Press.
Birch, T. H. (1993). Moral Considerability and Universal Consideration, *Environmental Ethics*, 15, 313–332.
Bourdieu, P. (1985). The Social Space and the Genesis of Groups. *Theory and Society*, 14(6), 723–744.
Bourdieu, P. (1989). Social Space and Symbolic Power. *Sociological Theory*, 7(1), 14–25.
Bourdieu, P. (1998). *Practical Reason*. Cambridge: Polity Press.
Boyd, D., and N. Ellison. (2007). Social Network Sites: Definition, History, and Scholarship. *Journal of Computer-Mediated Communication*, 13(1), 1–11.
Brabazon, T. (2005). *From Revolution to Revelation: Generation X, Popular Memory and Cultural Studies*. Aldershot: Ashgate.
Chapin, H. (1977). *Dance Band on the Titanic*. Elecktra.
Dillon, R. (2007). Respect: A Philosophical Perspective. *Gruppendynamik und Organisationsberatung*, 38 (2), 201–212.
Dillon, R. (2015). Respect, in E. N. Zalta (Ed.), *The Stanford Encyclopedia of Philosophy* (Fall 2015 Edition), http://plato.stanford.edu/entries/respect/
Eyerman, R., and Turner, B. S. (1998). Outline of a Theory of Generations. *European Journal of Social Theory*, 1(1), 91–106.
Fisher, M. (2012). What Is Hauntology? *Film Quarterly*, 66(1), 16–24.
Fiske, S. T., Cuddy, A. J. C., Glick, P., and Xu, J. (2002). A Model of (Often Mixed) Stereotype Content: Competence and Warmth Respectively Follow From Perceived Status and Competition. *Journal of Personality and Social Psychology*, 82(6), 878–902.
FitzSimons, P. (2013, October 17). Why Oh Why Does Gen Y Not Get It? *Sydney Morning Herald*. Retrieved from www.smh.com.au/sport/why-oh-why-does-gen-y-not-get-it-20131016-2vn4u.html

76 Adulthood

Fraser, G. (2003, June 21). The Bullshit Before the But. *The Guardian.* Retrieved from www.theguardian.com/world/2003/jun/20/gayrights.religion2 Retrieved 30 April 2016.

Garner, A. (1973). *Red Shift.* London: HarperCollins.

Goffman, E. (1956). *The Presentation of the Self in Everyday Life.* New York: Vintage Books.

Goffman, E. (1961). *Encounters: Two Studies in the Sociology of Interaction – Fun in Games and Role Distance.* Indianapolis, IN: Bobbs-Merrill.

Gosse, D. (2017, January 4). Transcript of Simon Sinek Millennials in the Workplace Interview. *Ochen.* Retrieved from https://ochen.com/transcript-of-simon-sineks-millennials-in-the-workplace-interview

Grenfell, M. (2008). *Pierre Bourdieu: Key Concepts.* Stocksfield: Acumen.

Illouz, E. (1997). Who Will Care for the Caretaker's Daughter? Towards a Sociology of Happiness in the Era of Reflexive Modernity. *Theory, Culture and Society,* 14(4), 31–66.

Lareau, A. (2003). *Unequal Childhoods: Class, Race, and Family Life.* Berkeley, CA: University of California Press.

Lawrence-Lightfoot, S. (2000). *Respect: An Exploration.* Cambridge, Mass: Perseus.

Macrae, C. N., Stangor, C., and Hewstone M. (1996). *Stereotypes and Stereotyping.* New York: Guilford Press.

McGarty, C., Yzerbyt, V. Y., and Spears, R. (Eds.). (2002). *Stereotypes as Explanations: The Formation of Meaningful Beliefs about Social Groups.* Cambridge: Cambridge University Press.

Nowotny, H. (1981). Women in Public Life in Austria, in Fuchs Epstein, C. and Laub Coser R. (Eds.), *Access to Power: Cross-national Studies of Women and Elites,* pp. 147–156. London: Allen and Unwin.

Padilla-Walker, L., and Nelson, L. (2012). Black Hawk Down?: Establishing Helicopter Parenting as a Distinct Construct from Other Forms of Parental Control during Emerging Adulthood. *Journal of Adolescence,* 35(5), 1177–1190.

Ramos-Oliveira, D., and Pankalla, A. (2019). Negative Stereotypes: An Analysis of Social Cognition in Different Ethnic Groups. Social Cognition of Stereotypes. *Psicogente,* 22(42), 196–210.

Reay, D. (2004). Gendering Bourdieu's Concept of Capitals?: Emotional Capital, Women and Social Class, in L. Adkins and B. Skeggs (Eds.), *Feminism after Bourdieu,* pp. 57–74. London: Blackwell.

Scheer, M. (2012). Are Emotions a Kind of Practice (and Is That What Makes Them Have History)? A Bourdieuian Approach to Understanding Emotion, *History and Theory,* 51 (2), 193–220.

Smetana, J. G., and Asquith, P. (1994). Adolescents' and Parents' Conceptions of Parental Authority and Personal Autonomy. *Child Development,* 65(4), 1147–1162.

Somers, P., and Settle, J. (2010). The Helicopter Parent: Research Toward A Typology. *College and University* 86 (1), 18–27.

Summers, A. (1975). *Damned Whores and God's Police: The Colonization of Women in Australia.* Melbourne: Allen Lane.

Tajfel, H. (Ed.). (1978). *Differentiation between Social Groups: Studies in the Social Psychology of Intergroup Relations.* London: Academic Press.

Tajfel, H., Billig, M., Bundy, R. P., and Flament, C. (1971). Social Categorization and Intergroup Behaviour. *European Journal of Social Psychology,* 1(2), 149–178.

Tajfel, H., and Turner, J. C. (1979). An Integrative Theory of Intergroup Conflict, in W. G. Austin and S. Worchel (Eds.), *The Social Psychology of Intergroup Relations*, pp. 33–47. Monterey, CA: Brooks/Cole.

Trzesniewski, K. H., and Donnellan, M. B. (2014). "Young People These Days … ": Evidence for Negative Perceptions of Emerging Adults. *Emerging Adulthood*, 2(3), 211–226.

Van Dijck, J. (2013). *The Culture of Connectivity: A Critical History of Social Media*. New York: Oxford University Press.

Woodman, D., and Bennett, A. (2015). *Youth Cultures, Transitions and Generations: Bridging the Gap in Youth Research*. Houndsmills: Palgrave MacMillan.

Woodman, D. and Wyn, J. (2015). Class, Gender and Generation Matter: Using the Concept of Social Generation to Study Inequality and Social Change. *Journal of Youth Studies*, 18(10), 1402–1410.

Wordsworth, W., and Coleridge, S. T. (2013). *Lyrical Ballads 1800*. Abingdon; Oxon: Routledge.

Zembylas, M. (2007). Emotional Capital and Education: Theoretical Insights from Bourdieu. *British Journal of Educational Studies*, 55 (4), 443–463.

Zukin, S. (2010). *Naked City: The Death and Life of Authentic Urban Places*. New York: Oxford University Press.

5 Memory, Certainty, Significance

We're annoying (Eliza, 16).
We seem to be all thugs (Joe, 19).
Ignorant, really self-absorbed (Karen, 22).
Doesn't know anything (Susan, 23).
Thought I was trouble (Neil, 35).
Constantly made derogatory comment (Lucille, 40).
Devalued (Alexandra, 51).
Going out now … . At this hour of the night? (Fred, 73).

These comments from research participants are their reflections on the kinds of labels applied to them when young. They demonstrate how adult misrecognition of young people occurs across generations. Each generation has been misrecognised by the adults who preceded them – their parents, their teachers, media commentators, adults in their social sphere. Yet each generation, when they reach adulthood, in turn proceeds to denigrate ensuing youth generations. The misrecognition is patently evident in these self-descriptions as 'thugs', of being 'devalued', the subject of 'derogatory comment', or of being categorised as 'trouble'. The negative stereotyping is apparent and has obviously struck home. However, this stereotyping appears to make little or no difference, or is discarded, when newly arrived-at adults reflect upon and assess the behaviour and attitudes of the young people that follow them. It is as if their own denigration by adults never happened. This capacity to ignore their own experiences, and importantly to fail to empathise with those young people following them, appears to begin at a relatively early age. How does this occur?

One of the most frequent memories of childhood is the interminable waiting that punctuates the lives of children and young people. In the Australian summer, stiflingly hot December and February afternoons are often spent anticipating the 3pm end of school bell. The incessant wait for Christmas Day presents and the long summer school holidays is interminable.[1] As is the endurance required for the five-year period of teenagehood – 13 to 18 years – time spent in anticipation of gaining a driver's licence, of

DOI: 10.4324/9781003427476-5

being able to drink legally, of being able to move into autonomous living; and above all of not being restricted by parental and adult mandates as to when and with whom they go out and how late they can stay up at night. Rundell describes this period as 'a boundary condition between the past, the present and the future' (2009: 45). And for that period between 13 and 18 in particular, it is a boundary condition characterised by acquiescence and passivity (often aggressive passivity) caused by the seemingly total paucity of agency (see Hage, 2009). Teenagers, still under the legal sway of their parents, teachers and other adults, eagerly await with anticipation their eighteenth birthday. They have spent their life gradually, incrementally, acquiring agency, yet, although tantalisingly close, they are still not fully independent until they achieve the magical number of 18. Waiting involves the passage of time, a passage that is invariably slow except when engaged in pleasurable activities. Punctuating this seemingly endless process of waiting are oases of activity, of excitement, discoveries, experimentation, as the metamorphosis from childhood to teenagehood and young adulthood sees new opportunities, new modalities as new experiences become available. As each of these new experiences is incorporated into an individual's habitus, that experience is reflected upon and synthesised as part of what Giddens refers to as: 'a particular narrative ... [which] integrate[s] events which occur in the external world, and sort[s] them into the ongoing "story" about the self' (1991: 54). The notion of time itself becomes part of the reflexive modalities which make up the ongoing personal narrative that increasingly distinguishes 'past from the present, and the future from both in increasing complexity' (Rundell, 2009: 42). Yet this ongoing narrative of the evolving self relies increasingly upon memory which, as we have seen, can be unreliable.

Music and other cultural forms experienced during formative years have a profound impact in terms of later adult preferences for music and cultural products. As Furlong and Cartmel (2007) have indicated, our present-day behaviours emerge from, and yet exist simultaneously with, those of the past in an amalgam of past and present. In adulthood, past and present merge. The adult, having incorporated their youth experiences into their persona, then synthesises those experiences into their adult sensibilities. They view the world from the perspective of their recently acquired adult status, but this is simultaneously seen through the prism of experiences and understandings acquired as a young person. Although the past influences and shapes the present, as Goodwin and O'Connor observe, 'somehow everything is separate from and different to the past' (2017: 23). So, although present understandings are shaped by the past, they nevertheless exist in the present. The past influences and shapes, but reflections are constantly taking place in the present. The adult persona is separate from, and different to, that adult's young person identity. Although the childhood/teenage self exists within them, is integrally part of them, they are not their childhood/teenage self in adult clothes.

As we will see in Chapter 7, the teenage and young adult experience of music is crucial in the young person's journey to self-discovery – the process of *grounded aesthetics*. As such, the engagement with cultural product in their youth accrues greater cachet and is more deeply rooted within their habitus. Most will have shared experiences with their peer group: educational, cultural, sporting, recreational, media and, increasingly, social media experiences. Most will have suffered adult denigration. Most will be aware of the zeitgeist of their generation via various forms of interaction with each other and engagements with various forms of media. The young person emerges into adulthood as part of a wider cohort of young adults who have shared the zeitgeist of the generational experience of growing from childhood to adulthood in roughly the same timeframe. This generational sharing acts as an indelible bond linking them to each other and separating them from those that went before and those that come after.

Social In-Groups and Ownership

Music and other youth cultural forms provide understandings that go beyond an aesthetic engagement. Pauline's example of 'Russians' (Sumner, 1985) as an illustration of her understandings about the world of international politics centred on the politics of the Cold War between East and West. She posed the question: 'How did you know what was going on?' Here, Pauline employs the second person singular pronoun 'you' as the signifier (de Saussure, 1959) in that sentence. But the intent of the pronoun is the inclusive 'we': her generation of demographic peers. This collective collegiality of young people 'sharing' specific generational experiences was echoed by others in the interviews and focus groups. Anthony (65) talking of his teenage years and the experience of collectives said, 'We grew up with that'. Similarly, Max (65) talked of the collegiality of his and his generation's experience:

> At the time in England we had new radio stations come out for youngsters. Pirate radios, Luxemburg. So, they were pumping out this music all the time. So that was a huge influence on teenagers in our time.

As we have seen, Melissa (65) also used the reflexive 'you' to refer to her generational experience: 'you'd run home from school to go and watch Top of the Pops'. Paul (65) identified 'Ready Steady Go, so good for us' as the show that he and his friends enjoyed, and by extension, his generation. This sense of a generational community extended to a sense of collective ownership of the music of the age. That generation felt like it was *their* music, *their* bands. They owned not only the individual experience but the *collective* experience, the shared knowledge of all listening to the same radio stations, of all rushing home to watch Top of the Pops and Ready Steady Go. Their collective ownership was proprietorial. The music was collectively theirs. The bands were collectively theirs. Above all, the experience was collectively theirs. As they moved through their teenagehood into adulthood, they took those shared experiences with them as they progressed through life. It helped to define them: 'We ended up with our own generation of musicians and we still love it. Because that's from your teenage years' (Melissa, 65).

Generational social identity, shared with others who passed through the period of childhood and teenagehood to young adulthood at approximately the same time, exemplifies this embrace, this absorption of the zeitgeist cultural forms of the age. The process of social identity and social categorisation allows those who share that same social identity to function as a 'social in-group'. Social identity links members of the social in-group, enabling them to see themselves and other in-group members as 'interchangeable exemplars of the group prototype' (Hornsey, 207). The afternoon audience of 'Ready Stead Go' formed the interchangeable exemplars of that particular group prototype. Membership of the group goes further than mere shared experiences to the shared understandings emerging from those experiences. It encompasses the totality of the engagement involving shared 'attitudes, emotions and behaviours ... appropriate in a given context' (209; see also Rabbie and Lodewijkx, 1996). The group prototypes in the case of this research reflect generational commonalities: Baby Boomers, Gen X and Millennials.

Individual members of an in-group identify other social in-groups as separate from their own. Importantly, how they identify attitudes, emotions and behaviours of other in-groups different to theirs is exclusionary. Differences, perceived as qualitative, allow the in-group to stereotype both themselves and other identified social groups. This capacity to stereotype plays an important role in the way an in-group makes sense of their world and particularly the way that each in-group interacts with other in-groups:

> Stereotypes have a social function, in the sense that they help explain the social world and to legitimize the past and current actions of the in-group.
> (Hornsey, 2008: 209)

Inherent in the qualitative judgements made about themselves and other in-groups is the elevation of the attitudes, emotions and behaviours of their own group when compared with those of other groups. Hornsey points out that these relationships between groups are structural, involving 'status and competition' (210) with those other groups. Each in-group privileges the experiences of their own in-group over those of other in-groups – in this case generations that follow theirs. Upon attaining adulthood, each generational in-group collectively, qualitatively, assesses each following generational in-group as inferior. The cultural products and the ephemera associated with those following generational in-groups can then be trivialised and stereotyped as part of the ongoing process of misrecognition. As Bourdieu might have put it: each generational in-group is its own *field*, with its own *doxa*. And for once the rules of the game are determined by the young people who are members of that generational in-group.

The Process of Embodiment and Investment

Young people's respect for adults reflects what Darwall (1977) calls 'recognition respect'. Adults expect and often demand respect because of their social position, their life experience, indeed their 'adulthood status'. Their resultant pre-eminence (Bird, 2004) demands an appropriate deferral to their adult status. Adults expect to be accorded *recognition respect* as one of the accrued benefits of the outcomes of their rite of passage to adulthood. When that respect is not forthcoming from young people who are oblivious to, or choose to ignore, the exalted status of their (the adults') generational achievements, the newly arrived adults find themselves cast into Bourdieu's social death of *has-beens*.

As we have seen with Pauline and Matthew in particular, respect, and lack of it, was a theme running through the interviews and focus groups: either on the part of the older informants, with regard to lack of respect towards them by their youngers; or on the part of the younger informants in the form of both the respect demanded of them by adults simply because of their age and seniority, or the lack of respect given to them by those same elders. Lack of respect was a constant point of generational difference amongst informants. As each generation passes through their teenage years, respect for their elders was a necessary condition of entry to many of the fields they operated within. This demand for conformity reflects what Cullity (2019) refers to as 'paternalistic interference'. Upon reaching maturity, they feel it is now their turn for respect to be shown to them by younger people. Their disappointment at this respect not being forthcoming is pronounced. As informant Betty put it: 'We were more or less indoctrinated to conform, whereas the younger people today don't' (Betty, 68). Here, Betty sees the act of conforming as being linked to respect: we conformed because we were expected to respect our elders. Importantly, Betty perceives that the current generation appears to have bypassed that indoctrination.

With age comes an expectation of respect. When that respect is not forthcoming, it does not dampen the expectations. As we have seen with Pauline, respect is not forthcoming from her students, but that does not alter the fact that she expects it to occur, and when it doesn't, misrecognition ensues. In any person's lifetime, they will experience the transition to adulthood. That journey begins as a young person with feelings of resentment at the demands made by parents, teachers and other adults for them to be deferred to as 'elders'. Upon attaining adulthood, it progresses to expecting that same respect be accorded to them, afforded by their status and authority as 'elders' – the same respect they begrudgingly, conferred on their elders.

As Giddens (1984) points out, social relations evolving and changing across space and time often involve waiting. Adolescent experimentation and engagement with youth cultural forms brings young people into conflict with parents, teachers and adults, conflict often centred around demands by adults to comply with their wishes.

As young people personally invest in the cultural products as part of the process of *Libido sciendi*, each investment comes with a dividend. The dividend from engagement with cultural forms is the ongoing enjoyment and sense of fulfilment resulting from that engagement – in all its forms. The investment in the acquisition of this embodied capital is often done unknowingly, unconsciously – a spontaneous engagement and reaction to the cultural product. And the greater the investment, the greater the dividend. The randomness of the rewards of this investment recognises its own *internal rationale* (see Bourdieu and Wacquant, 1992), its own reward. It is this internal logic which allows the misrecognition of the randomness of its embodiment. The joy at engagement with grounded aesthetics is often not shared by parents and adults. Responses can range from overt disapproval to banning of the 'offending' cultural product. Parents/adults demand that their judgements be respected and obeyed – be deferred to. Resentment at this inability of the adults to 'understand' causes young people to misrecognise the demands of adults that they be deferred to. This embodied misrecognition is then reflected in the form of an expectation, as they enter and pass through adulthood, that they too will be deferred to in much the same way that they were forced to defer to adults. This assumption, unspoken and often unrecognised, is that 'what goes around will come around'.

So, young people spend what seems like an eternity getting to and achieving their adult status. In doing so, they suffer and endure the seemingly endless misrecognition by their parents, teachers and other adults as part of that transition process. Finally, they transition to being an adult and enter the next stage of their lives as fully fledged (legal) adults. But they do so as members of a cohort of young people who have passed through similar experiences at approximately the same time and with whom they share a social identity. The bonds of this social identity draw individual members together. They share experiences, attitudes and emotions according to the zeitgeist of their generation which allows them to stereotype themselves and others of their generation who share their social identity. Subsequent generations cannot match the richness of their experience. Their investment in the *libido sciendi*, their engagement with the *grounded aesthetics* of their youth ensures that the dividend they reap as they age includes the certainty that their youth experience was superior to ensuing youth generations.

Expectations and Certainty at Risk

The embodiment of the knowledge that theirs was/is the only authentic youth experience is arrived at with the certainty adhering to the circumstances of its embodiment. If each generation 'knows' that theirs was the authentic youth experience, then it follows naturally that the authenticity, 'their' authenticity, cannot be matched by that of other generations. This 'certainty', embodied as *illusio*, conferring the capacity to infallibly *voir* and *savoir*, does not require analysis, does not require interrogation. It remains, locked in the habitus as an unimpeachable 'truth' emboldened by the double language of (the now) *generational* disinterest.

As part of the interviews and focus groups, informants were asked to imagine whether their teenage self could envisage what they would become as adults. They were invited to reflect on their teenage self and how they came to acquire their perceptions of young people today. For some, the source was personal experience: 'How you grew up. The experiences you went through. Did you have a hard time or not' (Richard, 31).

The claim that 'how you grew up' colours the way young people today are perceived by adults highlights again the axiom that the child is parent of the adult. Richard's reflections of his teenagehood from the perspective of his early thirties are undertaken from his concept of who he is now. This perspective was clearly informed by not only his capacity for real-time reflection, but by his capacity to reflect on, and analyse, how he got to where he is. That reflection has enabled him to develop and maintain the process of presentation of self to self: the ability to grasp and preserve a cogent image of who he knows he is.

There is an assuredness to the belief in the pre-eminence of adults' own cultural forms when compared with ensuing generations. That certainty is *doxic*. It serves to underpin their understanding of the way the world works. As young people transition to adulthood, that certainty becomes like a touchstone of their habitus: how could any following generation's youth experience match theirs when theirs was the pinnacle of youth experiences? But the emergence of new younger generations, each with their own set of *grounded aesthetics*, challenges that certainty. These newer generations are themselves interacting with their own cultural forms, and in the process, begin the process of disowning those of their parents' generations, or at least incorporating (a la Bennett) them as a kind of addendum to their own experiences. Adults respond to these challenges with mockery and trivialising as an attempt to maintain the infallibility of the certainty of the authenticity of their own youth experience. They misrecognise these challenges as inauthentic responses to their own authentic understandings.

This ongoing intergenerational interaction with following generations soon confirms that the 'rules of the game' that they understood to be set in stone, and that they were forced to adhere to, don't necessarily apply upon arrival at adulthood. The expectations that they entered adulthood with, that they too would be deferred to as they were forced to, aren't necessarily forthcoming. Just as they did in their own youth, young people have the temerity to question the cultural forms of them, their elders. Yet these recently arrived adults have been hardwired to believe their cultural forms are the gold standard for the authentic youth experience. Ensuing youth generations fail to show respect according to the ritual expectations of the older generation. The cycle begins again.

This is notably the case with Millennials. Adult understandings of Millennials centres on the trivia of young people's pre-occupation with

Memory, Certainty, Significance 85

phones and social media which seemingly provides them with the excuse to ignore others around them. This particularly applies to older adults, themselves struggling with the demands of the technological challenge of phones, social media and technology in general. The end result is a perception (if not the reality) that the young people are failing to pay due deference to them, to show them the respect as adults they have come to expect and deserve. The rules of the game that they felt compelled to play within, that they have carried with them as they entered and passed through adulthood, have seemingly lost their validity. Having waited out their teenage years, having survived the walled garden, having breached the future, having attained their maturity, having attained the sanctity of adulthood, they are confronted not by respect but by indifference to their adult status – an indifference in the form of Millennials' obsession with the ubiquitous mobile phone.

Millennial's obsession with technology is at the heart of what Beck[2] refers to as the 'risk society':

> As knowledge and technology race ahead we are left behind, panting in ignorance, increasingly unable to control the machines we depend on.
> (Beck, 1998: 13)

Here, Beck is very clearly referring to adults. Yet young people were born into a digital age. Technology framed their formative years. Their parents have had to adapt their analogue consciousness to the digital transformation of the last 30 years. The cosmos that young people function within is digital. They have grown up tuning their parents' TV sets, setting up their mobile devices and fixing their computer problems. The new rules of the game dictate that this is their role. As we saw with informant Helen: 'My grandma gets me to post everything on her Facebook … because she doesn't know how to' (Helen, 16). There is no more powerful example of this demographic technology demarcation than the cliché of the helpless adult relying on a young person to solve their digital incompetence.

Technology puts adults' sense of certainty at risk. To make matters worse, the young people who do understand technology are the same young people whose obsession with that same technology causes them to disdain providing due deference to the adults which those adults now believe they have a right to deserve.

The Media: Agents of Moral Indignation

The fragmenting of the media landscape over the past 30 years has resulted in the mainstream legacy media audience increasingly being comprised of older listeners, watchers and readers. George (30) was very conscious of this fragmentation:

> Commercial television, especially breakfast current affairs television, is now aimed squarely at a much older demographic much older than any of us in this room… Scare mongering … 'Oh those teenagers you know'. Most people they're talking about don't watch commercial television anymore so that kind of media has quite a monopoly on the beat up of young children. The people who noticed … are the old people.

Clearly mainstream media is becoming the source of choice for the older age cohort. And the traditional broadcast media is where they are more likely to have their generational misrecognition reinforced.

Bourdieu is unequivocal about the impact that mainstream media, and in particular television, has upon significant sections of the population:

> Television enjoys a de facto monopoly on what goes into the heads of a significant part of the population and what they think.
> (Bourdieu, 1984: 18)

Cohen identifies the media as a significant player in 'exploitative culture' (2002: 156). Goode and Ben-Yehuda (2006) characterise the tendency for the media to over-report as them becoming 'actors in the drama of moral panic' (24–25). This active participation is intrinsically linked to the potential benefit they can extract (in terms of ratings and sales/consumers). They may be as Cohen describes them 'agents of moral indignation' (2002: 9–10), but the motive is ultimately profit through maintaining popularity with the target audience. And increasingly, the audience for that mainstream media is older adults.

Fred (73), in initial discussions about the role of media, demonstrated his understanding of the way the media functions:

> It's not a newsworthy effort if you see a boy scout take a little old lady across the street. But you'd stand up and cheer for the boy scout. Would it make the news? NO! [But] if that boy scout threw a stone at the dog it'd probably be on the news.

Yet when challenged about where he gained most of his knowledge about young people, and particularly where he gained his negative attitudes towards young people, Fred responded: 'the media … to a large degree'. By his own admission, Fred's perception of young people was driven almost exclusively by the way young people are portrayed in the media. His concerns about the drug ice and young people in Chapter 3 reflected the moral panic about youth drug use that has raged across the mass media over the past 40 years (see Armstrong, 2007; Homan, 2003; Jenkins, 1994; Linnemann, 2010; Fredrickson et al., 2019). From his response, Fred is aware of the moral panic generated by the media, yet his endorsement of this moral panic was unquestioning. For Fred, ice and young people were inextricably linked. It was at the heart of his concerns ('appals me'). However, he relies almost exclusively upon information from the mass media. Despite the fact that some of the more serious media outlets have called into question the nature and scale of the 'ice epidemic' (Fitzgerald, 2015; Turtle, 2007), the mainstream 'drugs' moral panic continues to be largely accepted. This was unequivocally Fred's position.

For young people, the mainstream media, although not their source of choice, was very much within their consciousness because they were aware of and understood that 'they' (young people) were often the subject of much of that media's attention and focus. Joe (19), Elaine (21) and Sharon (23) were very conscious of the role that the mainstream media plays in the denigration of young people, that the field of mass media is all-pervasive in the way that young people are presented and represented:

> Bad news stories make good headlines... On a schoolies' trip, five kids ... hang over the balcony, that's a very, very small minority. But the media make it out that they're all going to the Gold Coast to hang over the balcony. They take the bad headlines because they know that the bad stories make good front-page news.
>
> (Joe, 19)

Sharon (23) saw media denigration of the youth generation as part of a wider tendency by society as a whole to focus on the negative:

> When you get given five good things about someone and the one bad thing will take it away from whatever it is, you'll always remember that one negative. Our human nature is drawn to the negatives always ... That's what is focussed on.

The media focus on the negative, on the creation and promotion of moral panics, is the reality that young people deal with on a daily basis (see Altheide, 2009, 2003; Holland, Blood, Thomas, Lewis, Komesaroff and Castle, 2011; Lumby and Funnell 2011; McRobbie and Thornton, 1995). The economic imperative to sell newspapers, to garner viewers and listeners, is a driving force to discover/expose/reveal that which will cause people to buy newspapers, watch television and listen to radio thereby putting pressure on journalists to create a story. Bourdieu highlights this pressure:

> The journalistic field produces and imposes on the public a very particular vision of the political [and other] field[s]... ruled by a fear of being boring.
> (Bourdieu, 1998: 2)

The past 30 years has seen a fragmentation of media from 'mass' status to increasingly fragmented 'niche' markets and distribution outlets (Giddens, 1984; Goldhaber, 1997; Davenport and Beck, 2001; Lanham, 2006) with young people in particular turning away from mass media outlets and relying increasingly upon online access.

Young people having vacated traditional media have abandoned it to their elders. Joe (19) works in the mass media and he has observed this transformation taking place at close quarters:

> There'll be no news read from the regional desk. It'll all be read from Sydney[3]. And, from the media's perspective, that's being driven by young people. That change is being driven by people of social media in that 18 to 30 bracket, who don't have any demand to buy the paper [or use television] any more.

Increasingly marginalised as young people desert it, mainstream media, conscious of the narrowing demographics of their audience, seek to tailor their output to that audience. A fundamental element of the media landscape going back to tabloid newspaper days and 'gutter press', mainstream media has increasingly resorted to sensationalism as its default mode of operation. The emergence since the turn of the century of Fox News in particular and similar clones of Fox in the UK and Australia is the 'highpoint' of this phenomenon. As Megan Garber puts it, Fox has two pronouns, *you* and *they*:

> Fox has two pronouns, *you* and *they*, and one tone: indignation. (*You* are under attack; *they* are the attackers.) Its grammar is grievance. Its effect is totalizing. Over time, if you watch enough *Fox & Friends* or *The Five* or Tucker Carlson or Sean Hannity or Laura Ingraham, you will come to understand, as a matter of synaptic impulse, that immigrants are invading and the mob is coming and the news is lying and Trump alone can fix it.
> (Garber, 2020)

Indignation is its tone and grievance is its grammar. It is this sense of outrage which is at the heart of mainstream media's 'appeal' to their older audience (that and cooking shows and house renovations and 'dating shows' and other 'reality' shows). Sensationalising young people and the threats they pose is one rung down from the level of hyperbole cited by Garber above, but the cry for young people to get their heads out of their mobile phones and 'man up', and other assorted young people misrecognitions, has been, and remains, a staple of mainstream media sensationalism.

Although it is no longer their main source of news, Joe, Elaine and Sharon were aware of the way mass media portrays young people.[4] Their explanations of the doxa of the way the media works incorporated an understanding of the motivation of Bourdieu's 'fear of being boring'. The rules of the game, they understand, dictate that 'bad news stories make good headlines' (Joe, 19). Older adults' denigration of young people follows on from their interaction with mass media because 'that's what the media's taught them and that's what they think's right' (Joe, 19). Joe's statement was laced with sarcasm and contempt.

Joe, Elaine and Sharon have arrived at the early adulthood stage replete with their own understanding of mass media's manipulation of the 'facts' to place young people in a negative light. They shared an understanding that being a young person meant being misrecognised by the mass media, and that the older audience were going to respond positively to this manipulation, even when it's not a young person involved:

> Even in stories regarding older people ... [a] P Plate crash. It's a 42-year-old person with their p plates. Straight away you're going to be thinking young person. Because p plates are when you're learning to drive.
>
> (Elaine, 21)

Joe followed up with an extension of the P plate scenario:

Joe: Car accident. Some man runs off the road into tree. Drink driving allegedly speeding. What's the first thing somebody thinks of? They go...
Sharon vociferously interjects: 20-year-old male!
Joe: Exactly! 20-year-old male who bought a high-powered ute.

This sequence happened spontaneously as if Joe and Sharon were speaking with the one voice. The sense was one of more than mere familiarity with the phenomenon they were describing. The subtext of that synchronised reaction was that they have seen this time and time again. Their acquired understanding of this media manipulation, and the resultant resentment, has become part of their habitus. Adult and media misrecognition of them and of young people in general is now part of the doxa of being a young person entering adulthood. Elaine recounted a personal story of the disconnect between the mass media 'spin' and the reality of her own experience:

> My father's a school principal and their school captain unfortunately dies in a car accident, hit by a truck driving on the wrong side of the road... The newspapers ... implied that it was the 'P plater's fault because it was late at night and he'd been out at a pub. The truth was he'd been working a gig ... a musician ... driving home from the gig and the truck driver's been irresponsible... That wasn't the story the media spun.
>
> (Elaine, 21)

For them 'the media is king' (Joe, 19); 'the media spins it' (Sharon, 23).

Joe, Elaine and Sharon have entered the legal and social world of adulthood. The memory shadows of their youth, recently exited from, are strong and clear. Even though their legal status has changed and they now wear the legal status of adult, the *garment* of 'young person' still enfolds them. Their sense of who they are remains very much in the category of young person. The bonds and the memory of their youth are still powerful enough to allow them to continue to define themselves as young person. The sense of hurt at their treatment by adults is still palpable: 'What's the first thing they think of... 20 YEAR OLD MALE'! The outrage is that of a young person. The resentment at the unfairness of it all is that of a young person. But as we have seen with the example of George, Neil and Joanne (ten years older) in Chapter 4, the persona and the attitudes and values of adulthood beckon, as does the capacity to view their former young person status from the accompanying vantage point of the double language of generational disinterest. Joe's pronouncements on the future of mainstream media, his adoption of the Adult Voice to frame his analysis, heralds this onset.

Identity: A Self-Reflexive Universe of References

The history of moral panics includes repeated examples of young people in their varying subcultural disguises wreaking havoc as 'folk devils' – from Mods and Rockers in the 1960s (Cohen, 2002) to threat of African gangs as a major issue in the 2018 Australian Victorian State election (Martin, 2018; Wahlquist, 2018; Ghazarian, 2018). Despite the fact that young people have effectively vacated the field of mainstream media, they nevertheless are conscious of the role that mainstream media plays as an active player in misrecognising young people. This has led to a kind of hybrid media engagement for young people. Their major engagement is with social media and online sources. But this does not deter them from a conscious awareness of how mainstream media continually misrecognises them and their generational cohort. Social media also thrives on sensation. 'Breaking' is one of the most common 'signal alerts' that one encounters on social media. News does not disappear on social media. It is played then re-imagined, re-focussed, re-propagated and then replayed – endlessly. Young people engage with news on their own terms, but they do engage.

Joanne 32, George 30 and Neil 35 work in the media. News is their bread and butter.[5] As part of their focus group discussion about how young people are reflected in the mass media Joanne, 32, George, 30 and Neil, 35 focussed on examples of moral panics and how the media might have treated them when they were teenagers. Joanne's recollection was of the *Daily Telegraph*'s January 8, 1997 front-page story of 'The Class We Failed'[6] (Morgan, Anderson, Dobson, Allon & Neilson 2006), the infamous Mt Druitt High School HSC story where photos of a class sitting for the end of school certificate were shown on the front page of a Sydney Tabloid newspaper. The headline read 'THE CLASS WE FAILED', but the story ruthlessly shamed those in the photograph:

> When I dig around in my head for media treatment of young people when I was young that's probably a memory.
>
> (Joanne, 32)

'The Class We Failed' article is an example of how the field of education, with its major focus on young people, is rich fodder for the mass media to exploit moral panics associated with 'that continual political minefield that is education' (Neil, 35). It is a case of:

> The same stories being told over and over again ... drugs ... killing teenagers at festivals ... young people getting drunk and making fools of themselves... the same bunch of stories and ad lines recycled every generation.
>
> (Neil, 35)

Why would young people bother with mainstream media when as Neil points out 'The same stories being told over and over again ... drugs ... killing teenagers at festivals ... young people getting drunk and making fools of themselves'? As George points out, young people in the main increasingly eschew mainstream media because for them 'trust' is the only currency they are interested in when it comes to news sources:

> They use social media as their media ... They have to trust people before they actually will bother reading a post, or even thinking about something because they're influenced by what their people who are in their friend group, who they trust to actually sort out what kind of interests them. And it's kind of brought to them. They don't really have to seek it out.
>
> (George, 30)

This is young people taking control not only of their news sources, but they are also taking control of their online presence. The process of curating your own media content, identified by George, reflects what Pariser identifies as the creation of our 'own unique information universe: the filter bubble' (2011: 1). The trust identified by George exists within this bubble. It is formed, shaped, by the dynamics of the interactions within the bubble: 'Your identity shapes your media, and your media then shapes what you believe and what you care about' (125). Abidin has identified that within the digital sphere, there are 'influencers' and 'followers', and the 'intimacy' (2013, 2015) established between the two contributes to this trust. Their chosen online media providing 'news that is pleasant, familiar and confirms our beliefs' (1). This filtering process leads to the creation of each young person's information universe. In effect this means:

> Being an individual (that is, being responsible for your choice of life, your choice among choices, and the consequences of the choices you chose) is not *a matter of choice*, but *a decree of fate*.
>
> (Bauman, 2008: 53–54)

The process of curating information simultaneously incorporates the curation of identity which, according to Hinkson, 'needs to be created, just as works of art are created' (2016: 37). And this is a two-way process: receiving and incorporating information into each person's habitus and reflecting back the incorporated information as the person's online and non-online persona. This process has been an ongoing one, preceding the 'digital age' as we have seen with *grounded aesthetics* and *introjection*. The advent of online personas has provided an immediacy to the arenas that each actor now engages in and with: a 'self-reflexive universe of references' (Rushkoff, 2013: 50). This is a process of synthesising the understandings resulting from the digital interaction along with the sources of that interaction. This reflects what Robards and Bennett refer to as 'the politics of the everyday, bound by issues of taste and belonging' (2011: 305). Online identity creation is a complex interaction of agency on the part of the young person and the demands and limitations imposed by online media corporations. Above all, unlike mainstream media, it reflects the two-way process of online engagement. Handyside and Ringrose in referencing Snapchat talk about 'online persona':

Curation of a finely edited version of one's life, through which truth is manipulated to present a specific impression through the temporal impermanence of snaps.

(2017: 352)

Further, encouragement of 'second guessing creates ambiguity and multiplicity' (352) in the curated online spaces. Similarly, Turkle (1996) and Boyd (2007) have all explored the notion of agency in the creation and evolution of identity. Woodman (2009) has specifically examined this discourse between the competing proponents of structure and agency (see also Kember and Zylinska, 2012; Papacharissi, 2014; Ringrose and Coleman, 2013; Bonanno, 2014). Evans' reference to 'bounded agency' (2010: 262) highlights the complexity of the agency/structure dichotomy and reflects Bourdieu's concept of habitus as 'structured and structuring structure'. In Evans' doctoral study, it was identified that, echoing (and foreshadowing) the futurists in Chapter 8, in the stereotyping of Millennials, there is a perception amongst adults that young people are not only engaged with digital technology but are both consumed and defined by it. And it is the ubiquitous mobile phone which is the iconic representation of their obsession.

Millennials are identified with digital technology because they are perceived to be the first generation to have grown up with it from birth – the ubiquitous digital natives. There has been critical discussion as to the efficacy of this label (see Bennett, Maton and Kervin, 2008). But again, whether the term is an accurate descriptor or not, the perception is that Millennials are 'digital natives'. They seamlessly engage with technology not just with ease but as though born to it – which of course they are. This perception has entered the lexicon. Elaine (21) self-identified as a digital native:

We're digital natives, so for us that's all part of our life and we know how to use [technology]. They don't understand what we're actually doing with it. They just think we've got our head in it, not paying attention.

The predominant doxa surrounding Millennials is that they are inextricably entwined with their digital nativity to the detriment of personal interactions, placing the future at risk.

The media then, in all its forms, serves to help frame the discourse around adult misrecognition of young people. As the media has fragmented, so has its audience. This demarcation of audience comes with its own stereotypes. In reality, many adults engage with social media and, as we have seen with informants in the Millennial demographic, they are aware of and engage with mainstream media. Nevertheless, these stereotypes are used to stigmatise young people and amplify moral panics. Each successive moral panic about youth behaviour, highlighted by mainstream media, serves to confirm adult perceptions. Perceptions that each successive youth generation commits some form of failure of respect for the authenticity of the generations that preceded them, thereby posing a risk to the future. From the perspective of young people, mainstream media recycles the 'same bunch of stories every generation', and those recycled stories will misrecognise them and their generational peers. Yet that pattern repeats. They will go on to take their turn to repeat that misrecognition as they move from teenager to young adulthood and then into full adulthood. Joanne, George and Neil are now well into that journey.

Having reached adulthood, adults find themselves in a situation where they feel increasingly alienated from the world of their children. Mainstream media has been abandoned by young people in favour of social media. Mainstream media reflects back to adults the interests, concerns and prejudices of the older demographic, creating a kind of echo chamber where those prejudices are reinforced.

From the time of birth, parents and other adults organise and control young people's lives. 'Respect' has been part of the currency paid as part of those imposed constraints. Young people learn that the code of growing up includes the knowledge that they will be paying that currency of respect either willingly or begrudgingly. Having paid their dues, an expectation is created that when they reach adulthood, they will have earned the 'recognition respect' from their own children and other young people. The 'respect investment' they have made as young people will produce the dividend of respect from ensuing generations. That certainty is put at risk when the respect they have expected and counted upon is not forthcoming. Misrecognition in the form of resentment ensues.

The following chapter will explore how habitus evolves with the addition and emission of material as each new life experience is encountered and engaged with. This engagement and the embodiment of those experiences – what is accepted and what is rejected – is facilitated by the process of the *aesthetic solera*.

Notes

1 Northern hemisphere countries would experience something similar prior to and following their midyear long summer break.
2 Both Giddens (1984) and Beck (1998) have sought to explore the notion of risk in response to radical global change taking place from the 1980s. Both sought to provide theoretical understandings of the uncertainty created by the rapid social, economic and cultural changes brought about by globalisation – that in a time of uncertainty, 'risk is a way of controlling ... the future' (Beck, 1998: 11). While Giddens and Beck sought to explain the effect of uncertainty operating on a global scale, nevertheless uncertainty as a phenomenon functions at both the global and the local level.
3 The interviews for this research were conducted in and around Newcastle and the Hunter Valley where the author lives. Newcastle is about 130 km north of Sydney, the largest city in Australia.
4 Mainstream media is a staple of gyms and airports and roadside truck stops and cafes and shopping centres and the family home when they visit. It is difficult to escape at least being aware of its ubiquity.
5 One only has to walk into any radio newsroom in the country to find it chaotically littered with that day's morning papers as journalists and presenters mine the dailies for content with which to fill their programs.
6 The Class We Failed was a story promoted by Sydney's Daily Telegraph which referenced very poor HSC results from Mt Druitt High School, a low socio-economic area in Sydney's Western Suburbs. A photograph of the class was published on the front page resulting in defamation proceedings against the Telegraph and a subsequent award of damages against the paper. This created a sensation when first published. The awarding of damages against the paper for defamation did not produce anywhere near the same amount of coverage.

Bibliography

Abidin, C. (2013). Cyber-BFFs*: Assessing Women's 'Perceived Interconnectedness' in Singapore's Commercial Lifestyle Blog Industry *Best Friends Forever. *Global Media Journal: Australian Edition*, 7(1), 1–20.
Altheide, D. (2003). Notes towards a Politics of Fear. *Journal for Crime, Conflict and the Media*, 1(1), 37–54.
Altheide, D. (2009). Moral Panic: From Sociological Concept to Public Discourse. *Crime Media Culture*, 5(1), 79–99.
Armstrong, E. (2007). Moral Panic over Meth. *Contemporary Justice Review*, 10(4), 427–442.
Bauman, Z. (2008). *The Art of Life*. Cambridge: Polity Press.
Beck, U. (1998). The Politics of Risk Society, in Franklin, J. (Ed.), *The Politics of Risk Society*, pp. 9–22. Cambridge: Polity.
Bennett, S., Maton, K. and Kervin, L. (2008). The 'Digital Natives' Debate: A Critical Review of the Evidence. *British Journal of Educational Technology*, 39(5), 775–786.

Bonanno, E. R. (2014). The Social Media Paradox: An Examination of the Illusion Versus the Reality of Social Media. *Sociological Imagination: Western's Undergraduate Sociology Student Journal*, 3(1), Article 3.

Bourdieu, P. (1984). *Distinction: A Social Critique of the Judgement of Taste*. London: Routledge & Kegan Paul.

Bird, C. (2004). Status, Identity and Respect. *Political Theory*, 32(4), 207–232.

Bourdieu, P. (1998). *On Television*. New York: New Press.

Bourdieu, P., and Wacquant, L. (1992). *An Invitation to Reflexive Sociology*. Chicago, IL: University of Chicago.

Boyd, d. (2007). Why Youth (Heart) Social Network Sites: The Role of Networked Publics in Teenage Social Life, in D. Buckingham, (Ed.) *Youth, Identity, and Digital Media*, pp. 119–142. Cambridge, MA.: MIT Press.

Cohen, S. (2002). *Folk Devils and Moral Panics: The Creation of the Mods and Rockers* (New ed.). London; New York: Routledge.

Cullity, G. (2019). *Concern, Respect, and Cooperation*. Oxford: Oxford University Press.

Darwall, S. (1977). Two Kinds of Respect. *Ethics*, 88, 36–49.

Davenport, T. H., and Beck, J. C. (2001). *The Attention Economy: Understanding the New Currency of Business*. Boston, MA: Harvard Business School Press.

de Saussure, F. (1959). *Course in General Linguistics*. New York: McGraw-Hill.

Fitzgerald, J. (2015, May 18). Don't Panic: The 'Ice Pandemic' is a Myth. *Sydney Morning Herald*. Available from www.smh.com.au/comment/dont-panic-the-ice-pandemic-is-a-myth-20150515-gh2plm.html

Fredrickson, A., Gibson, A. F., Lancaster, K., and Nathan, S. (2019). "Devil's Lure Took All I Had": Moral Panic and the Discursive Construction of Crystal Methamphetamine in Australian News Media. *Contemporary Drug Problems*, 46(1), 105–121.

Furlong, A., and Cartmel, F. (2007). *Young People and Social Change: New Perspectives*. Maidenhead : McGraw-Hill/Open University Press,

Garber, M. (2020, Sept. 16). Do You Speak Fox? How Donald Trump's favorite news source became a language. *The Atlantic*. Retrieved from www.theatlantic.com/culture/archive/2020/09/fox-news-trump-language-stelter-hoax/616309/

Ghazarian, Z. (2018, November 19). Victoria Election: The Scandals Sloganeering and Key Issues to Watch. *The Conversation*. Retrieved from https://theconversation.com/victoria-election-the-scandals-sloganeering-and-key-issues-to-watch-105495

Giddens, A. (1984). *The Constitution of Society: Outline of the Theory of Structuration*. Cambridge: Polity Press.

Giddens, A. (1991). *Modernity and Self-identity: Self and Society in the Late Modern Age*. Cambridge: Polity Press.

Goldhaber, M. (1997). The Attention Economy and the Net. *First Monday*, 2(4). Retrieved from https://doi.org/10.5210/fm.v2i4.519

Goode, E., and Ben-Yehuda, N. (2006). *Moral Panics: The Social Construction of Deviance*. Cambridge, MA: Blackwell.

Goodwin, J., and O'Connor, H. (2009/2017). Youth and Generation in the Midst of an Adult World, in A. Furlong (Ed.), *Handbook of Youth and Young Adulthood: New Perspectives and Agendas*, pp. 21–30. London: Routledge.

Hage, G. (2009). *Waiting*. Carlton: Melbourne University Publishing.

Handyside, S., and Ringrose, J. (2017). Snapchat Memory and Youth Digital Sexual Cultures: Mediated Temporality, Duration and Affect. *Journal of Gender Studies*, 26(3), 347–360.

Hinkson, M. (Ed.). (2016). *Imaging Identity: Media, Memory and Portraiture in the Digital Age*. Canberra: ANU Press.

Holland, K., Blood, R. Warwick, T., Lewis, S., Komesaroff, P., and Castle, D. (2011). Our Girth Is Plain to See: An Analysis of Newspaper Coverage of Australia's Future 'Fat Bomb'. *Health, Risk & Society*, 13(1), 31–46.

Homan, S. (2003). *The Mayor's a Square: Live Music and Law and Order in Sydney*. Newtown: Local Consumption Publications.

Hornsey, M. J. (2008). Social Identity Theory and Self-categorization Theory: A Historical Review. *Social and Personality Psychology Compass*, 2(1), 204–222.

Jenkins, P. (1994). 'The Ice Age': The Social Construction of a Drug Panic. *Justice Quarterly*, 11(1), 7–31.

Kant, I. (1991). *The Metaphysics of Morals*, M. Gregor (trans.). Cambridge: Cambridge University Press.

Kember, S., and Zylinska, J. (2012*). Life after New Media–Mediation as a Vital Process*. Cambridge, MA: MIT Press.

Lanham, R. (2006). *The Economics of Attention*. Chicago, IL: University of Chicago Press.

Linnemann, T (2010). Mad Men, Meth Moms, Moral Panic: Gendering Meth Crimes in the Midwest, *Critical Criminology*, 218 (2), 95–110.

Lumby, C., and Funnell, N. (2011). Between Heat and Light: The Opportunity in Moral Panics. *Crime, Media, Culture*, 7(3), 277–291.

Martin, L. (2018, October, 31). Victorian Election Gang Violence at Centre of Law and Order Debate. *The Guardian Australia*. Retrieved from www.theguardian.com/australia-news/2018/oct/31/victorian-election-gang-violence-at-centre-of-law-and-order-debate

McRobbie, A., and Thornton, S. (1995). Rethinking 'Moral Panic' for Multi Mediated Social Worlds. *The British Journal of Sociology*, 46 (4), 559–574.

Morgan, G., Anderson, K. J., Dobson, R., Allon, F., and Neilson, B. (2006). A City of Two Tales: Distinction, Dispersal and Dissociation in Western Sydney. *After Sprawl: Post-Suburban Sydney: E-Proceedings of 'post-Suburban Sydney: The City in Transformation' Conference, 22–23 November 2005, Riverside Theatres, Parramatta, Sydney*. Retrieved from www.uws.edu.au/__data/assets/pdf_file/0019/7174/Morgan_Final.pdf

Pariser, E. (2011). *The Filter Bubble: What the Internet Is Hiding from You*. London: Viking/Penguin Press.

Plato (1921). *Theaetetus*, H. N. Fowler (trans.). London: William Heinemann Ltd.

Rabbie, J. M., and Lodewijkx, H. F. M. (1996). A Behavioral Interaction Model: Toward an Integrative Theoretical Framework for Studying Intra and Intergroup Dynamics, in E. H. Witte and J. H. Davies (Eds.), *Understanding Group Behaviors, Vol. 2: Small Group Processes and Interpersonal Relations*, pp. 255–294. Mahwah, NJ: Lawrence Erlbaum.

Ringrose, J., and Coleman, B. (2013). Looking and Desiring Machines: A Feminist Deleuzian Mapping of Affect and Bodies, in B. Coleman and J. Ringrose (Eds.), *Deleuze and Research Methodologies*, pp. 125–144. Edinburgh: EUP.

Robards, B., and Bennett, A. (2011). MyTribe: Post-subcultural Manifestations of Belonging on Social Network Sites, *Sociology*, 45(2), 303–317.

Rousseau, J. J. (1997). *'The Discourses' and Other Early Political Writings*, V. Gourevitch (trans.). Cambridge: Cambridge University Press.

Rundell, J. (2009). Temporal Horizons of Modernity and Modalities of Waiting, in Hage, G. (Ed.), *Waiting*, pp. 39–53. Carlton: Melbourne University Publishing.

Rushkoff, D. (2013). *Present Shock: When Everything Happens Now*. New York: Current.

Sennett, R. (2003). *Respect: The Formation of Character in a World of Inequality*. London: Allen Lane.

Sumner, G. (1985). Russians [Recorded by Sting]. On *The Dream of the Blue Turtles*. Saint Phillip, Barbados and Morin-Heights, Quebec, Canada: A & M Records.

Turkle, S. (1996). *Life on the Screen: Identity in the Age of the Internet*. London: Orion.

Turtle, M. (Reporter). (2007, February, 1). Ice Hysteria Clouds Alcohol Epidemic: Expert. [ABC PM]. Sydney Australia: ABC Radio. Retrieved from www.abc.net.au/pm/content/2007/s1838522.htm

Wahlquist, C. (2018, October 26). Victorian Election Roundup Dutton Reprises Gang Fears As Liberals Run On. *The Guardian Australia*. Retrieved from www.theguardian.com/australia-news/2018/oct/26/victorian-election-roundup-dutton-reprises-gang-fears-as-liberals-run-on Accessed 10 January 2019.

Woodman, D. (2009). The Mysterious Case of the Pervasive Choice Biography: Ulrich Beck, Structure/Agency, and the Middling State of Theory in the Sociology of Youth. *Journal of Youth Studies*, 12(3), 243–256.

6 Appropriate or Inappropriate?
The Aesthetic Solera and Habitus

We are the products of editing not authorship.

(George Wald)[1]

As we saw with Joe, Elaine and Sharon, the perception of young people transitioning to adulthood, and indeed their own self-concept as an adult, does not immediately transform with the advent of their adult legal status. The progression to adulthood does not cease at age 18. Participation in further education, employment, significant relationships, moving out of home and even family, and home purchases are all part of the transition process usually beyond 18 years (see Wyn and Woodman, 2006; Furlong, 2009; Furlong, Woodman and Wyn, 2011). The process of relinquishing their young person status and achieving adult status is gradual and ongoing (see Danesi, 2003). In any event, eventually (at some indeterminant time which is unique to each individual) their self-concept will metamorphose from young person to adult. But before, during and after that transition, it is Wald's truism that holds for the adult we become. And with the passing of time, like the bones and muscles of an ageing body, the editing becomes increasingly inflexible and hardwired.

Transition from youth to adult involves a process of adjustment – letting go the reins on the part of parents/teachers/associated adults, and a testing of the waters on the part of young people. Many adult signposts, such as relationships, experimenting with alcohol, and other de facto rites of passage, are often part of a young person's life experience prior to 16, 17 or 18. Côté refers to these as the 'decline in normative social markers in the transition to adulthood' (2009: 379).

As young people enter and progress through their teenage years, parents, having nurtured their children from infancy to teenager, adapt to, and attempt to manage, this transition process. Their children's increasing independence, and the pace of that increasing independence, occurs in concert with, and sometimes simultaneously in conflict with, their personal preferences. Emerging independence may or may not conform to what parents had

DOI: 10.4324/9781003427476-6

envisioned, but eventually parent(s) will need to come to terms with the fact that their formal control over their children is receding and will shortly disappear (see Baumrind, 1978, 1991; Darling and Steinberg, 1993; Smetana, 2005; Spera, 2005) .

As the young person approaches adulthood, their evolving status as adult is incorporated into their habitus, and their doxic understandings of what they can and cannot do evolve. For parents, relinquishing control and (direct) responsibility is gradually incorporated into their habitus. Adapting to the changed rules of the game can be problematic as their children no longer require permission; indeed the young person may no longer remain within the geographical confines of the family home or the home town. These generic transitional changes collectively reflect each individual change, each individual set of attitudes of parents, and each individual set of levels of maturity of each young person. Each legal transition point mirrors a myriad of informal individual transition points, often unrecognised as such. And with each transition point, each individual young person's concept of themselves transforms from child/teenager into 'emerging adult' (Arnett and Tanner, 2006).

Parents, seeing this change, have to deal with their own concept of self. As their child approaches legal adult status, they have to come to terms with their child's evolving independence and their own relinquishing of control. They come to rely upon their own experience of teenage and young adulthood to assess and to create expectations about how their children will behave. These 'predetermined expectation[s]' (Dwyer and Wyn, 2001: 78) inform both their attitudes and their responses to what happens in the lives of their children and other young people.

Any predetermined expectations however fail to take into account that young people are growing into maturity in a world that is significantly different to that of their parents. More importantly, as Furlong, Woodman and Wyn (2011) have pointed out, it is a world that young people experience as different from the world in which their parents grew up. As such, expectations very quickly come into conflict with the reality parents confront. This plays out both at a strategic level in terms of realisations and understandings and in terms of daily encounters/confrontations (see Buchanan, Eccles and Becker, 1992; Smetana and Asquith, 1994). These encounters combine with previous encounters to create new understandings and acceptances. This is an ongoing and constant process. New ground rules are negotiated and renewed constantly. In the process, they unconsciously move the parent/child lines of demarcation until both parent and child emerge as evolved individuals, their habitus changed by the process and with new understandings of the rules of the game that apply individually, and to their relationships.

Young people arrive at adulthood having undertaken ongoing negotiation of their rights and responsibilities with a view to establishing themselves as fully autonomous individuals. Like a moth emerging from a chrysalis, their new self carries much of their predecessor with them but is identifiably different from its previous stage of development. The parent too has to incorporate into their habitus the understanding that being a parent has changed. Both child and parent now find themselves in a binary paradigm based upon changed roles. Firstly, the young person is learning to play by the new rules of adulthood, unconstrained by parental responsibility (the doxa of adulthood). Secondly, the parent, aware of their child's changed status, now has to come to terms with the fact that their role in the game has changed – their status is now much closer to one of equal rather than parent/child and incorporating the doxa of being a parent of adult children.[2]

Although their child may be on the verge of adulthood, the parent has been the carer for that child's entire life. At birth, their responsibility was 100 per cent. As their child approaches adulthood, that responsibility (at least in a legal sense) will eventually be zero. But the parent/child relationship accrues rituals, practices and understandings which have been ingrained over the period of the child's development. The parent's habitus incorporates these collective practices and understandings: they are the parent; the young person does what they are told; the young person is provided for; the young person's behaviour reflects the values and positions of their parent; respect is demanded. Each individual parent/child relationship will play out with their own variations of these practices and understandings. These metamorphoses bring with them their own concerns.

The Psychologising of Miley Cyrus

In Chapter 5, Pauline's and Matthew's concerns were for young people's lack of respect for adults. They 'know their rights', and, importantly, act upon that knowledge. Yet increasingly, parents and adults deny that autonomy by a concern for their safety, seemingly at odds with the 'concerted cultivation' that they have applied since childhood. In doing so, they actually create the environment which encourages children to challenge their authority. The *walled garden* Pauline and Matthew have created for their children contains the seeds of disenchantment with the outcomes of their own parenting.

Michelle's (44) position regarding the 'walled garden' is arrived at by means of her accumulated symbolic capital based upon her experience of being part of a large family. Observing her mother, she learned to be competent, resilient and independent:

> My mother was one of nine and they all had to fend for themselves, and then she brought me up when I had to fend for myself but probably not as much, 'cause I was only one of three.
>
> (Michelle)

Michelle's working-class upbringing incorporates a 'sense of constraint' (Lareau, 2003: 6), which ironically embraces an acceptance of authority, but which nevertheless provides her with the skills, knowledge and understanding of how to parent. Michelle's adult persona has a 'feel for the game' of parenting. These parenting skills and her parenting practice, what Longhofer and Winchester (2013) refer to as the ingrained habits and dispositions that we possess due to our life experiences, are shaped 'to act or respond in certain ways ... without [her] being conscious of them or being directed to adhere to them' (English and Bolton, 2015: 92). Like Pauline, Michelle (44) thinks her kids have it easier than her and have had opportunities 'like music and sport'.

By contrast, informant Christine is 35 and without children. She is very conscious of the way helicopter parenting sows the seeds of its own demise by promoting the 'walled garden':

> Helicoptered, ... Just overprotected... Parents possibly compensate in other ways. Well, you can't go outside, so I'll buy you every gaming system that you want. Kids are used to getting everything that they want, this next generation coming through... . At the end of the day, it is the parents' fault, because they have given in.

Pauline and Michelle clearly link their own upbringing to not only their own parenting but also to their attitude towards young people in general. Christine, younger than Pauline and Michelle, viewed the process of helicoptering and (from her perspective) its consequences, unencumbered by personal parenthood. But all three acknowledged that helicoptering and the creation of the *walled garden* are parental attempts to protect young people from sites of anxiety and that in doing so, their Millennial children have had greater protections applied to their childhood and teenage years than they had applied to them.

As 16-year-olds on the verge of adulthood, Eliza, Gina and Iris were in no doubt as to the *walled garden* they inhabited. At the tail-end of their youth, adulthood beckoned both formally and informally. Each understood the social world they inhabited and functioned within, and the doxa inherent in that world. They understood that the rules of the game that underpin that social world determine how they and other young people function, and importantly how they are perceived by adults. The exemplar they focused on to illustrate this understanding was the US celebrity Miley Cyrus and her treatment by the media and, by extension, adults in general. The difficulties faced by young people dealing with adult expectations as they grow up are multiplied by a factor of ten for young people who happen to be celebrities. From Shirley Temple to Judy Garland to Drew Barrymore, young people growing up in the glare of their celebrity status have had to deal with the often irreconcilable tension between their on-screen persona and the reality of a living, breathing young person transitioning to adulthood.

From the outset, discussion was animated when the subject of Cyrus arose during the conversation. It was as if Cyrus was a touchstone, an avatar for their own sense of self. At the time of the focus group, Cyrus had recently been the subject of severe media attention for her music video 'Wrecking

Ball' (2013), and particularly for its 'raunch' style (see Levy, 2005; Oppliger, 2008; Zeisler, 2008; Powell, 2015).

Miley Cyrus began her career as a child star on the family friendly TV series *Hannah Montana* playing the central character Miley Stewart/Hannah Montana. The series as a whole played to a 'tween' (Hall, 1987) audience and reflected broad wholesome family values. And this wholesomeness of the series accrued to the characters and, by default, to the actors. The *walled garden* surrounding Cyrus' appearance in the show reflected this constructed wholesome public persona. The audience expectation was that the public persona of the character Hannah reflected the private individual – the actor. The *walled garden* of her public profile as a childhood series heroine (and no doubt the expectations of the producers) demanded that the private persona reflected the same values as the media image. When she behaved quite differently as an adult performer, there was a shock reaction. Iris, Gina and Eliza understood that process. They reflected a much clearer comprehension of the dynamics at play between the public and private persona than the wider mainstream media response to Cyrus' music video performance. They talked about how Cyrus progressed from being a 'Disney star' (Eliza, 16), a 'perfect little' girl (Gina, 16) to the poster girl for raunch culture.

Iris, Gina and Eliza saw through the celebrity façade with Cyrus. What they saw is Cyrus' *authentic* self – the self that she is really. For them, Cyrus plays out on the screen and on social media the dilemmas that they face on a daily basis. The wholesome persona of Hannah Montana is as fictitious as the wholesome persona their parents perceive them to be. What Cyrus has had the temerity to do is to leave her childhood, and her tweens, and her youth behind her. Like desiccated cicada husks lying on the ground, the shell of her Hanna Montana persona past lies as if frozen in aspic, forever in reruns, a reminder of what was and is no more.

To their mind, what Miley Cyrus has done since Hannah Montana is grow up: 'She's heaps grown up ... wearing all the really skimpy costumes' (Eliza, 16). The walled garden surrounding her as Hannah Montana was shattered by the process of transitioning from teenager to adulthood. But in the minds of much mainstream media and many adults, she had no right to do so: the walled garden is immutable, seemingly unable to be breached – until it is.

As a child star of a wholesome TV series, the 'Disney girl [has] become[s] [a part of] the main pop media' (Gina, 16). But rather than being an object of derision, Eliza and Gina and Iris instead concentrated on her (from their perspective) authenticity. They saw her as a role model. Her journey from Disney star to young adulthood reflected their own journey, their own struggles to break free of the walled garden. As Iris (16), reflecting on Cyrus' journey, said:

> She's brave and she's a feminist and she's all about change and equality for the genders and for the gay and lesbian and transgender community and ... a lot of the older ... generation don't like that change. They don't want

gays to have the same equal rights as we do... which I think is so stupid but I ... applaud her so much for everything that she's done.

At 16 years of age, the walled garden still existed for Eliza, Gina and Iris. It was part of what they understood determines how they are perceived by adults. The social world they inhabited incorporated the reality that, from an adult perspective, they are not yet allowed to progress to the next stage of their lives:

> She went away ... for a while and grew up, became ... an adult and they just expected her to stay the same and be the same little ... Hannah Montana, perfect little girl, ... not to grow up, even when she's a person.
> (Eliza, 16)

'Even when she's a person' is the most poignant ingredient in this sequence. It encapsulates from Eliza's perspective the dichotomy of the media-created social world that Cyrus inhabited as Hannah Montana and the real world that she exists in as a real person. For Iris Gina and Eliza, it is Cyrus as real person that they see. Cyrus inhabits the same social world facing the same trials and tribulations they face. Cyrus' journey reflects their own passage to adulthood being played out on the big screen in front of them. Eliza understood, both intellectually and viscerally, that adulthood will happen. She will not remain like the Disney girl. Her parents may understand this intellectually but from Eliza's perspective, they cannot come to terms with it emotionally:

> My mums' like you know [when] you're older you'll still be my baby. I'm like yeah but I'm gonna grow up, like it's gonna happen. I can't stop myself from... Like ... it's a thing that happens and a lot of people just don't like change... It's something that is inevitable, and you can't stop.

What Eliza, Gina and Iris have identified here is the moral panic applied by the media and assorted adults to the evolution of Miley Cyrus, a moral panic that sees Cyrus' metamorphosis from Disney girl to purveyor of raunch culture to represent a wider decline in moral standards of female youth. Public media commentators maintained that Cyrus had become a poor role model because her controversial and raunchy adult persona was at odds with the 'Disney girl' image cultivated for the TV series. We need to remind ourselves that the Hannah Montana character was a fictional construct designed and created to garner child and tween viewers for the series. The actor Cyrus, for the purpose of selling the series, accrued to herself cultural capital of childhood innocence based upon the Hannah Montana persona. That created expectations on the part of audiences with regard to the Montana/Cyrus persona. Cyrus and Montana became interchangeable. Cyrus was fourteen when she began filming the series and the legal walled garden surrounding her participation in that series would have been very much within the control of her parents.

The disconnect between the 'adult' Cyrus and her teenage alter ego, Hannah Montana was played out in an online 'spat' between the adult Cyrus and former pop notoriety, the late Sinead O'Connor. From the vantage point of middle age, O'Connor, now the voice of mature reason, 'counselled' Cyrus 'in the spirit of motherliness and with love' (2013) about the dangers of celebrity. She publicly advised her not to 'exploit your body or your sexuality in order for men to make money from you'. There followed a back and forth online skirmish, the details of which are not relevant here. But as part of her response, Cyrus countered O'Connor's 'motherly' advice with an argument that 'connected her performance of sexuality to feminist empowerment' (Brady, 2016: 431). It should be noted that singer Sinead O'Connor was once notorious for her own 'outlandish' behaviour, including tearing up a picture of the Pope on Saturday Night Live (O'Dowd, 2018). In short, O'Connor was an *enfant terrible* in her day. However, she feels, from the security of middle age, from that position of adult moral superiority, at liberty to excoriate Miley Cyrus: 'I'm suggesting you don't care for yourself. That has to change' (2013). O'Connor then followed up with a patronising post on her own website entitled 'Urgent! Does Anyone Know the Whereabouts of this Girl's Parents?' (2014). This is indeed the Adult Voice in full cry.

Eliza, Gina and Iris see Cyrus from a totally different generational perspective. The persona she projects to them is very much at odds with the raunch image many adults perceive. It is the act of growing up roughly contemporaneously with Cyrus that allows them to see her as a role model. It is her choosing to be who she wants to be, despite the haranguing of older celebrities like O'Connor, that provides the impetus and the inspiration for the agency that Eliza, Gina and Iris garner from her role as an exemplar:

> Much of celebrity culture centres on young females growing up, and the very transition these young females (such as Miley Cyrus) are making into young womanhood is a central part of their celebrity. Indeed, it seems that concerns regarding the nature of 'unachieved' celebrity, and concerns regarding the harm of young girls' consumption of celebrity, are both centred on understandings of 'appropriate' or 'inappropriate' femininity, and these concerns come together in a particularly heightened way in tween popular culture's constructions of celebrity, of which Hannah Montana is emblematic.
>
> (Kennedy, 2014: 226)

For O'Connor, Cyrus' female raunchiness was 'inappropriate'. For Eliza, Gina and Iris, it was not only appropriate but inspiring. For O'Connor, the 'psychologizing' of Cyrus sees her as a victim of pimps: 'Please in future say no when you are asked to prostitute yourself. Your body is for you and your boyfriend' (O'Connor, 2013). Yet for 16-year-old Eliza, Gina and Iris, Cyrus is a role model, a 'feminist ... a good person [who's] all about change and equality for the genders and for the gay and lesbian and transgender community', and who had the effrontery to grow up. Eliza, Gina and Iris, at the time of interview, were living through a similar transition process to that which Cyrus had been through. Their social worlds may have differed markedly but the challenges they faced in transitioning to adulthood mirror the same need to escape the walled garden of childhood. For 16-year-old Eliza, Gina and Iris, that escape was imminent.

A Sense of Entitlement

Youth leaders Joe (19), Elaine (21) and Sharon (23) interact on a regular basis with community leaders. Those community leaders constantly express their admiration for the maturity of behaviour and the thoughtful attitudes of the youth leaders they interact with. But Joe, Elaine and Sharon are not seen as exemplars of young people as a whole. They are viewed by the adults they interact with as the exception to the rule. Despite the evidence they see in front of them with the young people they interact with, adults share a capacity to classify all young people as threats. This was categorised by Sharon (23) as being 'like a sense of entitlement' – an entitlement to say whatever they want about young people.

Sharon has hit upon a key element that drives adult moral panics about young people. Cultural capital is acquired throughout one's lifetime. The store of that capital is added to and melds with experiences and existing symbolic and economic capital, as one's habitus constantly metamorphoses and evolves:

> Habitus is both a system of schemes of production of practices and a system of perception and appreciation of practices. And, in both of these dimensions, its operation expresses the social position in which it was elaborated.
>
> (Bourdieu, 1989: 19)

Social position is code for status. Adult cultural capital is embodied as status – as enhanced social position. The acquisition of status requires no screening process. Status is its own validation via its own self-referencing feedback loop. In any ensuing interactions with people, the (now) entrenched status will influence those interactions. Furthermore, entrenched status then helps to determine how those interactions unfold. If the interaction is positive, it serves to reinforce the adult's status, strengthening and embellishing the existing habitus. If the interaction is negative and the adult's status is challenged, they are quite likely to respond negatively – by misrecognising by 'getting their back up'. But in both cases, the effect is to shore up the status, further entrenching it.

Joe, Elaine and Sharon's experience as youth leaders has allowed them to practise in a range of social spaces that most young people would not normally frequent. As representatives of young people, they tend to interact in social worlds dominated by adults (service clubs, local government, and so on) where they occupy a relatively privileged position. Their status as youth leaders has been incorporated into their habitus. They are entitled to enter these social worlds because their status as youth leaders means they are not the vast majority of young people who would, in all probability, eschew entry. In the event that they were to attempt to do so, they would in all probability be made very quickly aware that they were not welcome. As youth leaders, they understand the rules of the game and adjust their behaviour accordingly to fit in. They know that they are playing the game on someone else's home turf in an arena which is dominated by, and reflects, the cultural capital and the doxa of the adults who welcome them into this social world. The youth leaders play the game of polite, slightly deferential young people operating as guests in the realm of their hosts. Meanwhile, the adults warmly welcome those that they would normally disparage into their social world. Unspoken in these exchanges are several assumptions: the young people put on hold their disdain for the fact that for the duration of the event they will be patronised; and the adults put on hold their implicit wish – 'if only all young people were like these'. These separate doxa function in concert with each other, with both the young people and the adults quite often aware of, but not making apparent, their knowledge of the other. In these homologous fields where youth leaders and adults interact, the net effect is to reinforce the status of the adults, because the youth leader's incorporated doxa equips them to play the game of deference and respect within the social world of the adults. Joe learnt the rules of the game early on when talking to members of the community:

> I know from experience presenting to... groups of older people... We went out into the community as the six school leaders and spoke and we got asked questions from the floor... one of the guys turned around and said: 'Oh you're out there throwing cricket balls through windows'. And it was sort of like: 'no we're out there in the park learning to play cricket'.
>
> (Joe, 19)

These presentations were undertaken in the community to groups of older people, on their turf. These older people, comfortable in familiar territory and surrounded by their age peers, felt at ease alleging that the young people before them were guilty of vandalism. The rules of the game denote that Joe can only respond by respectfully stating what they are actually doing. It would be outside of those rules for Joe to take a similarly aggressive stance and accuse the elders of being narrow-minded, insular and biased. Similarly, when talking of a leadership program, facilitated and supported by adults, Elaine lamented the fact that the leadership program is not seen as important by said adults who only turn up at the end to disparage young people:

> Disappointing, when you've reached the end of a leadership program and hear someone make those sorts of comments [as with Joe and the cricket ball] and you go well if you'd spent the whole weekend here and actually listened to what we had to say you'd realise that we weren't just talking about, from our point of view but from ... the young people around us who make the same sorts of comments. We're giving them that voice. And you're not hearing that, and you're just coming here and going 'oh wow this is really cool that there's this group of 20 of you that are really interested'. And it's a frustration because it means that you're not actually being taken seriously because you're a young person. That you're just a novelty to them.
>
> (Elaine, 21)

Elaine is disappointed but she knows that to display her disappointment, let alone anger or rage at this treatment, is not the appropriate action because even though it's a leadership course for young people, it's supported by adults expecting deference and respect. The adult social world dominates the cultural capital and the doxa of the program.

Joe, Elaine and Sharon can function within those adult-dominated fields because they know and understand what Bourdieu has identified as the 'code' that is required to be at ease within those fields. They have the capability to *voir*, to *savoir*, which gives them the insight into the accompanying *doxa* which they are then able to bring to bear when they enter the adult-dominated arena.

Whether it be the field of family or education (the two fields they occupy most often during the process of growing up), young people learn the code they need to adopt in order to operate as a young person in those fields. Those few that opt to follow the quite narrow path of youth leadership learn that to operate effectively within adult home turf, it is the young people who need to make the adjustment, to incorporate into their habitus the capacity to be deferential and polite. If they don't, they know that access to adult fields will be denied to them. Elaine, Joe and Sharon grew up in middle-class households. Middle-class children are much better at being able to fit in a wider array of circumstances than those from more disadvantaged backgrounds. This is a result of social homology (Bourdieu, 1984: 16) where the social magic of having cultural capital means the capacity to fit in widely (Bourdieu and Thompson, 1991; see also Bourdieu and Wacquant, 1992: 209–210; Butler, 1999).

Adjustment is a one-way street. As we have seen in a previous chapter, Fred does not feel the need to do any adjusting. Being in his 70s, he has reached a position in life where his habitus is more rigidly structured, less flexible, less liable to change. Fred displays all the traits of an educated left liberal based upon his initial comments on the media and young people. But his habitus incorporates the status that accrues to a 70-plus legal professional. His left-liberal intellectual response to young people and media treatment of young people belies, or is subsumed by, his status as a professional senior male whose disposition is pretty much set in its ways. As we have seen with his music, Fred has determined where he sits – his position is set in stone. Scott McKenzie, Les Misérables, the Beatles are the musical representations of the wider ossification that has occurred as he has aged: 'My interest in music is what I like to hear' (Fred, 73). This rigidity applies across the doxa that informs his view on the world, his attitudes towards contemporary music, the ice epidemic and mobile phones that reflect that ossification. In his mind, Fred has earned the right to sit in judgement of young people. The use of terms such as 'Bonkers' and 'Vikings at the gate' are outward manifestations of the status he has acquired. He has earned the privilege of being able to sit in judgement of young people because of the status and privilege accruing to his 70-year-old habitus. The social worlds that Fred operates within, the people he interacts with daily, are mutually self-supporting, reinforcing his status. He has worked his whole life. He has achieved retirement age. That age and the social field of similarly aged retirees accrues to it the attendant status of 'elder' and the deference that complements that status. The social world that Fred inhabits, family and golf club, reflects back to him that status and attendant deference. That social world accrues to it as well the right to speak with the Adult Voice. This is what Sharon means when she refers to a 'sense of entitlement'.

For those reasonably well off in society, and particularly for males, the cultural and economic capital acquired as a result of living a long and prosperous life provides the entrance fee to this exclusive club, the *in-group* of comfortable retirement. This particularly applies to male seniors. Fred's sense of fixed status creates an interesting paradox. The social settings he occupies as a result of his life experience (family, golf club, legal profession and so on) all mutually reinforce the status he has acquired. His interaction with young people, either in person or in homologous fields he may share with them (family, public transport, the media), is undertaken from that position of privilege. But his response to outward manifestations of young people's behaviour (music, social media use, ice) reflects a position of relative weakness. His misrecognising of young people and their cultural forms is based upon his inability to understand the rules of the game of what young people are doing. He doesn't have the code. As far as music is concerned, Fred has not possessed the code since the days of the Beatles.

In a similar way, Jo Heywood, Principal of all-girl Heathfield School in Ascot, reflects this sense of privilege – this entitlement to sit in judgement. Heywood took it upon herself when quoted in an article, by Graeme Paton in the *London Daily Telegraph*, to publicly take Miley Cyrus to task for her raunch persona depiction in the Wrecking Ball video. Heywood argues that

Cyrus is a poor role model for girls because her controversial and raunchy adult persona sits at odds with the 'Disney girl' image cultivated for the TV series. Heywood overlooks or is oblivious to the fact that the Hannah Montana character was fabricated, manufactured purely for entertainment purposes to attract television audiences. Hannah Montana does not exist except in the video mists. Heywood chooses to ignore this blatantly obvious fact and seeks to find fault in what is in reality a fictional TV contrivance.

> Celebrity role models such as Miley Cyrus are leaving schoolgirls 'manipulated and confused' by sending out mixed messages ... by launching themselves with clean-cut images before reinventing themselves ... the Olympics would provide teenage girls with a new generation of role models 'recognised for their achievements rather than their looks'.
> (quoted in Paton, 2013)

The title of 'celebrity role model' never accrued to Cyrus by choice. Heywood imposes this label from afar. Heywood is suggesting that Cyrus, upon accepting the role of Montana, should have been mindful of the fact that she was going to age. Furthermore, conscious of the impact that her ageing would have upon her younger audience, Cyrus should have then, for the sake of that audience, assumed the Hannah Montana persona as part of her habitus – for real. Because as far as Heywood is concerned, that's who she really is. Having embodied Hannah Montana, she should then have assumed the responsibilities of a role model for younger viewers because Cyrus and Montana are now interchangeable – one and the same. Heywood is cautioning Cyrus not to age – not to grow up. What Cyrus should have done was played the game. At fourteen years of age, Cyrus should have recognised her function, her obligations as a role model for girls, and should behave accordingly.

Principal Heywood, like Fred, does not have the code of the youth generation, but she and Fred still possess their status and privilege. It is incorporated in their doxa. For Principal Heywood, the mixed messages Cyrus is guilty of are that, from fourteen years of age, she should have behaved like an adult – should have bypassed, avoided, eschewed the remainder of her youth period, not pass GO, not collect $200, and transitioned at fourteen to an adult. By doing so, she would provide an example to all young people who saw her as role model and who could follow her example and bypass their youth. Above all, had Cyrus done as Heywood demands, Heywood would not have had to tilt at the windmill of young people behaving not as they should. Having not done so, Cyrus should immediately take heed of Principal Heywood's message, recant her raunch status and revert to her Hannah Montana picture perfect on the small screen persona. This in turn would have reinforced Heywood's status as a respected Adult Voice of reason.

Joe (19) and Elaine (21) were in no doubt as to who is in the better position – the adult or young person:

Elaine: it's a big disadvantage being a young person because everything's limited.

Joe: yeah you have that stigma attached to you, it's almost like you just can't shrug it off. You know you're always the younger person. You're the younger person in the workplace.

In the same way that Fred's status confers a sense of privilege and entitlement and Principal Heywood appropriates hers, so Joe, Elaine and Sharon are acutely aware of and reflect their lower status. That status manifests itself in their sense of frustration at the way they are treated. It will remain that way until they transition from young person to adult and older person, or as Sharon (21) put it: 'until you get wrinkles around your eyes'.

The Aesthetic Solera: Identity, Predisposition, Tendency, Propensity and Inclination

The act of curation involves the process of both selection and rejection, part of the yin and yang of the formation of identity: I like this, so I will select it; I don't like that, so I will reject it. But in rejecting this, the next process of selection will be informed by what I rejected. Similarly, my next process of rejection will be informed and shaped by what I have selected. This is:

> A temporally embedded process of social engagement ... informed by the past but also oriented toward the future (as a 'projective' capacity to imagine alternative possibilities) and toward the present ... to contextualize past habits and future projects within the contingencies of the moment.
>
> (Emirbayer and Mische, 1998: 962)

This process is undertaken constantly, both consciously and unconsciously, as each new aesthetic or digital interaction takes place – the process of selection and rejection acting as a kind of increasingly complex sieve: accepting, rejecting, ejecting, sorting and synthesising. As the young person ages, these curated interactions grow and meld like an aesthetic solera.[3] As each new experience is added, the solera 'base' of the habitus changes, modifying earlier experiences in order to accommodate the newer, yet all the while maintaining its coherence as it subtly changes over time. The effect is to simultaneously create within each person's habitus 'predisposition, tendency, propensity ... [and] inclination' (Bourdieu, 1977: 214; see also Conger, 1964; Erikson, 1968; Robards, 2012; Côté, 2005, 2006).

As a person ages, the aesthetic solera of the habitus becomes increasingly hardwired. The process narrows in terms of the types of material accepted, rejected and ejected. The base ejects less older material and accepts less new material as it begins to ossify. By this process, the individual habitus consolidates as the process of ossification proceeds. Open to the new in childhood and youth, it becomes increasingly less open as one ages.

Joanne (32), Neil (25) and George (30) have entered the stage of their life where the solera has begun to ossify. They were prompted to interrogate the notion of curation from the perspective of their status as recently arrived adults. George (30) began by refining his previous comments on curation:

> I do think it significantly impacts the mental state of people growing up in this culture... I'm a 16-year-old, my friend Jess curates her entire image, only posts the good shit, only posts the beautiful photo out of the hundreds and only posts that ... you get a skewed image of the great life Jess must have but she might be going through a billion terrible things but you as a person have almost this FOMO, fear of missing out, of why isn't my life like that?

Implicit in this imagined scenario is that Jess and her friend are representative of Millennials. George highlights the ease with which young people can curate their online persona. He explains the perceived dangers associated with that curation process. This imagined scenario presumes that Jess's friend will suffer FOMO. George argues that because the online persona of Jess is so 'positive', it significantly impacts upon Jess's friend's mental state. Implicit in this scenario is that social media enables FOMO as a new phenomenon. Having reached adulthood, George views the online activity of the imagined Jess and her friend as risky to the point where their mental health may be affected. This echoes the kinds of older generation fear projections that we have seen with Fred, Pauline, Matthew and Michelle and the work of Threadgold. George makes these assessments seemingly oblivious to the fact that he also has a curated online presence, probably since his teenage years. Yet the process of curation is not limited to the digital. Habitus is the totality of all curation. It's what we glean online, as well as from our engagement with education, fashion, music, social functions we attend, friends we have, and people with whom we have intense relationships. All that contributes to who we are. And George, like Jess and her friend, would have, in his teenage years, been curating his persona holistically, not just online. George's fears for the plight of Jess's friend misrecognise her as he projects his fears for her, based upon his now adult perspective. Principal Heywood's position is not that far removed from George's.

George's exemplar of Jess and her friend triggered a response from Neil (35) which identified his own apprehensions about oversharing:

> I think I've seen a few of the young people who are present on Facebook and actually crowd-source emotional support. They will put these long rambling posts about how terrible they feel and how they can't get out of bed and all this kind of stuff and then you see all the comments come through, it's just embarrassing.

This triggered an emphatic 'Oh yeah' response from George. Notably, Neil began with the conditional phrase 'I think', indicating a lack of certainty that he actually has seen this phenomenon. The group was then prompted to address the question of whether 'crowd-sourced emotional support' may have been behaviour also exhibited by previous generations. George responded by creating a 1983 version of Jess in order to make a comparison with the coping strategies of the two, outlining what he believed to be a qualitative difference in attitude between the Jess of 2015 and the equivalent Jess of 1983, brought about by the change in technology:

> In 1983 Jess might have … been crying that morning, but put on a cake of makeup, put on a bit more of a sassy attitude, put a scrunchy in her hair and gone 'Fuck you'. At school … she might have just thought … she's got a bit of an attitude, but you look at her she'll agree. It's the same thing in a different form.

George's response advocates toughening up; employing 'tough love' to deal with a mental health crisis. George's construction of both 1983 Jess and her contemporary counterpart serves to underline the process of misrecognition that he has undertaken. Contemporary Jess represents the 'softness' of young people today (echoing FitzSimons' criticism of Millennial sports people). In many respects, this reflects the denigration inherent in the futurist dismissal of Millennials as selfie and social media-obsessed, so that they can no longer function without the crutch of 'crowd-sourced emotional support'. By contrast, 1983 Jess is self-confident, assured. When she does encounter self-doubt or emotional turmoil, the solution is straight-forward: a 'cake of makeup, put on a bit more of a sassy attitude, put a scrunchy in her hair and [say] "Fuck you" to the world'. This coping strategy is straight-forward because George's impartiality, the capacity to objectively assess, has been embodied as he transitioned to adulthood. As such, the application of some 'tough love' will no doubt allow her to deal with her self-doubt and emotional turmoil. His incorporation of his Adult Voice has allowed him to construct a fictitious '1983 Jess'. And he does so with the absolute conviction, the entitlement of the generational double language of disinterest.

George's creation of the 1983/contemporary 'Jess personas' raises an interesting paradox. George frames 1983 Jess as tougher, more resilient than her contemporary counterpart. Contemporary Jess is somehow weaker, less capable to withstand slings and arrows than her 1983 counterpart. Research suggests Millennials are actually more resilient than their predecessors: being found not lost, optimists not pessimists, team players not self-obsessed, trustful and smart (Howe and Strauss, 2000). They bypass mainstream media, and are therefore less prone to the impact of mainstream media scrutiny than previous youth generations. So George, applying his own construction of 1983 Jess as more resilient than contemporary Jess, is at odds with what we know and understand from research. It is as if George has created a mythical 1983 Jess in order to facilitate his misrecognising of contemporary Jess. In terms of age, George is closer to 1983 Jess. 1983 Jess reinforces not only his own misrecognising of Millennials, it reinforces the authenticity of 1883 Jess's (read George) youth experience; an experience which is superior and more legitimate than contemporary Jess's. There was no malice or indifference evident in George's distinction between the two versions of Jess. He implies that the evolution of Jess 1983 to her contemporary counterpart was a natural outcome of changed digital availability; a fait accompli. In short, he proposes that social media was the catalyst for the transformation from resilient Jess 1983 to the weaker modern version.

George's anecdote about 'mythical Jess' was related with an air of absolute certainty. Let us remember that mythical Jess exists only because George brought her into being to illustrate his argument. Although her existence is illustrative in intent, nevertheless George permits her creation in order to illustrate his absolute certainty of the forces at work in her creation. George understands mythical Jess's habitus. He understands the doxa that drives her behaviour. His understanding is based upon the conviction that what he has proposed for mythical Jess, in the mythical universe she inhabits, is true. He is able to fully grasp the absolute certainty that mythical Jess 'lives'. And he knows this because the double language of disinterest, embedded as doxic understanding, provides him with the *voir* and the *savoir* to know with certainty that which he knows. George now speaks with the absolute certainty of his Adult Voice.

The Figure of the Profligate Millennial

As we have seen in previous chapters, the figure of the 'digital native' Millennial with the ubiquitous mobile phone and a seemingly infinite supply of cash with which to purchase the latest technology has become a recurring motif for older informants like Fred, Pauline, and Matthew, and commentators like FitzSimons and Sinek; it also was the initial response from Neil. The figure of the profligate Millennial has entered the wider consciousness as a descriptor in much the same way as 'dole bludger' (see Threadgold, 2018). It is now part of the wider doxa applied to young people, and a focus for commentators like the FitzSimons and Sinek to create moral panics about youth (I will explore this further in Chapter 8). The *social abjection* displayed towards the generic stereotype of young people, as the 'revolting figure of the profligate, criminalised welfare recipient' (Tyler, 2013: 193), has expanded to encompass the profligate Millennial with their mobile phones.

Informant George's then-and-now construction of the Millennial 'figure' of Jess serves as an illustration of the rapid technological and attendant social changes which have evolved over the past 35 years.

As we have seen throughout the interviews and focus groups, there was an underlying sense of resentment on the part of adults towards young people, and a corresponding understanding and acknowledgement by younger informants that they were the victims of that resentment against young people. The 'figures' of young people incited in the older informant responses reflected those feelings. This was brought into sharp relief by Neil's initial claim: 'they think they know everything, but they don't'.

Neil's statement illustrates how the process of misrecognition of young people evolves. The subtext of 'they think they know everything, but they don't' is that they think they know more than me, more than 'us' – my generation. Neil is making what he perceives to be an objective observation from his (now) position of adult. As we have seen, this double language of disinterest reflects the way that acquired symbolic capital manifests as 'understanding and describing notions of authenticity, coolness and distinction' (Threadgold, 2015: 54). The claim by Neil that 'they know everything' has been arrived at via his transition to adulthood. He now has the authority to pontificate on the attitudes of young people. His authority as an adult has been conferred by adult understandings enabling him to make this assessment from the position of apparent objectivity. The doxa of 'They know everything' is a truth that has been arrived at 'naturally' because as an adult, and as with George above, he has acquired the necessary 'detachment' to be able to assess young people objectively.

That younger people might potentially know more than Neil at 35 places his status as a mature male under threat. That status is integral to his habitus. His acquired embodied and materialised capital determines his place in the world, a place that is:

> Institutionalized in long-lasting social statuses, socially recognized or legally guaranteed, between social agents objectively defined by their position in these relations, determin[ing] the actual or potential powers within the different fields [they occupy].
>
> (Bourdieu, 1989: 4)

Neil's adult status has become a disposition enabling him to view today's young people from the perspective of one who has 'been there, done that'. Neil's statement 'they think they know everything, but they don't' is made from the perspective of someone who was young but is no longer. He has almost certainly arrived at an understanding that he once thought he knew everything but in transitioning to adulthood he realises this no longer applies. The symbolic capital accruing as part of his transition to an adult has endowed him with the objective certainty to confidently misrecognise the young people he now denigrates – and their capacity to know everything. Neil seemed unaware of the irony inherent in that certainty residing in this statement.

As Brabazon reminds us, notions of youth are inextricably linked to the concept of loss. The transition to adulthood is not without its emotional baggage. Self-awareness that one is now an adult (see Duval and Wicklund, 1972; Gilligan, 1989; Duval and Lalwani, 1999) incorporates the sense of achievement and freedom which accompanies most adult transitions. Yet it is also accompanied by the sense of new constraints that come with adulthood and are often accompanied by nostalgia (Boym, 2002; Fuentenebro de Diego and Valiente Ots, 2014; Davis, 1979) for a past that seemed simpler and more halcyon. The misrecognition that Neil and George display towards young people is tinged with the realisation that this viscerally remembered part of their life is behind them. From this point onwards, adulthood is increasingly their default position and the capacity for misrecognition grows.

The evolution of habitus is not linear. The subjective narrative that one creates, and which evolves over a lifetime, reflects this interaction between past and present to create at any one point in time:

> The temporary sum total of the young person's aspirations and assessments of past successes and failures and interpersonal recognition and rejection in the social arenas where autonomy and self-responsibility are expected.
> (Heinz, 2009: 8)

This process of 'self-socialisation' leads each of us to an understanding of self 'constructed by reflecting events and actions in terms of biographical memory' (49).

This capacity for reflection allows individuals to not only review and evaluate their own life experiences, but to also view their personal life experiences in the context of the wider socialising process. Their life experience can be assessed against the observed behaviour of the social world they inhabit. As George, Neil and Joanne observe and analyse behaviours of Millennials, they do so from the perspective of adults who have passed through the period of adolescence to arrive at their now adult status. Their assessment of those younger than them is arrived at via the prism of their own youth experience and their current world view as adults. They perceive not only the differences between their own remembered experiences of being a young person, but they feel they can analyse social and cultural changes which impact upon young people today. George provides a useful historical summary:

> It's come about through history and media and seeing people over the years die of addiction; seeing cultures change, seeing AIDS sweep through the 80s but also the fact you can google anything. Contraception. If you weren't told about it in 50s 60s 70s 80s, you just went out and think 'God I [hope I] don't get pregnant on the first time'. But it's so much easier to find out that stuff rather than having to wait for someone in your family or one of your friends to tell you, and eliminating a lot of misinformation.
> (George, 30)

For Joanne, George and Neil, their youth is very much still within their memories of recent experiences. In making comments about the new generation, they are observing and assessing from the perspective of recent experience. Their accumulated symbolic capital, and the symbolic capital acquired as a newly emerged adult, frames their analysis of young people. The adult is very much present and in control. And the young person is receding further into the depths of memory.

Taste and Discernment: Hopes, Dreams and Adult Disappointment

Bourdieu defines taste as the 'supreme manifestation of discernment' (1984: 11). Discernment, or distinction, is the process by which individuals and groups distinguish themselves from others. Implicit in any understanding of taste is the notion of preference which itself confers upon taste the notion of a hierarchy where something is favoured over another thing due to status. Taste privileges:

> Because it has the privilege of defining, by its very existence, what is noble or distinguished as being exactly what itself is, a privilege which is expressed precisely in its self-assurance.
> (Bourdieu, 2010: 85)

This is foundational for understanding the intrinsic prejudice inherent in adult misrecognition of young people. It is evident that notions of legitimacy (and taste) are determined by those making the distinction. In the same way that Willis interrogates notions of hierarchies of art by stating that ' "art" is in the "art gallery", it can't therefore be anywhere else' (1990: 1), so Millennials are what adults determine them to be. Millennials have not self-labelled themselves as selfish and self-centred. Yet as we have seen previously, that claim about their existence has taken on the mantle of received knowledge, a kind of 'communal wisdom'. Millennials may appear 'selfish and self-centred' because when adults enter their geographical space, they remain in their own social space, seeming oblivious and indifferent to any adults who are present. This indifference challenges the adult's status.

These classifications of Millennial are almost exclusively the domain of adults. They are not part of the self-analysis of young people themselves. Joe (19) was adamant about this:

> It's a conversation I've never had on social media. It's a conversation I've never had in real life. It's a conversation I've never had anywhere about what generation are we? We get stigmatised that we're ... Generation Y.

Joe's observation obviously struck a chord with the other two young people because it elicited a spontaneous laugh in recognition and agreement from Sharon, and Elaine interjected sarcastically and ironically: 'What generation am I?'.

Joe, Elaine and Sharon are at home in the digital social space that they share with other Millennials. When adults engage with social spaces that are homologous with Millennials, what many see is young people who seem in Fred's terms: 'bonkers'. And this negative assessment is imbued with the mantle of authenticity because of the age of those making the distinction and the conferring of the mantle of objectivity by that age and experience.

Since they are around the age of 20, the habitus of Joe, Elaine and Sharon is more fluid. They readily demonstrate their capacity for technological mastery. Elaine self-identifies as a 'digital native'. It is possible that their technical mastery online provides them with the flexibility to adapt and change. The perception, at least by those older than them, is that they are more able to adapt and change. As we saw previously, their status as youth leaders provides them with both passage into the adult world awaiting them and insight into the doxa of that world. Their forays into adult social fields prepare them for when they too will enter into that world. As youth leaders, their preparedness for that transition includes a much better understanding of the rules of the game.

Parental expectations and aspirations for their children reflect the emotional capital invested in their children since birth. This capital is 'banked' as the child grows. Young peoples' new-found freedom quickly comes into conflict with parental expectations. Parental disappointment, anger and frustration are matched by the sense of outrage and anger at not being understood on the part of the young person. The expected dividends from their emotional capital invested in their child may not be realised by the parents. The young person's disappointment at expectations of loosening of parental reins not being met is also manifest (see Symonds, 1939; Orlansky, 1949; Baldwin, 1955; Inhelder & Piaget,1955; Steinberg, Lamborn, Dornbusch and Darling, 1992; Baumrind, 1967, 1971, 1989; Glasgow, Dornbusch, Troyer, Teinberg and Ritter, 1997). Parental fear and distrust manifests itself in the misrecognition of their child's apparent refusal to conform to the expectations, hopes and dreams they had for them. As we have seen, many older informants referenced a halcyon past where young people apparently 'knew their place', where the status of parents/teachers/adults was recognised and deferred to. For Christine, 35, the difference between this Arcadian past and the reality of the present is typified by the issue of corporal punishment, an instance of actual rather than symbolic violence:

> You're not allowed to smack your children these days. You have to talk to them like an adult. So, I think kids have then learned to … They don't understand the consequences of something. They'll just keep fighting back or keep yelling until you put an iPad in their hand, and that's exactly what they wanted in the first place. Yeah, so I think kids can be a lot more manipulative these days.

Parents are now constrained from using corporal punishment. Yet from Christine's perspective, rather than young people being grateful for parents refraining from the use of corporal punishment, young people have instead taken advantage of this new parental restraint. Those opposed to the banning of corporal punishment, like Christine, deplore it as an example of 'political correctness' (Kimball, 1990; Bloom, 1987; D'Souza, 1991). Christine's resentment at parents not being able to inflict physical violence on children leads to that resentment being channelled into misrecognition. The irony of this misrecognition is that yet again parents and adults have created the circumstances where their parenting style has put in train the circumstances whereby their authority and status will be challenged when their children become teenagers. Paradoxically, Christine voices this failure:

> It is the parents' fault, because they have given in... It used to be, you were naughty when you were a kid, you get smacked and you're sent to your room. But now, just like all those choices to make once you finish high school, you've got all these different options on how to parent your child, and everyone's got an input. Yeah, there's constant pressure to be the perfect citizen.
>
> (Christine, 35)

Although Millennials are the current focus for this resentment, as Davis has pointed out (1997, 2010), Baby Boomers have also been the beneficiaries of changed parenting norms. As a member of Generation X, Christine seems oblivious to the fact that her generation was negatively stereotyped as the 'Latchkey Generation' (Coupland, 1991; Bower, 1991; Henseler, 2013). So it would appear that rather than being 'nurtured' by the use of corporal punishment to maintain her on the 'straight and narrow', she was actually a 'victim' of her 'working parents' neglect' left to her own devices with nothing but a set of keys (irony off). What Christine's response (and many of the other informant's responses) exemplify is that each generation looks back on their own upbringing with rose-coloured glasses and with disdain at the self-indulgent profligacy of ensuing generations. A significant characteristic of this nostalgia is that young people today are 'soft', 'snowflakes'[4] by comparison. This seemingly universal adult stance of 'we did it tougher in our day' is parodied mercilessly in the nonsensical hyperbole evident in the Monty Python Sketch: The Four Yorkshiremen[5] (The Full Monty Python, 2008). It is this nostalgia for a time when things were simpler, when as young people they had to confront and deal with adversity, which is another point of demarcation for adults when comparing their youth experience with ensuing youth generations (see Niemeyer, 2014; Routledge et al., 2011, 2012; Davis, 1979).

Engagement with Cultural Products

Earlier youth cultural theorists (Hall and Jefferson, 1976; Hebdige, 1979; Muggleton, 2000) associated interaction with cultural products with subcultural identification and used notions of subculture to analyse resistance to adult authority leading to explanations of various moral panics emerging from this interaction. At the centre of this analysis was the notion of youth subcultural practice providing the trigger for moral panics and negative adult judgements.

Notions of subculture have been problematic for some with McRobbie (1978, 1991) singling out the omission of family and females as major faults in subcultural theory. Similarly, Clarke (1982) pointing out that subcultures are heterogeneous and far from homologous. In order to better explain this complexity of young people and identity, Bennett's alternative of *neo-tribes* offered a more flexible and nuanced categorisation.

Neil's story of his youth growing up in a small town is illustrative of how young people's identity and membership of a *neo-tribe*, at odds with the mainstream, can elicit intolerance of that that difference. Growing up different in a small town is fertile ground for misrecognition and not just necessarily from adults:

> The chemist in the town thought I was trouble because I had purple hair and a nose ring and wore weird clothes. It was like [be] 'like the rest of us and you'll be ok. But if you're going to be different we're going to punish you for it'. The behaviour of other kids on the bus and just the way I was treated in sort of social situations – really rude treatment at the supermarket, that kind of stuff. There was that perception that 'Oh the future generation's in trouble if this is what they're sending [to school]'. I just got more determined to be different.
>
> (Neil, 34)

What Neil is pointing to in this experience is that he was not only misrecognised by the chemist and other adults but also misrecognised by his peers at school. His status as 'different', as 'other', caused his peers to misrecognise him as well. George's comment that 'I think that is a general teenage reaction' indicates that this peer rejection of difference was a typical response. The disparity between adult misrecognition and peer misrecognition arises because adult misrecognition is directed towards young people in general. Peer misrecognition ensues from young people seeing difference from the perspective of the acquired cultural and social capital that creates the accompanying doxa of 'normality' and is applied generally to individuals.

Innocence is a basic tenet of societal understandings of childhood. Young people's innocence is the major motivating factor for creation of the 'walled garden' to preserve and maintain that innocence. Ironically, the 'walled garden' thus created is the foundation for the evolution of misrecognition of young people. The act of parenting, of raising a child, raises parental expectations for their children. These expectations, founded upon the hopes, love and responsibilities inherent in the act of parenting, paradoxically create the conditions whereby misrecognition of their children and other young people will ensue because those expectations, hopes and aspirations clash with their fears for young people.

As young people mature, they increasingly roam further from the home to engage with situations where parental and other adult influences are at a minimum. As they do so, conflict emerges between parental and other adult expectations and young people's prising open of the 'walled garden'. This then provides fertile ground for the evolution of moral panics where young people are transformed from innocents to 'folk devils'. The figure of the profligate mobile phone and technology-obsessed young person has become part of the accepted doxa of Millennial behaviour. The following chapter will examine the role that music plays in the evolution of habitus and the touchstone function music has as grounded aesthetic and as memory trigger.

Notes

1 Wald G. (1964). THE ORIGINS OF LIFE. *Proc Natl Acad Sci U S A*. 1964 Aug;52(2):595–611.
2 And eventually an 'empty-nester'. Goren, J. A. 1983. "Now that the Children are Gone: A Phenomenological Study of the Empty Nest Transition." *Dissertation Abstracts International* 44: 901.
3 A solera is a process for making fortified wines where parts of a base spirit is gradually drawn off and bottled and replaced by newer spirit. In this way, the 'totality' of the mix, the base, is maintained yet subtly changes as some of the base is drawn off and newer spirit is added.
4 Derogatory term signifying lack of resilience.
5 There have been a number of iterations of this Monty Python sketch. The video cited is from the 1982 performance LIVE AT THE HOLLYWOOD BOWL and features Eric Idle, Graham Chapman, Michael Palin and Terry Jones.

Bibliography

Arnett, J. J., and Tanner, J. L. (Eds.). (2006). *Emerging Adults in America: Coming of Age in the 21st century*. Washington, DC: American Psychological Association.

Baker, S., Robards, B., and Buttigieg, B. (2016). *Youth Cultures and Subcultures Australian Perspectives*. London: Taylor and Francis.

Baldwin, A. L. (1955). *Behavior and Development in Childhood*. New York: Dryden Press.

Baumrind, D. (1967). Child Care Practices Anteceding Three Patterns of Preschool Behavior. *Genetic Psychology Monographs*, 75, 43–88.

Baumrind, D. (1971). Current Patterns of Parental Authority. *Developmental Psychology*, 4(1, Pt. 2), 1–103.

Baumrind, D. (1978). Parental Disciplinary Patterns and Social Competence in Children. *Youth & Society*, 9(3), 238–276.

Baumrind, D. (1989). Rearing Competent Children, in W. Damon (Ed.), *Child Development Today and Tomorrow*, pp. 349–378. San Francisco, CA: Jossey-Bass.

Baumrind, D. (1991). The Influence of Parenting Style on Adolescent Competence and Substance Use. *The Journal of Early Adolescence*, 11, 56–95.

Bell, E. (2008). From Bad Girl to Mad Girl. *Genders 48, August*. Retrieved from https://go.gale.com/ps/anonymous?id=GALE%7CA194279235&sid=googleScholar&v=2.1&it=r&linkaccess=abs&issn=08949832&p=AONE&sw=w

Bloom, A. (1987). *The Closing of the American Mind: How Higher Education Has Failed Democracy and Impoverished the Souls of Today's Students*. New York: Simon & Schuster.
Bourdieu, P. (1977). *Outline of a Theory of Practice*, R. Nice (trans.). Cambridge: Cambridge University Press.
Bourdieu, P. (1984). *Distinction: A Social Critique of the Judgement of Taste*. London: Routledge & Kegan Paul.
Bourdieu, P. (1989). Social Space and Symbolic Power. *Sociological Theory*, 7(1), 14–25.
Bourdieu, P. (2010). *Distinction: A Social Critique of the Judgement of Taste*. London: Taylor and Francis.
Bourdieu, P., and Thompson, J. B. (1991). *Language and Symbolic Power*. Cambridge, MA: Harvard University Press.
Bourdieu, P., and Wacquant, L. (1992). *An Invitation to Reflexive Sociology*. Chicago, IL: University of Chicago.
Bower, B. (1991). Home Alone: Latchkey Kids on Good Behavior. *Society for Science & the Public*, 140(4), 54.
Boym, S. (2002). *The Future of Nostalgia*. Basic Books. pp. xiii–xiv. ISBN 978-0-465-00708-0.
Brabazon, T. (2005). *From Revolution to Revelation: Generation X, Popular Memory and Cultural Studies*. Aldershot: Ashgate.
Brady, A. (2016). Taking Time between G-string Changes to Educate Ourselves: Sinead O'Connor, Miley Cyrus, and Celebrity Feminism. *Feminist Media Studies*, 16(3), 429–444.
Buchanan, C. M., Eccles, J. S., and Becker, J. B. (1992). Are Adolescents the Victims of Raging Hormones? Evidence for Activational Effects of Hormones on Moods and Behavior at Adolescence. *Psychological Bulletin*, 111(1), 62–107.
Butler, J. (1999). Performativity's Social Magic, in Shusterman, R . (Ed.), *Bourdieu: A Critical Reader*, pp. 113–128. Oxford: Blackwell.
Conger, J., (1964). The Evolution of Identity. *The Milbank Memorial Fund Quarterly* 42(4) Part 1, 36–44.
Coupland, D. (1991). *Generation X: Tales for an Accelerated Culture*. London: Little Brown Book Group.
Cyrus, M. (2013). Wrecking Ball. YouTube. August 25. Retrieved from www.youtube.com/watch?v=My2FRPA3Gf8
Danesi, M. (2003). *Forever Young: The Teen-Aging of Modern Culture*. Toronto: University of Toronto Press.
Darling, N., and Steinberg, L. (1993). Parenting Style as Context: An Integrative Model. *Psychological Bulletin*, 113(3), 487–496.
Clarke, G. (1982). *Defending Ski Jumpers: A Critique of Theories of Youth Sub-Cultures*. Discussion Paper. Birmingham: University of Birmingham.
Côté, J. E. (2005). The Postmodern Critique of Developmental Perspectives: Special Issue, *Identity: An International Journal of Theory and Research*, 5, 95–225.
Côté, J. E. (2006). Identity Studies: How Close Are We to Developing a Social Science of Identity? An appraisal of the Field, *Identity: An International Journal of Theory and Research*, 6, 3–25.
Côté, J. E. (2009). Youth-identity Studies: History, Controversies and Future Directions, in Furlong, A. (Ed.), *Handbook of Youth and Young Adulthood: New Perspectives and Agendas*, pp. 367–376. London: Routledge.

Davis, F. (1979). *Yearning for Yesterday: A Sociology of Nostalgia*. New York: Free Press.
Davis, M. (1997). *Gangland: Cultural Elites and the New Generationalism*. St Leonards: Allen & Unwin.
Davis, M. (2010). *Gangland: Cultural Elites and the New Generationalism* (3rd ed.). Melbourne: MUP.
D'Souza, D. (1991). *Illiberal Education: The Politics of Race and Sex on Campus*. New York: Free Press.
Duval, T. S., and Lalwani, N. (1999). Objective Self-awareness and Causal Attributions for Self-standard Discrepancies: Changing Self or Changing Standards of Correctness. *Personality and Social Psychology Bulletin*, 25(10), 1220–1229.
Duval, T. S., and Wicklund, R. A. (1972). *A Theory of Objective Self-awareness*. New York: Academic Press.
Dwyer, P., and Wyn, J. (2001). *Youth, Education and Risk: Facing the Future*. London: Routledge.
Emirbayer, M., and Mische, M. (1998). What is Agency? *American Journal of the Sociology*, 103(4), 964–1022.
English, F., and Bolton, C. (2015). *Bourdieu for Educators. Policy and Practice*. Los Angeles, CA: Sage.
Erikson, E. H. (1968). *Identity: Youth and Crisis*. Oxford: Norton & Co.
Fuentenebro de Diego, F., and Valiente Ots, C. (2014). Nostalgia: A Conceptual History. *History of Psychiatry*, 2014 Dec; 25(4):404–411.
Furlong, A. (2009). Revisiting Transitional Metaphors: Reproducing Social Inequalities under the Conditions of Late Modernity. *Journal of Education and Work*, 22(5), 343–353.
Furlong, A., Woodman, D., and Wyn, J. (2011). Changing times, Changing Perspectives: Reconciling 'Transition' and 'Cultural' Perspectives on Youth and Young Adulthood. *Journal of Sociology*, 47(4), 355–370.
Gilligan, C. (1989). *Mapping the Moral Domain: A Contribution of Women's Thinking to Psychological Theory and Education*. Cambridge, MA: Harvard University Press.
Glasgow, K., Dornbusch, S., Troyer, L., and Steinberg, L. (1997). Parenting Styles, Adolescents' Attributions, and Educational Outcomes in Nine Heterogeneous High Schools. *Child Development*, 68 (3), 507–529.
Goren, J. A. (1983). Now that the Children are Gone: A Phenomenological Study of the Empty Nest Transition. *Dissertation Abstracts International*, 44, 901.
Hall, C. (1987). Tween PowerZ: Youth's Middle Tier Comes of Age. *Marketing and Media Decisions*, outubro, 56–62.
Hall, S., and Jefferson, T. (Eds.). (1976). *Resistance through Rituals: Youth Subcultures in Post-War Britain*. London: Hutchinson.
Hebdige, D. (1979). *Subculture, the Meaning of Style*. London: Methuen.
Heinz, W. R. (2009). Youth Transitions in an Age of Uncertainty, in A. Furlong (Ed.), *Handbook of Youth and Young Adulthood: New Perspectives and Agendas*, pp. 3–13. Abingdon: Routledge.
Henseler, C. (Ed.). (2013). *Generation X Goes Global: Mapping a Youth Culture in Motion*. London: Routledge.
Howe, N., and Strauss, W. (2000). *Millennials Rising: The Next Great Generation*. New York: Knopf Doubleday.
Inhelder, B., and Piaget, J. (1955). *The Growth of Logical Thinking from Childhood to Adolescence*. New York: Basic Books.

Kennedy, M. (2014). Hannah Montana and Miley Cyrus: 'Becoming' a Woman, 'Becoming' a Star, *Celebrity Studies*, 5(3), 225–241.
Kimball, R. (1990). *Tenured Radicals: How Politics Has Corrupted Our Higher Education*. New York: Harper Collins.
Lareau, A. (2003). *Unequal Childhoods: Class, Race, and Family Life*. Berkeley, CA: University of California Press.
Levy, A. (2005). *Female Chauvinist Pigs: Women and the Rise of Raunch Culture*. New York: Free Press.
Longhofer, W., and Winchester, D. (2013). *Social Theory Re-wired*. New York: Routledge.
McRobbie, A. (1978). *Jackie: An Ideology of Adolescent Femininity*. Birmingham: Centre for Contemporary Cultural Studies.
McRobbie, A. (1991). *Feminism and Youth Culture: From 'Jackie' to 'Just Seventeen'*. Basingstoke: Macmillan Education.
Muggleton, D. (2000). *Inside Subculture: The Postmodern Meaning of Style*. Oxford: Berg.
Niemeyer, K. (2014). *Media and Nostalgia Yearning for the Past Present and Future*. United Kingdom: Palgrave Macmillan.
O'Connor, S. (2013, October, 3). Sinéad O'Connor's Open Letter to Miley Cyrus, *The Guardian UK*. Retrieved from www.theguardian.com/music/2013/oct/03/sinead-o-connor-open-letter-miley-cyrus
O'Connor, S. (2014, October 26). Urgent! Does Anyone Know the Whereabouts of this Girl's Parents? *The Sinéad O'Connor Site*, October 26. Accessed June 12 2019. www.sineadoconnor.com/2014/10/does-anyone-know-the-whereabouts-of-this-girls-parents/
O'Dowd, N. (2018, August, 22). Sinead O'Connor Was Booed Off Stage at Bob Dylan Concert over Tearing Up Pope's Picture. *Irish Central*. Retrieved from www.irishcentral.com/culture/sinead-oconnor-bob-dylan-pope
Oppliger, P. (2008). *Girls Gone Skank: The Sexualization of Girls in American Culture*. Jefferson, NC: McFarland & Company.
Orlansky, H. (1949). Infant Care and Personality. *Psychological Bulletin*, 46(1), 1–48.
Paton, G. (2013, November 5). Miley Cyrus is a Poor Role Model to Girls and Gives them Mixed Messages, Says Headmistress. *Telegraph, UK*. Available at: www.telegraph.co.uk/education/educationnews/10427622/Miley-Cyrus-is-a-poor-role-model-to-girls-and-gives-them-mixed-messages-says-headmistress.html
Powell, A. (2015). Young Women, Raunch and the Politics of (Sexual) Choice: Is Australian Youth Culture Post-Feminist?, in S. Baker, B. Robards and B. Buttigieg (Eds.), *Youth Cultures and Subcultures: Australian Perspectives*, pp. 215–28. Surrey: Ashgate.
Robards, B. (2012). Leaving MySpace, Joining Facebook: 'Growing Up' on Social Network Sites. *Continuum: Journal of Media & Cultural Studies*, 26(2), 385–398.
Robards, B., and B. Buttigieg (Eds.). (2016). *Youth Cultures and Subcultures: Australian Perspectives*, pp. 53–64. Burlington: Ashgate.
Routledge, C., Arndt, J., Wildschut, T., Sedikides, C., and Hart, C. M. (2011). The Past Makes the Present Meaningful: Nostalgia as an Existential Resource. *Journal of Personality and Social Psychology*, 101(3), 638–652.
Routledge, C., Wildschut, T., Sedikides, C., Juhl, J., and Arndt, J. (2012). The Power of the Past: Nostalgia as a Meaning-Making Resource. *Memory*, 20(5), 452–460.

Smetana, J. (2005). Patterns of Parental Authority and Adolescent Autonomy, in J. Smetana (Ed.), *New Directions for Child Development: Changes in Parental Authority during Adolescence*, pp. 61–69. San Francisco, CA: Jossey-Bass.

Smetana, J. G., and Asquith, P. (1994). Adolescents' and Parents' Conceptions of Parental Authority and Personal Autonomy. *Child Development*, 65(4), 1147–1162.

Spera, C. (2005). A Review of the Relationship among Parenting Practices, Parenting Styles, and Adolescent School Achievement. *Educational Psychology Review*, 17(2), 125–146.

Steinberg, L., Lamborn, S., Dornbusch, S., and Darling, N. (1992). Impact of Parenting Practices on Adolescent Achievement: Authoritative Parenting, School Involvement, and Encouragement to Succeed. *Child Development*, 63(5), 1266–1281.

Symonds, P. W. (1939). *The Psychology of Parent-Child Relationships*. Oxford: Appleton-Century.

The Full Monty Python. (YouTube). Four Yorkshiremen – Monty Python. 2008. www.youtube.com/watch?v=ue7wM0QC5LE

Threadgold, S. (2015). (Sub)cultural Capital, DIY Careers and Transferability: Towards Maintaining Reproduction When Using Bourdieu in Youth Culture Research, in Baker S., Robards B., and Buttigieg B. (Eds.), *Youth Cultures and Subcultures: Australian Perspectives*. Farnham: Ashgate, pp. 53–64.

Threadgold, S. (2018). *Youth, Class and Everyday Struggles*. Routledge: London.

Tyler, I. (2013). *Revolting Subjects: Social Abjection and Resistance in Neoliberal Britain*. London: Zed Books.

Wald, G. (1964). The Origins of Life. *Proceedings of the National Academy of Sciences USA*. 1964 Aug; 52(2), 595–611.

Willis, P. (1990). *Common Culture: Symbolic Work at Play in the Everyday Cultures of the Young*. Milton Keynes: Open University Press.

Wyn, J., and Woodman, D. (2006). Generation, Youth and Social Change in Australia. *Journal of Youth Studies*, 9(5), 495–514.

Zeisler, A. (2008). *Feminism and Pop Culture*. Berkeley, CA: Seal Press.

7 Music

The Past in the Present

Vikings at the Gates.

(Fred)

As Webb, Scirato and Danaher (2002) remind us, at the core of the process of misrecognition is the capacity to forget. Upon arrival at adulthood, we somehow manage to forget, or at least park to one side in a hidden corner of our memory, the denigration and mockery by adults during our youth and adjust to, and embrace, the doxa of being an adult. Because we get embroiled in, are consumed by, the rules of the game of the world we now inhabit as an adult, we (ironically) lack the objectivity to scrutinise the how and the why of who we are and how we got here. We wear the present like a cloak – Bourdieu's garment. This is the natural order of things: respect resides with the adult and is duly expected; young people know their place; authenticity resides with the adult's youth experience; and by extension inauthenticity must reside with young people from ensuing youth generations. This process of forgetting allows us to ignore, or at least re-categorise, the misrecognition we endured as young people. The garment of the natural order of things allows us to 'unsee' the opportunities to empathise with young people from ensuing generations who are experiencing what we experienced during our youth. It allows us to put aside the emotional capital we embodied while ourselves enduring adult misrecognition as a young person. It allows us, with the mantle of authenticity and hubris which accrues to our now adult status, to misrecognise young people from ensuing youth generations. It also allows us to misrecognise the music of ensuing youth generations; Fred's labelling of 'Vikings at the gate' is at the more extreme symbolically violent cusp of this denigration.

Upon attaining adulthood, what is gradually forgotten is that the collective understandings, the doxa acquired in their youth, was specific to that particular time period. The privileging of those understandings allows adults to forget, or at least ignore, the circumstances surrounding their acquisition of their collective doxa. The privileging of our own youth experience

DOI: 10.4324/9781003427476-7

denies the possibility that any such youth experience could be repeated in any subsequent youth generations. Ours is a 'one-off'. Their 'reality', the doxa accumulated over a lifetime, cannot encompass any challenge to this 'truth'. This 'truth' legitimises and vests the authority of the double language of disinterest in each adult. This truth, once embodied is presumed, intuitively understood, arrived at via those 'special moments' indelibly remembered from our adolescence. These doxic understandings assume that the social world which enveloped our youth experiences will remain static. It assumes that our perceptions of the privileged centrality of our position within that social world derive from a teenage experience that cannot be matched. We know this to be true because as Melissa has told us: 'We ended up with our own generation of musicians and we still love it. Because that's from your teenage years'. When the fixed, immovable status of the adult's teenage social world is challenged by young people claiming legitimacy for *their* youth experience, misrecognition of ensuing generations results.

For young people emerging into adulthood, conflict with older generations is determined by the 'principles of division' (Bourdieu, 2000: 186) which reflect their emergence from the fields of youth and education into the fields of employment and adulthood. The outward manifestations of the social, cultural and economic capital acquired during their youth place them at odds with their elders. Conscious of, and reacting to, the misrecognition directed at them by their elders, they push back. This conflict leads to attempts at subversion of the social space occupied by their elders which in turn leads to further push back by their elders.

Symbolic violence relies upon subtext, irony, sarcasm and denigration to convey the intended violence implicit in the misrecognising of young people. Many, if not most, adults have ongoing relationships with young people – as employers, teachers, sports coaches and, most intimately of all, as parents and relatives. Much of this engagement takes place over a long period of time where the young person's growth and maturity is seen either first hand or from a near proximity. In addition, adults have an engagement with young people via young people's representations in various forms of media (a la Hannah Montana). Misrecognising the behaviour of young people takes place within the context of shared experiences and degrees of intimacy and familiarity of the adult with the young person and vice versa.

We have already met Fred (73) several times: early Baby Boomer, university educated, retired law professional. He had adult children whose teenagehood occurred in the 1980s and early 90s. Throughout the interview, he indicated a breadth of knowledge and experience, and a reflexive understanding of both his place within his demographic profile and the place of that demographic within the wider society. His responses reflected if not a sense of empathy, then at least a broad understanding of the forces at work (sociological, cultural and economic), which may impact upon the way young people function within their cultural milieu. His understanding ran to being able to see negative responses from his age contemporaries as not only lacking in a rational basis but as a result of intergenerational misrecognition. He talked about, 'ongoing whinges, moans and complaints ... a lack of patience by some older people towards younger ones'.

His 'considered' responses served to create the sense of someone with (to his mind) a clear understanding of young people: 'generational matters will continue to happen whilst ever there are human beings on this earth... . [Young people are] intelligent with a capacity to astound' (Fred, 73). To this reasonable assessment, he then added the rejoinder: 'and on other occasions appals me', referring specifically to the problem of drugs and young people: Drug abuse 'leads them to behave towards other members of our community ... in... an appalling manner'.

In discussing drugs and young people, Fred acknowledged parallels with his own generation, especially experiences with alcohol, which he made repeated references to:

> In earlier generations there were young people who did dreadful things like drinking too much ... possibly [you] and I were involved with the same activity.
>
> (Fred, 73)

In outlining the differences between young people today and his own teenage experience, he provided the following definitive statement: 'We didn't have drugs available to us'.

Fred states categorically: 'We didn't have drugs available to us'. This is not a conditional response as in 'I didn't use drugs'. Fred's use of the collective 'we' presumes that his personal experience was a collective generation-wide experience. His implied inclusion of the author, who is himself within the parameters of Fred's Baby Boomer age demographic, presumes the author to have had the same or similar remembered experiences. Yet the inference was at odds with the actual lived experience of this author.

Fred's understanding of generational difference in substance abuse indicates a dislocation between accepted understandings of the historical Baby Boomer youth experience and Fred's 'remembered' youth generational experience. Fred's apparent unawareness of drugs[1] 'being available to us' may represent his own individual experience. This again parallels Mark Fisher's reflections on the way time is out of synch with our present. What we see here is Fred manifesting 'the virtual agency of the no longer' (2012: 21) – 'reversing into tomorrow based on a nonexistent past' (Petit, 2010). For Fred, drugs never happened. His present does not countenance a past that included drugs. Here he demonstrates his being part of what Edmunds and Turner refer to as a 'self-conscious age stratum' (2002: 12) of Baby Boomers. His awareness of the wider social and cultural milieu within which he transitioned from childhood to adulthood ensured 'an active generational consciousness' (Thomson, 2016: 45; see also Frisch, 1979; Raleigh, 2012). This would have enabled him to see his own experience within the ambit of a wider social and cultural environment which, for baby boomers, would have included illegal drugs.

Fred's remembered experience was very much central to his doxa, a doxa in which in his remembered past, drugs did not exist. His lived experience would have encompassed the wider 'counter culture' of his generation even if he personally did not experience it. There is a dislocation between his remembered past and the generational consciousness with which he transitioned to adulthood. Fred's class disposition may also have contributed to his 'amnesia'. His position within the law community may very well have influenced and shaped his attitude towards drugs. In any event, it is this dislocation in his remembered past which allows him to use his 'imagined' past as a benchmark by which current youth generations can be judged.

Fred's habitus is the accumulation of the symbolic and economic capital he has acquired during his lifetime. It is ongoing and continues throughout his life. This evolution is 'in a state of constant flux' (Bourdieu, 2000: 131). No doubt Fred was aware of drug taking among his fellow young people during his youth. He was after all emerging from his youth stage during the era of Woodstock, Timothy Leary, Haight Ashbury, Jimmy Hendrix, Janis Joplin and so on. But with the passage of time his recall of actual history has been transformed as the experiences and 'understandings' of 40 years of living are embodied. His doxa is now at odds, via his 'remembered youth', with the social world he actually inhabited in his youth. The airbrushing of drugs from his youth experience now influences the way that he views young people today. For him, unlike his own now 'remembered' youth generation, young people today are captured by, and are the victims of, drugs – very much the makings of a moral panic. Fred has very much entered his *Billy Pilgrim* phase: now 'lost in time', cloaked in the *garment* of his *collective faith in the universal*.

Nostalgia's Not What It Used to Be

Fred's mis-remembered youth experiences are privileged by the lapse in time between the experience and the present, colouring the way he perceives young people today. Compared to the Elysian experiences of this remembered past, the experiences of young people of today appear flawed. They cannot match the apparent innocence and the good-natured experience of Boomers, because young people today are at risk of (evil) drugs.

Fred's *nostalgia* for a remembered past that doesn't exist represents what Phillips (1985) calls the process of 'desire's distortions and reorganisations…. memorialised' (66). Hutcheon and Valdes refer to this process as:

> The simple, pure, ordered, easy, beautiful, or harmonious past is constructed (and then experienced emotionally) in conjunction with the present—which, in turn, is constructed as complicated, contaminated,

anarchic, difficult, ugly, and confrontational. Nostalgic distancing sanitizes as it selects, making the past feel complete, stable, coherent, safe.

(2000: 20)

It is this *memorialisation* that ennobles the past within the habitus of adults. That which was 'complicated, contaminated, anarchic, difficult, ugly, and confrontational' has had the memory of these elements sanitised. In their place exists an idealised past, memorialised with the imprimatur of authenticity. Nostalgia distances, makes the past feel safe, stable. The allure of the past glows in comparison with the immediacy of dissatisfactions with the present. Mitchell and Thomson refer to this as *rosy retrospection* (1994). Rosy retrospection enables adults to re-cast their past as simultaneously arcadian and character building. The demands and rigour of their youth experience enables them to face their adulthood toughened by their experience and able to face the future.

Music is a central element in the way young people make meaning in their lives. And that central role extends to the part it plays in the evolution of habitus as the music from our past, embodied at such a crucial time in our lives, then memorialised. The process of grounded aesthetics locates this teenage musical cavalcade as the central plank in the soundtrack of our life (Owen, 2006). Latching on to these musical experiences and then embodying them influences and informs the way adults misrecognise the music of young people of ensuing generations. The garment that our youth musical experience enfolds us in unmasks yet another paradox in the way that the child is the parent of the adult. The euphoria of the youth musical experience remains with us as treasured memories, memorialised in our habitus with the authenticity of the sheer exhilaration of the actual experience and embodiment. But the accompanying misrecognition of 'turn that down', 'you call that music?' 'you're not listening to that!' 'no you can't go to that concert' is somehow forgotten, banished from our memory – or more appropriately set aside, transformed into the nostalgia of quaint memories of 'being disciplined'. These memories can take their place alongside assorted anecdotes from their youth – curios of what it was like to be a young person in their day. It is the capacity to treat their misrecognising by adults when young as an off-handed 'nod' to the 'we did it tough in our day' that serves to discount this misrecognition. In their day they were tough. They knew how to deal with it. The alchemy of consecration has transformed the angst, and the disappointments, and the storming off to their rooms, of their teenagehood into nostalgia. This nostalgia converts the trials of teenagehood into a rite of passage – a rite of passage that they traverse, and pass with flying colours, on their journey to adulthood. This is the 'tough love' that they now advocate for ensuing youth generations to buttress them in preparation for adulthood. Mirroring 1983 Jess, all that is required is for them to simply 'put on a bit more of a sassy attitude, put a scrunchy in their hair and gone Fuck you'. To their mind, what they endured was much worse than young people today. But they

130 *Music*

knew how to deal with that denigration and humiliation and frustration. As young people back then, those now adults weren't snowflakes like the young people today. That 'were real misrecognition' that they suffered. Their misrecognition from their youth can now take its place alongside the hyperbole of the *Four Yorkshiremen* – You think you were misrecognised? That were looxury! WE were the ones who were misrecognised – cause that was from our teenage years.

You Can't Stop the Music

The relationship we experience with music is one of the more intimate (Turino, 1999; Sugarman, 1997; Pacini Hernandez, 1995) of artforms we engage with. It's music's semiotic capacity to directly allow us to 'know' (Turino, 1999) that makes it special. The core of music's intimacy is the emotion it can evoke within us. It's the sublime joy and exhilaration of discovery at the very first time you listened to Dark Side Of The Moon, made even more memorable because it was on headphones; the raw energy of the Beatles' Twist And Shout; and the deeply felt poignancy and pathos of Randy Newman's Old Man. These are but three examples from the soundtrack of my life but each of us can quote manifold examples from our own life soundtracks. Tia De Nora (2000) has explored this intimate relationship in detail and particularly how that process of intimacy weaves its way into and through our consciousness. The complexity of that relationship entwines and enfolds itself into our being when we encounter music that we 'connect' with; that 'speaks' to us; that penetrates our core. At the centre of this analysis is the way music and 'self' interact, an interaction intrinsically interwoven with the function of memory – who we are is arrived at by how we got here. Central to that process is how earlier youth musical experiences secure themselves to our habitus fusing, amalgamating with our self to seamlessly become part of who we are. De Nora defines this process as *self-programming* (2000: 49). These musical experiences from the past become like a series of continuous and evolving identity signposts as past seamlessly folds into present and into future. When one re-experiences that music as an adult, the experience acts as a 'trigger' activating the memory of the youth experience of the music. These nostalgic memories act to prime a series of 'mood relationships and systemic correlations' (65) which become the foundation for the link between the memory of those experiences and what De Nora labels the *embodied awareness* (85) which mediates and encompasses the physical linking of the environment with the original musical experience.

Music by itself is just part of the encounter. Memory is about the entirety of the experience: the music, the environment, the presence of others, the ambience. In this way, the totality of the experience is subsumed as embodied awareness. Equally important is the temporal environment: the conditions in which the musical tastes and preferences were acquired. The 'what' and the 'how' and the 'where' and the 'with whom' are located in time. It is this temporal location that has the capacity to colour and influence an individual's ongoing interaction with music and identity. Temporal embodied awareness serves to contextualise the way we respond to the later re-living of musical and cultural experiences. Implicit in the process of latching is an identification with the music as a visceral engagement, what De Nora refers to as *sonic patterns* (85) that are linked to specific times of a person's life.

De Nora draws a distinction between *traditional* music (community practice) and *modern* musical practice (individualised) (155). Music in traditional societies is deeply ingrained within meaningful and essential practices and traditions often associated with ceremony and ritual. Modern music by contrast is reflective of the sterility of modern industrial life. Implicit in this perceived contrast is the notion of decline in standards. It is this judgement of a decline in standards which draws parallels with moral panics applied to ensuing youth generations. The communal latching of a particular generation with the music of that time is where members of a particular generation, who may not share an identification with a particular musical genre, do share the musical generalities of the zeitgeist. That shared musical experience, viewed as superior to the music of ensuing generations, is a generationally shared introjection of musical experience of the zeitgeist which draws them together in generational fraternity and sorority.

Participants in this research time and again demonstrated the role that music plays in 'reflecting self to self'. Adam (69) was adamant about this significance explaining his teenage years as 'one of the greatest periods of my life… . I had the freedom to do whatever I liked'. Adam's account of being a teenager is tinged with nostalgia. He recalls the freedom to listen to and embody whatever musical and other cultural experiences he chose. For the older informants, their nostalgia for that period of life was tinged by understanding of the social and historical circumstances in the process of introjection.

The process of reflecting self to self is not static. Memories of teenage experiences both recall the experience from the past and reflect upon that experience in the present. Music is both an experience and an accompaniment to experience and the two are inextricably linked. Louise (65) articulated that link:

> We'd only really heard 40s and 50s music that was our parents, like you know your Frank Sinatras and they were all too old for us as teenagers sort of thing, so we ended up with our own generation of musicians and we still love it. Because that's from your teenage years.

This defining of self can be both positive and negative. An individual's habitus can sometimes be defined by the absence of a particular characteristic. Joanne (32), when responding to the music of Nirvana, referred to the band's 'coolness' factor, and talked of her lack of coolness at school. Her reflection of self to self, her defining of herself was in the negative: 'Well I was never cool enough to like that kind of music'.

The Process of Latching – I Know What I Like

The visceral process of latching is recognised and understood, even though it may not be a conscious understanding in terms of formal analysis. Nevertheless, as 16-year-old Sarah and Rebecca demonstrate, music is seamlessly understood and incorporated into each person's disposition during teenage years while the process of *latching* is at its most active. In response to hearing Nirvana's track 'Smells like teen spirit' in the focus group, Sarah and Rebecca spontaneously began singing. When it got to the 'hello, hello, hello, hello, hello' sequence they made eye contact and began singing to each other in an exaggerated style. The visceral linking of music and occasion was conspicuous:

Sarah: Oh I remember ... Ellie and Chloe for the first time and when they'd been dancing ...
Rebecca: Was so good.

That moment in time lives in their memory. The awareness of the totality of the experience is embodied: Smells Like Teen Spirit; Ellie and Chloe for the first time; was so good. The recollection of these embodied understandings triggers a whole range of responses – far more than just the music experience. Although the experience and the memory of the experience are embedded, the remembering is an impromptu response, spontaneous. And the spontaneity of the shared remembering makes the memory of that experience live in the present. The response is essentially intuitive. And it will live on in their collective memory as a visceral moment, almost overwhelming in the totality of the experience, permanently etched in this shared memory. All that is required for it to repeat is a similar trigger to make it live again in the present.

In their youth, the Boomer generation experienced what Leech calls a 'youthquake' (1973). Rock music set the Baby Boomer generation apart from their forebears. At that time, rock music and young people were inseparable (Frith, 1981: 9). Rock and roll, in many versions, has dominated popular culture since the 1950s (Martin and Segrave, 1993; Bennett and Taylor, 2012; Bennett, 2013). Generations following have grown up within a popular culture still dominated by rock music. The soundtrack of their lives has incorporated much of the music played by their parents. This wider soundtrack was reflected in the response of younger informants. They showed general acquaintance with, and even strong recognition of, most of the older songs played to them as discussion stimuli reflecting the environment in which they grew up.

Almost all the iconic songs from each decade chosen as musical stimuli for this research were recognised even by the youngest informants. Clearly, they had latched on to these songs. Sixteen-year-old Sarah cited specific examples of how the Sex Pistols was incorporated into her habitus:

> I've grown up with [them]. That's the kind of stuff that I grew up listening to and like I was in the car with dad and there was an interview about them on the radio 'cause there was something to do with an anniversary of an album of theirs happened not long ago.

However, the process of latching reflects the inexact nature of acquisition. This inexactitude sometimes includes the incorporation of incorrect information into memory. This occurred in one focus group of 18–25-year-olds. The Bruce Springsteen song 'Born to Run' was a secondary source used. As part of the discussion about 'Born to Run', Springsteen's 'Born in the USA' arose as a comparison. Lola (21) raised the issue of the President at the time attempting to appropriate 'Born in the USA' as an election ad. We know that it was in the 1984[2] Presidential campaign that Ronald Reagan attempted to do this and that Springsteen refused permission (Griffiths, 2016). Lola had heard the story but had somehow appropriated the song from Reagan in 1984 to Richard Nixon in 1972:

> That's what Bruce Springsteen was actually famous for and Richard Nixon should never have used that song, it was very funny.

For Lola, 'Born in the USA'[3] exists within the ambit of The Nixon administration – somewhere in the period 1968–1974 and almost certainly in the election of 1972. In her mind, it is forever associated with Nixon's campaigning. Until she is disavowed of this, it will continue to exist for her within this timeframe. That Lola has made this error is neither here nor there. The incorporation of inaccuracies into our memory is very common. But what Lola has done here has *latched* onto a piece of information which has now been incorporated into cultural memory, part of her embodied awareness. Along with the myriad examples of pop ephemera she has encountered, it will inform her disposition towards later musical products she encounters.

Latching is neither static nor uniform in its operation or effects. For Paul (65), the music incorporated into his habitus is locked in a time warp: 'I'm still in the sixties, seventies, I admit it'.[4] Fred (73) was adamant about not only his love of the music of his youth but the superiority of that music over later musical forms. His tastes very much reflected his middle-class persona of retired lawyer. He said that current popular music:

> Does nothing for me. My interest in music is what I like to hear. I don't care who plays it or who sings it … but that one [Nikki Minaj] does nothing for me. I love folk music. Folk music over generations I like. A lot of the Mersey stuff I like.

Paul and Fred's responses reflect the fact that the process of latching has been virtually completed. For Fred, he has ceased to incorporate new musical product into his habitus. The aesthetic solera base is accepting no more additions.

Melissa's response was more nuanced. The signature role that her youth played in acquiring and incorporating the soundtrack of her life into her persona is central to her understanding. She also acknowledges later *latching* has taken place but with the qualification of (in her mind) the qualitative difference inherent in this later latching:

> We ended up with our own generation of musicians and we still love it. Because that's from your teenage years. But we also love a lot of other music as well. This is like the thing of we can appreciate but it's not the same.
>
> (Melissa, 65)

'Appreciate' but not the same. We can 'appreciate' what is theirs, but 'that from our teenage years' is OURS. Latching is a particularly active process during the youth stage of life, linking the newly encountered musical and other cultural experiences to a specific time and place in the form of grounded aesthetics and is incorporated corporeally, as part of the ongoing habitus of each individual.

Embodied Awareness

For Sarah and Rebecca, 'Smells Like Teen Spirit' exists in their habitus as the experience itself and the circumstances surrounding the experiencing of the music. This is *embodied awareness*. The process of introjection links musical experiences to an environment – links music to specific places, specific experiences and importantly specific times in each person's life. Embodied awareness is more than just memory. De Nora talks of music having a visceral relationship, of 'corporeal ordering' (2000: 77). Thus, the music experience incorporates the context of that experience embodying the music. Importantly, the temporal context includes the age at which it happened. As they age and move into their teenage years, a young person gains ever-increasing autonomy over the music selected. Via this agency, they become the actor in the play, their personal soundtrack no longer organised and chosen at the behest of adults. They engage through the process of active selection with the grounded aesthetics of their generational music which they use to give meaning to their lives. They now are in control of the aesthetic solera. That aesthetic solera is now evolving into the soundtrack of their life.

Young peoples' taste in music is influenced by the myriad of individual characteristics of their life (relationship with parents, peers, teachers, as well as aesthetic preferences). Musical experiences are entrained and integrated into their habitus along with the wider environmental experience occurring contemporaneously with the musical experience. Each individual's life contains a series of these seemingly countless corporeal experiences. Once embodied, they are reflected upon and utilised to gain greater understanding of themselves. This aesthetic reflexivity provides the basis for associating with musical subcultural groups. Examples of such groups exist across the generations: 'surfie', 'mod', 'rocker', 'punk', 'goth', 'grunge', 'riot grrrl', 'emo' and the like. These subcultures can function as group identity (Hall and Jefferson, 1976; Hebdige, 1979). But the cultural forms which identify a young person as a punk or a goth not only allow entry to, and membership of, the subculture, but also provide each member with an individual identity. Subcultural membership is conferred because of who they are as individuals, which has been arrived at via the process of aesthetic reflexivity. For those not identifying with a particular subculture, the identification may be with a particular genre or specific band, or their tastes may be more neo-tribal.

Aesthetic reflexivity and the corporeal linking of music and environment was very apparent among the informants. The visceral association of music to the experiences of a wider environment was a constant point of reflection in discussion of the stimulus musical pieces. For Iris (16) and Eliza (16), that link was to specific time and place:

Iris: We have memories of these songs.
Eliza: I feel like … when we were in Primary school …at a school disco and like somebody acts songs like Soulja Boy I hear that and like cool … school disco like that [emphasis] and like oh yeah.

Primary School; School disco; Soulja Boy; Cool; Oh Yeah. The music is the trigger. Primary school and school disco are the corporeal environment that makes these memories so real, so poignant, so cool.

For Melissa (65), it was regular events that melded the music into the environment:

> It's all memories I think. There'll be certain songs that might remind you of your first date … we used to go to particular dance halls in our little town. Youth clubs and things.

For Pauline (49) and Matthew (55), the music referenced a particular social environment, a film, a band or a year:

Pauline: There was a sexual revolution. You know when John Travolta and his tight pants hit the dance floor.
Matthew: Oh, and Skyhooks … around about the same time.
Pauline: Skyhooks! Yeah 'You just like me cause I'm good in bed'. Yeah 1975.
Matthew: A revolution.
Pauline: REVOLUTIONARY! That is the word. It makes me want to be revolutionary.

Paul and Melissa made a corporeal link between music and the advent of television:

Paul: It was on the radio and television. We were just getting used to TV and they were on the top of the pops. That was a great time in our lives.

Melissa: You'd run home from school to go and watch Top of the Pops.

The energy and the animation in these anecdotes is immediately discernible. The totality of the teenage experience of music and other popular cultural forms has become embodied, made more special by the circumstances under which the experience occurred. This specialness, part of who we are, is seamlessly enmeshed in the complexity of the totality of who we are. Although we are more than conscious of the composers of the soundtrack of our lives, the arrangements of this internal symphony remain random, incidental, contingent upon memory and happenstance – Bourdieu's conductorless orchestration.

Traditional versus Modern Music

From Theodor Adorno to Camille Paglia, the decline in the standard of music has been an ongoing theme in the analysis of High and Popular culture. In popular music, this decline has been mooted since the 'golden age' of rock music in the 1960s into the 1970s was superseded by the emergence of Disco and Punk Rock. The advent of Hip Hop and computer-generated music has only served to engender greater animosity among those raised on, and committed to, the halcyon days of The Beatles and Bob Dylan (see Hesmondhalgh, 2022; Gracyk, 1993; Hennessey, 2020; Fang, 2019; JoanCA, 2023; Coyne, 2022).

These concerns mirror De Nora's demarcation between traditional and modern music which offers a parallel with adult generations misrecognising the music of following generations. Musical representations of the 'hierarchy' of quality of the music of the past vs the present, adult vs young people, create fault lines based on notions of authenticity. Modern music's absence of authenticity when compared with music from earlier times is caused by the influence of the modern world relying as it does upon 'rational, calculative modes of consciousness' (De Nora, 2000: 155). The increasingly rational and calculating function of modernity has corrupted music so that it now represents nothing more than 'commercial product' (see Hennessy, 2016). This concern with modernity is reflected in Melissa's concern about the quality of modern music being debased by the employment of technology by recording artists: 'and I think their musical tastes are influenced by the videos not necessarily by the talent of the artists' (Melissa, 65).

It is this perceived devaluation of musical quality that adults, and particularly Boomers, apply to the music of generations following them. They do so based upon the pretext that the authenticity of the music they grew up with grants them the absolute certainty that the music of ensuing generations is inferior. For Boomers, this is self-evident, a truism as Brabazon has pointed out. Baby Boomers, encountering the music identified with ensuing generations, see and analyse that music through the prism of their own authentic musical experience, bearing the cachet of the inherent excellence accruing to its hallowed place in the pantheon of popular/rock music.

Baby Boomers enjoy a status as the first generation inextricably bound to rock music (Frith, 1983: 9). Post-war prosperity fostered both the market and the disposable income necessary for the emergence of a range of popular cultural forms. Simultaneously, post-war prosperity saw the rapid expansion of secondary and tertiary education which meant that number of young people engaged in full time education instead of work expanded. Baby Boomers were the first television generation, the first to see themselves reflected back to them on TV and wider media (Bodroghkozy, 2001). Rose and Ross (1994) have argued that the amplified 'romanticisation' of the Boomer youth experience entitles it to be referred to as the 'golden age' of youth culture.

Being the first rock generation, part of this *golden age*, entitled Boomers to a sense of proprietary ownership of the entirety of the rock/popular music genre. This was an entitlement that was reflected back at them because Baby Boomers, the generation that produced rock music, also originated the genre of rock music journalism (see Lindberg et al., 2000; Trammell, 2003). This rock journalism in turn seamlessly validated not only the music of the generation but the generation itself. The legitimacy of rock journalism turned the journalism into the gold standard of music criticism via publications such as *Rolling Stone*, *New Musical Express* and *GoSet*. This set of acquired cultural capital, accruing as it did to a generation as a whole, served to privilege sixties and seventies rock music. In doing so, it established a 'journalistic' benchmark against which all subsequent music criticism could be compared and judged. And this benchmark continues to exist, as Brabazon points out, as 'talisman and shaman' (2018: 69) at the altar of their youth cultural experience. Bennett (2013) takes a more nuanced position pointing out examples of music genre aficionados keeping pace with developments and changes in the field, such as middle-aged punks. This is particularly the case with regard to genres and bands with a 'multi-generational fan base' (124). He cites an example of a review which instances the varied age of the fans attending a Pink Floyd concert (124). Nevertheless, Bennett does acknowledge the existence of conflict between generations over authenticity. In another echo of De Nora's thesis, he talks of the role that popular music plays as a 'cultural resource in everyday life' (4).

This multi-generational theme of musical preferences identified by Bennett was very much present during the interviews and focus groups. It was evident that since the 1960s, each succeeding youth generation has grown up listening not only to their own musical preferences, but to the musical soundtrack of

138 *Music*

their parents, played when they were younger and before reaching the age where they could control their own selection of music. They also grew up listening to their parents reminding them of the importance of the quality of the music of their generation. Aged 21, Elaine's comment, 'I feel trapped in the 70s and 80s since birth', provides an example of how the process of musical osmosis can embed itself within an individual's cultural repertoire. Nineteen-year-old Joe's musical tastes very much reflect this process of cross-generational embodiment:

> I've sorta grown up and my parents thought that I was better listening to Cold Chisel and Midnight Oil and Paul Kelly and Icehouse and stuff like that. And that's how I've been shaped as an individual and that's still what I listen to. ... I don't go to my mates – 'let's go and see Parkway Drive at Panthers'.

Twenty-three-year-old Sharon, obviously a fan, interjected: 'I'll go'. For Joe, Elaine and Sharon, their musical tastes are influenced by this early acquisition of the parental music playlist.

Nevertheless, they all agreed that their own musical playlist, their unique generational soundtrack, had brought them into conflict with their parents. Elaine, for example, in response to the musical prompt of a Kanye West song, talked about her guilty pleasure of listening to Kanye's music while at school and beyond the disciplinary limitations of her parents:

> In 2004 I was in Year 5 at the time. My parents didn't know about it. So it was one of those things where the parents tried to keep that sort of thing away from me. But I was already there.
>
> (Elaine, 21)

She referred to this same process as accessing 'forbidden fruit' when discussing Eminem. Joe (19) concurred: 'You borrowed the CD off your mates, so you could listen to it in your room'.

Echoing Brabazon's identification of the 'transcendent' link between music and dance where 'popular culture always affects the body' (2005: 81), Sharon (23) emphasised the sheer exhilaration of music and being in the moment:

> Being with friends, dancing, having fun, having a good time really, yeah. I'm with my friends, I'm having fun, I'm forgetting about everything else that's going on, I'm here in this moment and I'm going to have fun, whether anyone else wants to read into it that I'm being rebellious and all that kind of stuff, that's up to them.

Sharon has corporeally embodied the youth musical experience. Newer generations of young people such as Elaine, Joe and Sharon share a 'hybrid' compilation personal soundtrack derived from experiencing forbidden musical pleasures hidden from their parents combined with their parents' soundtracks.

The generational incorporation of popular music did not swing both ways. For Fred, the music of Eminem, Kanye West and particularly Nikki Minaj was an affront to not only his aesthetic values but to his sense of propriety. He used terms such as 'noise', 'rush' and 'invasion'. He explained, that the music was 'too much in your face ... rushed at you'. At one point, Fred asked the interviewer how the music was chosen for use in interviews. In response to the answer that the music was chosen in consultation the PHD supervisor, Fred commented in an off-the-cuff manner: 'who is obviously a sadist'.

A familiar refrain in Fred's criticism of the music of later generations played in the interview was that music had become faster, had speeded up due to the advent of modern technology, especially post-1990s music. In the space of one page of transcript, he repeated the word 'frenzied' five times:

> It was more jumping around more frenzied ... I don't like it frenzied ... unless it's something like Les Mis [Les Misérables] as being frenzied which I don't think it is ... [in reference to hip hop] it was spoiled by the vocal which turned rather frenzied ... [in defence of music from his era] they weren't frenzied.
>
> (Fred, 73)

Finally, as a kind of summary of his position, Fred invoked the analogy of the already mentioned Viking hordes.

Fred's responses to the musical stimuli were at the more extreme end of older generation informants. In the main, Baby Boomer responses were measured and understanding. Many were aware of, and even familiar with, musical styles and notable musicians and groups that their children and even grandchildren were listening to. Nevertheless, the underlying perception of their music as more authentic would enter the conversation at a subtextual level, where the misrecognition inherent in the superiority of their musical experience over later musical representations was apparent.

In response to the Sex Pistols song 'Anarchy in the UK', Pauline's immediate response was 'I find it really inspiring, ... it was written about the state of England, what was happening at the time'. The clear inference from this statement is that critical political commentary is absent from contemporary music.[5] The claim for authenticity emerged even stronger slightly later in the focus group when she referred to the mid-1980s Australian band 'Midnight Oil[6] ... writing political messages'. She then asked the focus group: 'Is there still a lot of messaging, political and social comment through music?'

The capacity to confer authenticity on something is not only self-defining, it also is self-justifying. Anything deemed not authentic is consigned to the status of not measuring up. Authenticity confers privilege and status. All musical expressions of ensuing youth generations must, by definition, be inauthentic.

In one of the focus groups, Paul (65) was at pains to explain how he enjoyed music from all generations. He said his friend Max (66) had exceedingly eclectic taste in music across all generations and had introduced him to a wide variety of music. Paul was appreciative of the new music and praised it. He recognised the musical examples played as focus group stimulus and was quite knowledgeable about the music of later generations. He spoke with authority on many of the musicians and groups and their musical output. However, misrecognition of later musical examples crept into the conversation. Paul revealed that when they were growing up, his son and daughter would often have friends around for parties. His son's friends were invited to his (Paul's) own birthday party. His son informed him on that occasion that they would be playing his (the son's) music:

> 'We're putting our music on dad, I've invited my friends around' And I'd say: 'Yeah, right.' So we did. We [were] standing around the house chatting away ... and in the end me and me mates just had a gutful: 'Nah that's it.' I put my own music on and guess what, they all started dancing. And we were gobsmacked.

The night's activities may or may not have played out as he recounted them in the focus group. But Paul's recollection of the event begins from the premise of his own generation's music garnering a better reaction than that of his son's. His doxa, his acquired understandings, place his musical and aesthetic values at the centre of his consciousness. Implicitly, his own generational musical experience accrues to it the mantle of the authentic; and the vote of approval from his son's friends proves just that – much to the chagrin of his son.

Curation of the Soundtrack of Your Life

Introjection functions in different ways at different times of life. As an individual's habitus develops, so does the process of curation of each individual's personal soundtrack which has evolved as technology has evolved. George (30) talked extensively about the process of curation. In his analysis, he reflected on how technology and social media affected and drove the process of curation. Technologies opened up this process to young people on a scale and across media unparalleled before now: 'Curating what you want to see ... everything that interests you and nothing that doesn't'.

The sources available to young people for accessing and curating their cultural products, including music, have expanded exponentially through technology whereas previous generations had much more limited choices of sources. Radio stations and specialist rock music shows on television provided most of the freely available material for the Baby Boomers generation and even for Gen X. They would have bought records from specialist music stores and gained information from arthouse movie theatres or the few music journals of the time. By contrast, young people today have the widest choice of musical genres and styles available to them in their handheld devices.

Increased availability of sources for music and other cultural products provides younger people with the capability to ever-expand their playlists. Having grown up with digital technology, most Millennials are both fluent and entirely comfortable with it. Yet older people, Baby Boomers in particular, are not nearly as comfortable with this technology. It is a point of demarcation. The propensity for Millennials to seamlessly move from one digital device to another and to be constantly engaged with technology was identified as a source of annoyance for older generation informants. In this excerpt, Melissa (65) expands on her previous concerns about the effect of modernism:

> With the music now, they have access to YouTube and TV … But [when] they get a really good video with this beat going, it becomes a hit sort of thing because they're getting the visual sort of thing as well. We didn't have that so much. We just went by the music.

Melissa perceives her curatorial process to be superior. Her curating did not have to rely upon 'a really good video'. 'We just went by the music'. Implicit in the statement 'it becomes a hit sort of thing because they're getting the visual sort of thing as well' is that they didn't need that kind of embellishment. Their music was unadulterated. Their music was pure. Their music was bore the mantle of authenticity. Michelle (44), who was not quite a full generation younger than Melissa, displayed a similar understanding when talking about music from the eighties: 'It was authentic yeah, by real people playing real instruments'. 'Real people'. 'Real instruments'. The mantle of authenticity makes it 'real'. No affectations. No ornamentation, no excess. REAL! This is De Nora's differentiation between traditional (real instruments) and modern (computer generated with video).

The process of curation is not constant. At various stages of life, different factors impact upon what is appropriate to be listened to. Personal aesthetic tastes and preferences are not the only factors. The process of self-censorship regarding what is appropriate to listen to also influences the curation process. Joanne (32), a recent mother of two children, was reticent in her response to Nikki Minaj. Her aesthetic response was positive, but hesitant. The following exchange illustrates this conflict:

George: I love Nikki. Nikki's amazing.
Joanne: I feel too old to like that song but…
George: but you like it.
Joanne: it's like a guilty pleasure like I'm too old for this and it's … . It's not real music and … . But I like it anyway.

Joanne's age and the conflict with her perceived responsibilities and the conflict with her attendant perceived parenting musical suitability was brought into sharper relief with the music of Eminem:

> I just feel conflicted around Eminem because I'm a respectable grownup person who is raising human children and how can I listen to something like that and bop along to someone who's joking about child molestation and rape or whatever? And it's just [whispers guiltily] it's like catchy but it makes me feel guilty.

Joanne likes the music of Eminem. But her perception, her concern, is that the lyrics conflict with her role as mother. The process of responsibilisation (Foucault, 1991) has placed her role as mother ahead of her pre-motherhood self who may have curated Eminem's music into her playlist without guilt. Eminem's place within her personal playlist now and into the future will be a site of conflict between her enjoyment of the music and her perception of what is an age-appropriate feeling towards his music. In short, the guilty pleasure associated with liking Minaj and Eminem will be ongoing as introjection, the process of presenting self to self. But that presentation of self to self has itself become blurred, compromised by her parental status.

Joanne's doxa now incorporates being a responsible adult and mother who should be 'above' liking the music of artists like Minaj and Eminem. That conflict over age suitability will almost certainly serve to influence her assessment of future music she encounters from younger generations. The selection process and the selection criteria she uses to determine additions to her aesthetic solera have begun to narrow.

Authenticity Trolling

For many of the older informants, the theme of authenticity was never too far from their focus when it came to comparing the music of their generation with that of later generations. As Brabazon (2005) has noted, authenticity is a point of subjective differentiation between the Baby Boomer generation and the Gen X dance generation which followed. As Cobb (2014) has noted, objective criteria for determining the *authenticity* of music, or indeed any artform, is difficult to identify let alone delineate. However, it is the perception of authenticity not the concept itself which reflects the authority inherent in the term. Perceptions of authenticity bear the cachet of legitimacy, of validity, of genuineness. Notions of authenticity are very much the domain of the rock journalism industry. It is rock journalists who adjudicate as to a particular band or artist's authenticity within the canon of rock music. Texts and acts lacking authenticity are relegated to the metaphorical remainder bin as fakes or sell-outs. Examples of this abound in the music industry, from the actual hoax of Milli Vanilli[7] (1990) to the artificially manufactured nature of The Monkees (1966–1971) when compared with the earlier established authenticity of The Beatles (1960–1970).

The question of authenticity has become one of the underlying tenets of contemporary music. The Monkees versus Beatles example is a case in point, as was the reaction to bubblegum music in the sixties, and the artificial distinction between pop (artificial, trivial) and rock (serious, authentic) music (Keightley, 2001: 111). This is not a recent phenomenon. But since the advent of social media in particular, the capacity for authenticity outrage has multiplied as the immediacy of the social media response has emerged as a social media phenomenon (Brady et al., 2021; Crockett, 2017; O'Callaghan, 2020). The Canadian Grunge band Nickelback is an example of a band at the forefront of this phenomenon. The mere mention of Nickelback has become synonymous for non-authentic music, as Hiatt points out:

> There are Nickelback jokes, Internet memes, even a web browser plugin concealing all information involving Nickelback. Nearly 40,000 people signed a petition in 2011 to ban Nickelback from performing at the half-time show of a high-profile football game in Detroit .... More pressure on Nickelback came when the American duo The Black Keys attacked the band in Rolling Stone, one of the dominant magazines in rock culture, accusing them of ruining rock 'n' roll with their 'watered-down, post-grunge crap, horrendous shit'.
>
> (Hiatt, 2012)

That nearly 40,000 people bothered to sign a petition to prevent them playing at an event indicates that the perceptions of their 'phoniness' was not an isolated occurrence. Nickelback was almost universally panned by critics and grunge aficionados. As Finnish researcher Salli Anttonen has noted: 'rock critics see themselves as the protectors and arbiters of authenticity and originality' (Silverman, 2016). They were described as 'deadly boring' (Schildt, 2014), dull and repetitive (Pekkala, 2003), the 'eternal bad band' (Vuoti, 2008) playing 'horrendous shit ... tailored for playlists' (Romppainen, 2008). A similar response has greeted the music of James Blunt (see Murphy, 2013; O'Sullivan, 2013; Berkkman, 2015). 'Blunt haters' know that:

> The music we hate follows us around like a stray dog. If we stand still for long enough, it'll cock its leg and piss on our trousers. There's no escaping it.
>
> (Berkkman, 2015)

In short, Nickelback and James Blunt have become a kind of shorthand for the antithesis of authenticity in the field of contemporary popular music.

The claim of authenticity acted as a kind of touchstone for Baby Boomer informants in this study. They used it to differentiate their music from that enjoyed by later generations. Paul's anecdote about his son's friends enjoying his music in preference to that of their own generation is a case in point. However, authenticity as a trigger-point for misrecognition was not exclusively the domain of the Baby Boomer informants. The response to Bruce Springsteen's iconic song 'Born to Run' (1975), one of the stimulus pieces used, was sprinkled with some mocking but in the main it was respectful:

George (30): I love the bells but if you'd left it off it'd be a little more timeless.
Joanne (32): it's a classic... speaks of its time ... Was it Barack Obama that used it in his campaign? So it's kind of tinged with that for me now but even that campaign was about hope and growth and change so I guess it comes with that.
Neil (35): Yeah. I like it.

Clearly, Springsteen has attenuated to himself the garment of credibility. His was deemed to be an authentic voice.

The Bon Jovi song 'Livin' on a Prayer', released in 1986, a decade after 'Born to Run' (1975), was also used as musical stimulus in the focus groups. Like 'Born to Run', it has a driving rhythm underpinning its working-class angst. In another of the focus groups, Elaine (21) positively described it as a 'power anthem'. Elaine, Joe and Sharon all expressed their liking of this song, and for Joe (21) it was an iconic musical element in the soundtrack of his life:

That's one of those songs ... so many people can listen to, no matter their age or demographic, and they can find something that makes them go 'I want to achieve'. We did a 36 km walk from Stockton beach and I remember getting about 25 Ks along the beach and singing that song. We could see the end, we were almost there.

For Sharon (23), the song reminded her 'about mateship, people coming together, to have a good time'. Although 'Livin' on a Prayer' was not of their time, all three had latched onto this song. It had been incorporated into their habitus. It had, in their eyes, the mantle of authenticity.

George (30), Neil (35) and Joanne (32) saw Springsteen's 'Born to Run' as having the stature borne of authenticity. 'Livin' on a Prayer' on the other hand they equated more with the falsity more closely associated with Nickelback. For them, Born To Run exuded authenticity. Livin' On A Prayer failed this test. Neil began this criticism by describing the Bon Jovi track as a 'cheesy cash-in on a genre that was already bloated by the time Jovi got there'. Neil drew on the similarity with Springsteen:

Life's pretty hard in Jersey, I mean he's just taken over from Bruce Springsteen. It's a similar theme: we're all fucked.

Irony and sarcasm followed:

Joanne (32): It's more of like life's so hard for the little ... ['person' – unspoken].
[George: sings a line from the song in a mocking tone]
Joanne: which is just made to sell records 'cause people feel like they're bankrupt.
George (): it's exactly the same as every, you know, post grunge singer songwriter band that came after. Pearl Jam mocks singing in that mumbled style.

The Pearl Jam analogy underpins and distinguishes their (Pearl Jam's) authenticity. Singing in that 'mumbled style' is authentic because it is self-reflexive. Pearl Jam are aware of the parody element in the way they mimic Bon Jovi. Any bands following and attempting a similar style to Springsteen are merely imitating. The three then proceeded to initiate an impromptu improvisation built around the lyrics from 'Livin' on a Prayer'. This was a completely extemporaneous response:

George: They worked *on the docks* and they were *down on their luck*.
Joanne: So down so down [laughter]. They wanted to feel like there were other people in the same boat as them. Doin' it *tough* [mimics the song]
Neil: And it still has. There's still hope there you know.
George: Oh yeah [enthusiastically]
Joanne; And it's like an epic sing along song
Neil: Yeah
Joanne: It's got the key changes.
Neil: And the guitar.
George: [mimics] fall in *'looove'*
Neil: people felt like their life was *tough*.
George: At least they were *halfway there* and they'd started and they'd got somewhere. They're *livin' on a prayer*. But they were *halfway there*.

Spontaneous, all three were 'riffing' freestyle, playing off each other, enjoying the sequencing and enjoying the competitive 'feel' of trying to outdo each other in their one-upmanship. The spontaneity of the moment delighted them as they, in turn, took up the challenge to outdo the other. The misrecognition inherent in this moment was directed at the song and Bon Jovi (despite the fact that they knew the lyrics). But the subtext of the misrecognising was that the real target of the misrecognition were aficionados like Elaine, Joe and Sharon. Obviously, they were not aware of those three. They had never met. But Neil, George and Joanne had obviously encountered Bon Jovi acolytes and their target was the naivete of those Bon Jovi fans for being taken in by Bon Jovi's façade of authenticity. After all 'It's got the key changes ...And the guitar ... fall in *looove*.

Joe, Elaine and Sharon's 'power anthem' is a pale imitation in the eyes of Neil, George and Joanne. There is only ten years difference between George, Joanne and Neil's age and that of Joe, Elaine and Sharon. But in that ten years George, Joanne and Neil now embody enough cynicism to be able to distinguish between the genuine authenticity of the 'authentic working-class struggle' of Bruce Springsteen and the 'bloated… cheesy cash-in' of Bon Jovi. The cultural distinction they make relies on a binary classification: authentic and non-authentic. There is no objective criterion for them to reach these conclusions. But for George, Joanne and Neil, the binary classification of Springsteen as authentic and Bon Jovi as derivative is doxic. For them, the process of *introjection* of the musical output of Springsteen and Bon Jovi has been completed. In principle, the new generation (Elaine, Joe and Sharon) that likes the Bon Jovi song can be dismissed, misrecognised, by those with the superior knowledge of what is and isn't authentic. And for George, Joanne and Neil, it is notions of taste that determine the hierarchy that privileges Springsteen over Bon Jovi. Bon Jovi can consider himself well and truly trolled.

The process of introjection allows individuals to make conscious and unconscious connections between music listened to and acquired during teenage years, and the environment, physical and temporal, within which the music is experienced. The use of grounded aesthetics allows the young person to make sense of their world. For Baby Boomers, the process of latching has been a unique experience owing to their status as the first rock and roll generation, and as the first TV generation. Latching for later generations has become a more complex process as they have grown up with the pop and rock music of their parents forming part of the soundtrack of their lives.

As each generation latches on, they apply the mantle of legitimacy to their own soundtrack, which is deemed more authentic than the music of subsequent generations. Although this notion of authenticity applies across generations, older people have appropriated to themselves the mantle of the most authentic cultural product. However, this has not prevented subsequent generations from self-styling as the custodians of authenticity. It is the recognition of authenticity by those who are in the know and the lack of capability to recognise authenticity by those who are not in the know (in most cases, ensuing youth generations). This forms a significant component of the misrecognition applied to the cultural products of those subsequent youth generations. The following chapter will examine the way misrecognition becomes institutionalised via the way Millennials have been stigmatised by their status as the first 'internet generation'. Their obsession with technology and their association with the mobile phone makes them ripe for misrecognition.

Notes

1 Illegal drugs as opposed to his already acknowledged use of alcohol.
2 Born in the USA was itself released in 1984 so could not possibly have been available for the 1972 campaign.

3 The song used in the focus group was Born to Run (1975).
4 Despite this definitive statement, Paul in the focus group did demonstrate both an awareness of and appreciation of music from later decades.
5 'Russians' from The Dream of the Blue Turtles (1985).
6 Australian group Midnight Oil released their hit single 'Beds are Burning' in 1987.
7 See Philips, C. (1990). www.latimes.com/archives/la-xpm-1990-11-16-ca-4894-story.html

Bibliography

Adorno, T., and Simpson, G. (1941). On Popular Music. *Zeitschrift für Sozialforschung*, 9(1), 17–48.

Bennett, A. (2013). *Music, Style, and Aging: Growing Old Disgracefully?* Philadelphia, PA: Temple University Press.

Bennett, A., and Taylor, J. (2012). Popular Music and the Aesthetics of Ageing. *Popular Music*, 31(2), 231–243.

Berkkman, M. (2015, February 7). James Blunt's Sense of Entitlement Is So Palpable You Could Wear It as a Hat. *The Spectator*. Retrieved from www.spectator.co.uk/2015/02/james-blunts-sense-of-entitlement-is-so-palpable-you-could-wear-it-as-a-hat/

Bodroghkozy, A. (2001). *Groove Tube: Sixties Television and the Youth Rebellion*. Durham, NC: Duke University Press.

Bourdieu, P. (2000). *Pascalian Meditations*. Stanford: Stanford University Press.

Brabazon, T. (2005). *From Revolution to Revelation: Generation X, Popular Memory and Cultural Studies*. Aldershot: Ashgate.

Brady, W. J., McLoughlin, K., Doan, T. N., and Crockett, M. J. (2021). How Social Learning Amplifies Moral Outrage Expression in Online Social Networks. *Science Advances*: Aug 13; 7(33).

Cobb, R. (2014). *The Paradox of Authenticity in a Globalized World*. New York: Palgrave MacMillan.

Coyne, J. (2022, Dec. 10). More Evidence for the Decline of Rock/Pop Music. *Why the Revolution Is True*. Retrieved from https://whyevolutionistrue.com/2022/12/10/more-evidence-for-the-decline-of-rock-pop-music/

Crockett, M. J. (2017). Moral Outrage in the Digital Age. *Nature Human Behaviour*, 1, 769–771.

De Nora, T. (2000). *Music in Everyday Life*. Cambridge: Cambridge University Press.

Edmunds, J., and Turner, B. (2002). *Generations, Culture and Society*. Buckingham: Open University Press.

Fang, L. (2019, March 21). An Analysis of Why Modern Music Is So Awful. *Stereomonosunday*. https://stereomonosunday.com/2019/03/23/why-modern-music-is-so-awful/

Fisher, M. (2012). What Is Hauntology? *Film Quarterly*, 66(1), 16–24.

Foucault, M. (1991). Governmentality, in G. Burchell, C. Gordon and P. Miller (Eds.). *The Foucault Effect: Studies in Governmentality*, pp. 87–104. Chicago: University of Chicago Press.

Frisch, M. (1979). Oral History and Hard Times, *Oral History Review*, 7, 70–79.

Frith, S. (1981). *Sound Effects: Youth Leisure and the Politics of Rock'n'roll*. Pantheon Books: New York.

Gracyk, T. A. (1993). Romanticizing Rock Music. *Journal of Aesthetic Education*, 27(2), 43–58.

Griffiths, M. (2016, February 19). American Presidential Campaign Songs that Have Backfired on the Candidates. *The Independent.* Retrieved from www.independent.co.uk/arts-entertainment/music/features/american-presidential-campaign-songs-that-have-backfired-on-the-candidates-a6883811.html

Hall, S., and Jefferson, T. (Eds.) (1976). *Resistance through Rituals: Youth Subcultures in Post-War Britain.* London: Hutchinson.

Hebdige, D. (1979). *Subculture, the Meaning of Style.* London: Methuen.

Hennessy, T. (2016). *Beyond Authenticism: New Approaches to Post War Music Culture.* Doctoral thesis, Birkbeck, University of London.

Hesmondhalgh, D. (2022). Streaming's Effects on Music Culture: Old Anxieties and New Simplifications. *Cultural Sociology,* 16(1), 3–24.

Hiatt, B. (2012, January 19). The Rise of the Black Keys. *Rolling Stone, online edition.* Retrieved from www.rollingstone.com/music/music-news/the-rise-of-the-black-keys-180489/

Hutcheon, L., and Valdés, M. (2000). Irony, Nostalgia, and the Postmodern. Methods for the Study of Literature as Cultural Memory. *Studies in Comparative Literature,* 30, 189–207.

Joan, C. A. (2023, March 13). Why Did Rock Music Decline, and Can It Make a Comeback? *Spinditty.* Retrieved from https://spinditty.com/genres/rock-music-comeback

Keightley, K. (2001). Reconsidering Rock, in S. Frith, W. Straw and J. Street (Eds). *The Cambridge Companion to Pop and Rock,* pp.109–142. Cambridge: CUP.

Leech, K. (1973). *Youthquake: The Growth of a Counter-Culture through Two Decades.* London: Sheldon Press.

Lindberg, U., Gudmundsson, G., Michelsen, M., and Weisethaunet, H. (2000). *Amusers, Bruisers and Cool-Headed Cruisers: The Fields of Anglo-Saxon and Nordic Rock Criticism.* Arhus: Eget forlag.

Martin, L., and Segrave, K. (1993). *Anti-Rock: The Opposition to Rock'n'roll.* Hampden: Da Capo.

Mitchell, T., and Thompson, L. (1994). A Theory of Temporal Adjustments of the Evaluation of Events: Rosy Prospection & Rosy Retrospection, in C. Stubbart, J. Porac and J. Meindl (Eds.), *Advances in Managerial Cognition and Organizational Information-Processing,* pp. 85–114. Greenwich, CT: JAI Press.

Murphy, L. (2013, October 11). James Blunt The Most Hated Man in Pop. *Irish Times.* Retrieved from www.irishtimes.com/culture/music/james-blunt-the-most-hated-man-in-pop-1.1556345

O'Callaghan, P. (2020). Reflections on the Root Causes of Outrage Discourse on Social Media, in M. Navin and R. Nunan (Eds.), *Democracy, Populism, and Truth,* pp. 115–126. Chatham: Springer.

O'Sullivan, C. (2013, October 30). James Blunt on Twitter: How the Most Hated Man in Pop Is Fixing His Image. *The Guardian.* Retrieved from www.theguardian.com/music/shortcuts/2013/oct/29/james-blunt-twitter-most-hated-man-pop-fixing-image

Owen, D. (2006, April 10). The Soundtrack of Your Life: Muzak in the Realm of Retail Theatre. *The New Yorker.* Retrieved from www.newyorker.com/magazine/2006/04/10/the-soundtrack-of-your-life

Pacini Hernandez, D. (1995). *Bachata: A Social History of a Dominican Popular Music.* Philadelphia, PA: Temple University Press.

Pekkala, T. (2003). Nickelback: The Long Road. *Rumba,* 19, 33.

Petit, C. (2010). Content [Film]. Illumination Films.
Philips, C. (1990, November 16). It's True: Milli Vanilli Didn't Sing: Pop music: The duo could be stripped of its Grammy after admitting it lip-synced the best-selling 'Girl You Know It's True'. *LA Times.* Retrieved from www.latimes.com/archives/la-xpm-1990-11-16-ca-4894-story.html
Phillips, J. (1985). Distance, Absence, and Nostalgia, in Don Ihde and Hugh J. Silverman. (Eds.), *Descriptions.* Albany: SUNY P.
Raleigh, D. (2012). *Soviet Baby Boomers: An Oral History of Russia's Cold War Generation.* Oxford: Oxford University Press.
Romppainen, H. (2008, December 5). Dark Horse. *New York Times, online edition.* Retrieved from http://nyt.fi/a1353045544613
Ross, A., and Rose, T. (1994). *Microphone Fiends: Youth Music and Youth Culture.* New York: Routledge.
Schildt, S. (2014, November 14). Nickelback's Newest Is a Blob of Blandness. *New York Times, online edition.* Retrieved from http://nyt.fi/a1305897545353
Silverman, C. (2016, April 2). This Academic Figured Out Why So Many Critics Hate Nickelback. Prepare for some Nickeldiscourse. *Buzzfeed.* Retrieved from www.buzzfeed.com/craigsilverman/is-it-the-chad
Strausbaugh, J. (2001). *Rock 'til You Drop: The Decline from Rebellion to Nostalgia.* London; New York: Verso.
Sugarman, J. (1997). *Engendering Song: Singing and Subjectivity at Prespa Albanian Weddings.* Chicago; London: The University of Chicago Press.
Thomson, A. (2016). Australian Generations? Memory, Oral History and Generational Identity in Postwar Australia, *Australian Historical Studies*, 47(1), 41–57.
Thornbush, M., Golubchikov, O., and Bouzarovski, O. (2013). Sustainable Cities Targeted by Combined Mitigation-Adaptation Efforts for Future-Proofing. *Sustainable Cities and Society*, 9, 1–9.
Trammell, J. Y. (2003). Pop Music and the Press. *Journal of Communication Inquiry*, 27(3), 316–319.
Turino, T. (1999). Signs of Imagination, Identity, and Experience: A Peircian Semiotic Theory for Music. *Ethnomusicology*, 43(2), 221–255.
Vuoti, S. (2008). Nickelback: Dark Horse. *Soundi*, 12, 66.

8 Feeding the Moral Panic
The Millennial Shorthand Portrait

Put your f---ing phones away.

(Peter FitzSimons)[1]

One doesn't have to be a Baby Boomer or even a Gen Xer to misrecognise young people and their cultural forms. Moral panics centring on young people range much more widely than the relatively limited focus of youth cultural forms. But I contend that all adult misrecognition of young people materialises from, and is rooted in, the deeply felt and deeply seated, indelible belief that the adult's life experience is superior to that of the generations that follow. Moral panics with regard to young people emerge from the doxic understandings emanating from, and constructed with, the profound conviction that their life experience up to the present has had bestowed upon it the mantle of authenticity. The alchemy of consecration has concocted and infused that mantle of authenticity and it is lodged, embedded in the adult habitus – immutable. Each engagement with young people is informed by, and gives voice to, the those doxic understandings. In each of those engagements, it is the *illusio* of the commitment to the rules of the game which entitles the adult to pontificate about the inadequacies of young people with absolute certainty. The absolute clarity to *voir* and *savoir* transforms those pontifications into intuitive and instinctive responses to their interactions with ensuing youth generations. These intuitive understandings manifest themselves as the authority to dogmatise and harangue, give voice to, and articulate their misrecognition via the dominion of the double language of disinterest – a language that will brook no defiance, no questioning. The quote above from Peter FitzSimons succinctly summarises the absolutism of adult haranguing of Millennials and it is delivered via the Adult Voice.

What we have seen thus far are examples of misrecognition of young people operating at very much a personal level – individual and small groups: personal experiences and anecdotal remembrances. It remains to place misrecognition of young people within a wider context to explore how that misrecognition becomes 'institutionalised', absorbed into the wider

DOI: 10.4324/9781003427476-8

societal consciousness, in order to amplify the wider social and cultural environs within which misrecognition of young people takes place. It does so by concentrating on published 'critiques' that formulate aspects of the contemporary public discourse of the Millennial generation characterised by the stereotyping that appears in previous chapters. These critiques take the form of online newspaper columns, blogs, and material from interviews with prominent commentators.

Although adults misrecognising young people can be observed and understood generically, the emergence of the Millennial generation has seen an intensification of that misrecognition. It is not just young people per se that are the 'problem', but Millennials in particular are cause for particular and specific criticism and denigration. Millennials' emergence as the first generation of 'digital natives' is the focus for much of the adult angst and insecurity. Older adults in particular view Millennials' mastery and intuitive understanding of technology as a compelling reminder of their technological inadequacies. The cliché of their reliance on their children and grandchildren to set up their phones and TV sets is a constant reminder of their increasing irrelevance as they age – the realisation dawning that they are becoming *has-beens*. And each encounter with a phone wielding young person, engrossed in their 'digital world', is another reminder of their technological impotence. As we have seen, a typical response to young people's technological competence is to question the authenticity of the young person's cultural engagement. Melissa's denigration of youth music being 'influenced by the videos not necessarily by the talent of the artists' highlights this authenticity deficiency.

Over the past 20 or so years, a cohort of entrepreneurial media players and 'specialists' have placed the understanding of the 'Millennial mindset' at the centre of their business plan. These specialists include Simon Sinek, Mark McCrindle and Bernard Salt. They market their skills variously as 'corporate refocusing' (Sinek), 'social researchers … [taking] … the pulse of the nation', 'research-based futurist' (McCrindle) 'media commentator and business analyst' (Salt). Because much of their commentary is linked to consultancy advice to businesses and government departments as to how to deal with Millennials, I have chosen to link them under the umbrella title of 'futurists'.

The three 'futurists' play the role of *moral entrepreneurs* in fostering misrecognition of young people. It is the specific stereotyping applied to Millennials, and which is fostered in the wider community, that is elemental to the futurists' business plan.

As we have seen, misrecognition of Millennials centres on their continuous and seemingly endless engagement with technology, oblivious to the complexity of the societal and political environment the Millennials have grown up in. Stereotyped as 'digital natives' living out their 'choice biography', it is this notion of choice, and the associated freedoms, and the perception of licence to do as they please, that are the basis for the stereotyping of the Millennial lifestyle. Perceptions of the 'unique' nature of Millennials, when compared with previous youth generations, are both specific (applied to Millennials) and generic (as part of an ongoing paradigm of misrecognition). But first to sport.

Generational Dislocation of the Social Structure – It's Got to Hurt Inside

For Australians with their reputation for a seemingly boundless obsession with sport, Millennials' perceived failure to measure up to the courage and commitment of previous youth generations of sports people hits a particular nerve, striking at the heart of Australian sporting mythology. Ex-Australian representative Wallaby and now newspaper columnist, media commentator and writer of populist biographies, Peter FitzSimons was at the forefront of this assault on the lack of sporting courage and endurance of Gen Y.[2]

FitzSimons' 'shtick' is his down-to-earth approach and 'blokey' style. His writing for newspapers as a regular Fairfax (now Nine Newspapers) columnist has a strong sporting focus. As previously noted, his October 2013 column took to task Gen Y for not living up to the standards of generations that went before:

> There seems to be truth to the notion that something is missing in the current generation when it comes to what is expected of them when accorded the sacred privilege of 'playing for Australia'.
> (FitzSimons, 2013)

There is something missing in Gen Y. They're not 'up to it'. Previous generations of Australian sporting representatives by contrast made the country proud. In Australian sporting mythology, when a match was lost, players hurt badly. Quoting former Wallaby Michael Lynagh:

> It's fine to be a good sportsman and shake hands [at the end of the match] and say 'well done' [to the winning team], but it's got to hurt inside. And I don't think these Australians … hurt enough.
> (FitzSimons, 2013)

Unlike previous sporting heroes such as Lynagh, Rafter, Newcombe, Ponting, who 'cherish the baggy green cap',[3] FitzSimons tagged the entire generation as afflicted by a 'sense of entitlement that would kill a brown dog'[4] (FitzSimons, 2013). FitzSimons cites Australian representatives cricketer Michael Clarke, rugby union player James O'Connor; swimmer Nick d'Arcy; tennis players Nick Kyrgios, Bernard Tomic and Mark Philippoussis; and for special mention Olympic rower 'lay down Sally' Robbins[5] infamous for her 'unforgiveable' failure to compete to the end as part of the Australian Rowing Eight at the 2004 Olympics. But for FitzSimons, these are not just examples. The entire generation is worthy of condemnation. The very future of the pre-eminence of sport in Australian culture is threatened. This is what Cohen refers to as the 'dislocation of the social structure' (2002: 47). For

FitzSimons, previous sporting generations knew how to behave. Previous generations knew where and how they fitted in to the Australian sporting traditions. Previous generations knew:

> That way back when the culture of playing for Australia was set, honour was pretty much the only thing you got out of it ... so you honoured that.
> (FitzSimons, 2013)

For FitzSimons, Gen Y don't 'get' this. The 'sacred privilege'[6] of achieving national honour has been replaced by 'a more important consideration ... the immense riches on offer in sport' (FitzSimons, 2013). FitzSimons' own representation for Australia provides him with its own cachet of symbolic status. The 'symbolic profits' (Bourdieu, 1986: 84), acquired and integrated by him as an honoured member of the Baby Boomer sporting generation, permit him to sit in judgement of the entirety of Gen Y.

The impetus for FitzSimons' column was a remark by the then Australian Socceroo (the Australian national football team) captain Lucas Neill following Australia's (then) recent soccer losses to Brazil and France:

> [If] you dream of playing for Australia ... show me the hunger and the desire. I think that's where we are lacking now.
> (FitzSimons, 2013)

FitzSimons distils the reason for these losses down to a single cause – Gen Y. FitzSimons uses this sporting incident to amplify his own misrecognising of Gen Y. It is the ubiquitous mobile phone which FitzSimons identified as putting Australia's sporting reputation in peril. And unless and until Gen Y put down their phones and get back to giving it 'absolutely everything you had in you' (FitzSimons, 2013), the country's sporting reputation nay future will remain in peril.

The two football losses could be viewed as an isolated incident with specific causes. But for FitzSimons, the two consecutive losses by the Socceroos are a symptom of a wider malaise.[7] Gen Y tennis players also fail to live up to expectations:

> Both Poo [Mark Philippoussis] and [Bernard] Tomic the Tank Engine have been reluctant to play [tennis] for Australia. Unimaginable, during the era of Newcombe, Laver, and so on.
> (FitzSimons, 2013)

The heading of the article 'Why, oh why, does Gen Y not get it?' attributes a single sporting failure over a week in 2013 to the shortfalls of the whole generation. All Gen Y, by association, are guilty of and responsible for, the 6–0 drubbing in both cases. FitzSimons takes on the role of *moral entrepreneur* when he speaks on behalf of all of the older Australians who are not Gen Y. The traditional values that he lauds were/are (in his mind) typical of previous generations. Each of those generations in turn, when called upon on the sporting field, rose to the occasion. This is an implicit understanding in FitzSimons' analysis. The doxa of adult stereotyping of Gen Y requires no analysis, no questioning. Adults get it. Ricky Ponting in cricket and Lleyton Hewitt in tennis 'got it' despite the fact that they were themselves *enfant terribles* in their younger days and received similar denigration. The infamous photo of Ponting black-eyed and incoherently drunk on a newspaper front page (Cricinfo, 1999) and Lleyton Hewitt's calling an umpire a 'spastic' (Vincent, 2001) are conveniently omitted from FitzSimons' analysis. FitzSimons artificially creates a generational fault line, based upon a set of mythically perfect sporting values honoured and upheld by previous generations, in contrast to degenerate Gen Y competitors. Gen Y is deemed not worthy of those who have gone before. The result is the symbolic violence inherent in the directive: 'put your f---ing mobiles away' (FitzSimons, 2013). As a remedy for the problem he identifies, however, this seems an improbable leap of logic. This is the Adult Voice in full cry.

FitzSimons' article tars an entire generation with the same brush. This reflects what Cohen refers to as the process of *sensitisation* (2002: 80–89) which transforms a single occurrence into a pattern of deviant behaviour. FitzSimons' targeting of certain Australian sporting failures by younger players serves to confirm a deviant pattern of behaviour for an entire generation, while simultaneously mythologising previous generations.

FitzSimons implies the problem of Gen Y's lack of commitment to be a kind of disease and a form of addiction to technology. Moreover, he has embodied in his habitus the understanding that Gen Y is afflicted with the pathology of being unable to commit. He cites the case of convicted drug cheat Nick D'Arcy being picked to swim for Australia in the London Olympics. For him, the example of D'Arcy is symptomatic of a broader problem – a disease: 'the malaise spread much wider than that' (FitzSimons, 2013).

FitzSimons then goes on to chide Gen Y for their lack of commitment by choosing the 'evidence' of Australian cricketer Michael Clarke's sullenness after a game. Quoting Ricky Ponting's autobiography, he cites Ponting taking Clarke to task for not sticking around 'for a chat and a laugh' after the game. In fact, Clarke's admitted reason for avoiding post-game chat was his inability to keep his moods in check. FitzSimons then offers his own interpretation of Clarke's failure to socialise. It happened because he was a 'selfish prat who thought only of himself' (2013). As a younger player, Clarke is constructed as not behaving the way he 'should'. He is generationally condemned for not conforming to the accepted understandings, the doxa, of how Australian sports people should behave.

Threatening the Future – Dealing with the *Millennial Shorthand Portrait*

Adult stereotyping fixates on Millennials' seemingly endless obsession with technology. Their 'choice biographies' revolve around mobile phones and social media. This understanding of Millennials has been made more prominent by the emergence of a group of *moral entrepreneurs* that have gained prominence over the past twenty years – 'futurists'. Their underlying thesis is that unless we (adults) come to terms with Millennials and unlock our understandings of what motivates them and how they function, the future itself may be under threat.

Threadgold has acquainted us with the concept of *temporal youth*, the process whereby young people act as surrogates for adult anxieties about the future. These anxieties centre around young people being the hope for the future. But adult anxieties can only be allayed and hope fulfilled if the young people 'do their duty' and perform to adult expectations. The future has become an increasingly important component of public discourse as the rate of technological change in particular has accelerated over the past century, headed by the digital revolution and contiguous globalisation. Businesses and governments are concerned to ensure that they can respond to the rapidly changing environment in which they function – to manage this 'future shock'. The emergence of the futurist commentator as a social phenomenon has coincided with these changes as firms and governments seek to ensure they 'future-proof' (Rich, 2014) their organisations. They want to ensure that the organisation has the skills, knowledge and organisational structure to meet the challenge of the rapid changes and the need to re-invigorate and/or preserve infrastructure (see Rich, 2014; Coley, Kershaw and Eames, 2012; Kerr, 2010; Lawson, 1997). Increasingly, these technological changes are seen to have wider sociological implications. This particularly applies to Human Resources Departments concerned as they are with responding to the way technological change affects and moulds human interaction and attitudes towards work (see Boston, Wanna, Lipski and Pritchard, 2014; Meng, 2009; Kahn & Wiener,1967; Masini, 1993; Dator, 2002; Bell, 1997; Slaughter, 1996).

Academic interest in the future has been accompanied by the parallel development of a niche 'futurist' industry in response to government and commercial demand for information and strategies for dealing with rapid change in the work and market place.[8] A number of consultant firms and individuals have emerged to meet this demand. Much of the work of these futurists centres on how firms and government deal with Millennials – as employees and as consumers. This has led to the emergence of the cover-all model of the *Millennial Shorthand Portrait:* phone and technology-obsessed, inattentive, profligate and self-absorbed. It is the capacity to deal with the Millennial Shorthand Portrait that the futurists sell as the response to rapid technological changes. This is the futurist consultancy.

The role of the 'futurists' follows the pattern contained in Cohen's paradigm of how moral panics appear and take root and how the stereotypes emerging from this paradigm are exploited by futurists. The elements central to Cohen's paradigm of moral panic are *Deviance*; the role of *Moral Entrepreneurs* in promoting moral panic; and the concept of *Cabalism*, whereby a kind of 'group think' sense of conspiracy emerges as a result of the specific concerns raised by the emergence of the Millennial generation.

Sensationalism Attracts Attention

Deviance, the process whereby a 'group of persons emerges to become defined as a threat to societal values and interests' (Cohen, 2002: 1) is the basis for the particular concerns at the heart of moral panics about Millennials. Millennial informants were very conscious of the stereotyping of them by the wider adult community. Reactions to adult stereotyping of them ranged from a kind of 'shrug of the shoulders' acceptance to annoyance. Similarly, reactions to Millennials by adult informants demonstrated tacit acceptance of the place that Millennials occupy within society as a generation of miscreants.

The fracturing of traditional media over the past 20 years, along with the emergence of alternative delivery technologies and the convergence of technologies (Stöber, 2004; Everett and Caldwell, 2003; Rogers, 1993), has seen a narrowing of the market occupied by mainstream media. In the 1990s, Angela McRobbie and Sarah Thornton (1995) proposed a re-thinking of the concept of moral panics particularly as they related to media-driven moral panics. Their thesis revolved around the fact that as the sophistication of dealing with media expanded, representative organised pressure groups, acting on behalf of the targets of moral panics, organised to respond to the 'deviance claims'. McRobbie and Thornton posited that media-inspired moral panics had become routine, standardised, and were losing their effect because of the seemingly endless sequence of moral panics and the capacity of those targeted by moral panics to respond in an organised manner. Although, in many respects McRobbie and Thornton's thesis still holds true, the advent of social media has served to sidestep, bypass, McRobbie and Thornton's contention because young people, invariably the moral panic target(s), have deserted mainstream media. Mainstream media have been consigned to an audience of the middle-aged and elderly (see Bennett, 2013; Domingo et al., 2008; Creeber and Martin, 2009; Newman, 2011; Van Dijck, 2013). The futurists recognise this mass media rump as their market, their domain – ripe for their moral entrepreneurship.

Cohen talked of information arriving 'already processed by the mass media' (2002: 9). This 'processing' can be both organised and spontaneous. Given the already existing widespread perception of Millennials as reprobates, the mainstream media in particular has over the past twenty years used the 'futurist' as an acknowledged expert to reinforce existing negative Millennial stereotypes. Thus, a symbiotic relationship between mainstream media and the futurist has emerged. The media relies upon the futurist to create 'news' by reinforcing existing prejudices and the futurist uses the media to create cultural capital, as part of business model, which can then be converted into economic capital via promotion of their futurist commercial services. Cohen talks about *movement advocates* (2002: 20) who promote a particular cause. The futurists are movement advocates who promote the need to treat Millennials in particular ways in order to mediate the disparity between Millennial preoccupations and the needs of employers. In order to gain access to morning television and tabloid current affairs shows and other populist media, it is necessary for the futurists to attract the attention of those as Bourdieu refers to them: the ones with the 'eyeglasses' (2001: 247) that they use to filter material presented on these shows. The futurists' 'research' on Millennials is tailor-made fodder for the content demands of producers of radio and television programs and press editors. The futurists provide their Millennial shorthand portraits in a handy easy to consume package. The Millennial Shorthand Portrait simultaneously condemns and constructs Millennials as special, requiring special 'understandings'. And 'specialness' acts as code for deviance.

Moral Entrepreneurs of the Millennial Moral Panic

One of the dynamics of how futurists function as moral entrepreneurs is their capacity to gain media attention for their findings via the cultural capital acquired as television 'talent'. The extent of this cultural capital (and its capacity to convert to economic capital) is evidenced by their four-page separate listing on the website Celebrity Speakers (2019, see endnote 7). The following are three examples of futurists as moral entrepreneurs who are influential in Britain and Australia.

Simon Sinek

Simon Sinek is an American leadership consultant, a professor at Columbia University, founder of Sinek Partners (Corporate Refocusing) and author. He is also an adjunct staff member of the RAND Corporation. In writing for a popular audience, Sinek offers a paradigm for the causes of the 'Millennial phenomenon' that is circuitous in its analysis. His published interview with David Gosse in December 2016 illustrates his methodology in stereotyping Millennials. Sinek begins the interview with a kind of faux-discovery of the concept of Millennials:

> Apparently, Millennials as a group of people ... born from ... 1984 ... who are tough to manage. They are accused of being entitled and narcissistic, self-interested, unfocused and lazy – but entitled is the big one.
> (Gosse, 2017)

Sinek's opening gambit – the use of the word 'apparently' – implies naivete and disinterest as does the suggestion that Millennials may provide fruitful new cause for investigation.[9] Yet this disinterest is quickly jettisoned since what Millennials are accused of 'apparently' becomes accepted fact in the interview. He firstly asserts that it is parental failure that has led to the Millennial self-concept of being special:

> They were told they can have anything they want in life, just because they want it.
>
> (Gosse, 2017)

Sinek's negative generational analysis reflects the *embodied structures* he has acquired. In his categorisation of Millennials as lacking attention span and commitment, Sinek assumes a variation of the role of *rule creators*. The rule creator's role is as a crusader for moral reform (Cohen, 2002). For the futurists, their role as crusaders is to frame the argument. Discomfort, suspicion and fear of, and for, ensuing generations[10] exists as an observable phenomenon and is constituted in their discourse. What Sinek provides to mainstream media outlets is a voice of authority derived from the cultural capital he has accumulated as an expert in 'corporate refocusing'. Sinek presents as an 'expert' when contributing to debate and mainstream media outlets – on a fee-for-service basis. Appearances in mainstream media promote the services he provides. Futurists are aware of the doxa created by stereotyping of Millennials and exploit that doxa by framing their companies as being able to assist businesses in dealing with the Millennial 'problem'. This process follows the typical moral panic pathway of the creation of 'inventories', outlined by Cohen. The inventory of Millennial attributes is outlined in simple formulaic form – the *Millennial Shorthand Portrait.*

Bernard Salt

Salt writes regularly for the mainstream media and is often a guest on free to air television current affairs and chat shows. His articles regularly appear as opinion pieces in the conservative national newspaper *The Australian*. Salt is very aware of his audience of fellow Baby Boomers and their prejudices against youth. In a series of two articles published in 2016, he focused on the proposed spendthrift nature of the Millennial character. In these articles, he uses the well-worn vehicle of satire as an affective device to engage his conservative adult readership.

The first of Salt's articles appeared in The Australian in October 2016 entitled *What's More Important, Living Within your Means or Taking Selfies from a Bali Swimming Pool?*. In it he sets up the 'savers versus the spenders' dichotomy and introduces the satirical vehicle of the faux fairy tale:

> Gather round, boys and girls, for I have a tale to tell that will touch your hearts. I want to talk about two tribes that inhabit this land, the money mortals and the money magicians.
>
> (Salt, 2016a)

Salt sets up a binary opposition between the 'money mortals', the adults, and their opponents the 'money magicians', the Millennials. The frugal mortals inhabit a 'money challenged place [called] "the real world" [and have] learnt how to eke out a living using a crude but effective mathematical device known as a budget'. By contrast the 'money magicians' are proponents of the 'IDI – I Deserve It' who complain of never having enough money yet will post on social media 'photographs of themselves in a pool in Bali!'. Money mortals are disciplined – 'That's right, they *save*'. Money magicians (Millennials) lack the discipline of their parents, preferring pools in Bali to saving.

The second piece, 'Moralisers We Need You' (Salt, 2016b), is the origin of Salt's infamous 'smashed avocado'[11] treatise which focussed on Millennials buying a daily dose of smashed avocado breakfast instead of saving that money for a deposit on a house. Again, adopting a satirical approach, Salt utilises the 'come in close so we can share a secret' style so favoured by Peter FitzSimons to talk to the older demographic:

> If you are under 40 … I politely suggest that you turn the page… Shhh … act natural and read this column without making a sound… Come close to the page. Closer!
>
> (Salt, 2016b)

Salt invokes a kind of faux self-deprecation by referring to himself as belonging to a 'sect known as the Middle-aged Moralisers … MAM'. He then entreats his readers to join MAM:

> We think you are one of us… Come to our next meeting. You'll find it liberating to know there are others just like you.
>
> (2016b)

The focus of this piece is the previously mentioned 'smashed avocado' thesis. Salt hypothesises that if Millennials would just forego their smashed avocado breakfast, they would save enough to accumulate a deposit for a house. Salt (and by extension the members of MAM) can themselves afford this deposit (and the house) 'because I am middle-aged and have raised my family'. But, he asks, 'How can young people afford to eat like this?'. Salt's 'humorous' style and faux self-deprecation serve to mask the symbolic violence of generational denigration behind a veil of satire and humour.

Mark McCrindle

Mark McCrindle is a prominent futurist and has vigorously marketed himself as a predictor of the future to businesses. His company makes the following claim:

160 *Feeding the Moral Panic*

Figure 8.1 List of McCrindle clients.

> Australia's social researchers, we take the pulse of the nation… commissioned by governments, leading brands and some of Australia's largest organisations because of our renown for conducting world class research and communicating the insights in innovative ways.
>
> (McCrindle, 2019)

One of McCrindle's services for clients is analysis of generational difference to support advice on dealing with Millennials. The McCrindle website boasts an impressive array of clients.[12] That analysis concentrates very much on what might be termed 'shorthand' attributes of generations. An example of the cursory nature of the analysis can be seen from the following table, an excerpt from New Generations at Work (2016):[13]

Table 8.1 Generations Sociologically Defined by Mark McCrindle (McCrindle Research)

	Baby Boomers Born 1946–1964 Aged 40s & 50s	Generation X Born 1965–1979 Aged late 20s & 30s	Generation Y Born 1980–1994 Aged: Teens and 20s
Prime Ministers	William McMahon Gough Whitlam Malcolm Fraser	Bob Hawke Paul Keating	John Howard
Iconic Technology	TV 1956, Audio Cassette 1962 Colour TV 1975	VCR, 1976 Walkman, 1979 IBM PC, 1981	Internet, Email, SMSing DVD, 1995 PlayStation/ Xbox
Music	Elvis Beatles Rolling Stones	INXS Nirvana Madonna	Eminem Britney Spears Puff Daddy
TV & Movies	Easy Rider The Graduate Jaws	ET Hey Hey Its Saturday MTV	Titanic Pay TV Reality TV
Popular Culture	Flare Jeans Mini Skirts Barbie Frisbee 1959	Rollerblades Hyper colour Torn Jeans	Body Piercing Baseball caps Men's cosmetics
Influencers Social Makers/ Landmark Events	Evidential Experts Decimal currency in Australia, 1966 Neil Armstrong walks on Moon, 1969 Vietnam War, 1965–73 Cyclone Tracy, 1974 *Advance Australia Fair* becomes Australia's national anthem, 1974	Pragmatic Practitioners *Challenger* explodes, 1986 Halley's Comet, 1986 Stock market crash, 1987 Berlin Wall down, 1989 Newcastle earthquake, 1989	Experiential Peers Thredbo disaster, 1997 Columbine shootings, 1999 New Millennium, 2000 September 11, 2001 Bali Bombing, 2002 Invasion of Iraq, 2003

(Continued)

Table 8.1 (Continued)

	Baby Boomers Born 1946–1964 Aged 40s & 50s	Generation X Born 1965–1979 Aged late 20s & 30s	Generation Y Born 1980–1994 Aged: Teens and 20s
Historical Figures & Iconic Leaders	Martin Luther King Jr. Superman	Mother Teresa of Calcutta Spiderman	John Paul II Saddam Hussein
Learning Environment	Classroom style Quiet atmosphere	Round-table style Relaxed ambience	Cafe style Music and Multi-modal
Financial Values	Long-term needs Cash and credit	Medium-term goals Credit-savvy	Short-term wants Credit-dependent
Ideal Leaders	Command & Control Thinkers	Coordination & Cooperation Doers	Consensus & Collaborative Feelers
Purchase Influencers	Brand-loyal Authorities	Brand-switchers Experts	No brand loyalty Friends

The Generations Defined Sociologically

In his talks and writings McCrindle uses these shorthand analyses to provide 'insights' into Millennials. The sophistication of this analysis of the generation as a totality is summarised by his exemplar of that generation in the instance of a single Gen Y tee-shirt observed by McCrindle: 'which says ... [eloquently]: "When I'm bored I Google myself!" ' (2018).[14] McCrindle's company is indeed 'Australia's Social researchers'!

Although the futurists follow the typical pathway outlined by Cohen (2002) there are subtle modifications. The exaggeration and distortion inherent in their descriptions of Millennials mutates into the generic Millennial – the Millennial Shorthand Portrait. In the interviews and focus groups, this same concept of a generic Millennial – phone-obsessed, unable to commit, easily bored, lacking focus, profligate – was a constant refrain from Baby Boomer and Gen X informants. Moreover, Millennial informants were aware of the generic Millennial stereotyping applied to them, self-identifying as 'digital natives'. When Salt's 'smashed avocado' claim emerged as a symbolic representation of Millennials, it played to and reinforced adults' existing doxic prejudices towards Millennials.

The three examples cited are all male. Their prominence as 'futurist experts' represents the marginalised position female 'experts' occupy within mainstream media, representing as they do perceptions of males being most credible. Weibel et al. saw male newscasters being most credible, with women being 'mostly ignored when it comes to prestigious news items' (2008: 471; see also Dudo et al., 2011; Cann and Mohr, 2001; Lumby, 1994) which focussed on the preponderance of male experts on TV talk shows. An indication of the male dominance of the 'futurist' collective is demonstrated by the fact that of the 138 'futurists' cited in the link at endnote 7, only 21 are women.[15]

Cabalism in Media Representations

One of the most noticeable aspects of the generational discourse observed in this study is the almost universally shared consensus amongst adult informants of just what makes a Millennial. It is as if these understandings are accommodated without the need for discussion, bestowed by the power of *social alchemy*. These shared understandings, which Cohen identifies as *cabalism*, reflect a 'tendency towards conspiratorial mythology' (2000, 64). For cabalism to function, a sense of shared experience or values needs to be present. These shared experiences and values serve to set apart those affected, from those undertaking, the conspiratorial action.

Salt's 'smashed avocado' claim against Millennials was significant not only because of the backlash against it, but because it played to already existing understandings of Millennials. A seemingly endless housing boom in most capital cities, in particular Sydney and Melbourne, since the turn of the century, has led to challenges for new home buyers. Prevailing economic discourse is that Millennials are locked out of the housing market. This has become an ongoing theme in both mainstream and social media (see Koukoulis, 2016; Faruqi, 2016; Collier, 2017).[16] Much commentary on housing affordability has focussed on the challenge for Millennials of saving enough for a home deposit. Salt (2016a) has been at the forefront of directing criticism at Millennials, rather than acknowledging other factors, such as low youth wages and the precarious labour market, and massively inflated house prices substantially created by government policies since 2001. For Salt, all this is ignored and the cause is distilled down to Millennials' failure in their dedication to thrift. He points to their predilection for social media and accuses them of refusal to apply themselves to the task of saving. He ties this to their fixation on the peripheral and the ephemeral – their complete generational lack of commitment, almost as if it was they who had created the housing affordability crisis. Central to his condemnation is the reinforcement of the understandings that accrue to Baby Boomers as a result of their shared experience of growing and reaching their adulthood during the 1960s and 1970s (see Brabazon, 2005; Cheung, 2007; Bennett, 2013) when housing was far more affordable.

What Salt taps into at a deeper level is the uniformity of opinion on the failings of Millennials. As we have seen with Cohen's analysis, much community concern with regard to moral panics has tended to focus on subcultures: specific components of the wider youth demographic, represented most famously by his interrogation of moral panics surrounding the mods and rockers in Britain. The moral panic and the accompanying media focus has concentrated upon these specific subgroups of young people who represent the immediate threat. The sub-group may play into wider unease about young people in general, but throughout, the moral panic is almost exclusively specific to one group. The list of these specific threats from specific subgroups of the youth demographic are numerous (mods and rockers, punks, drugs, nasty girls etc.) – particular threats to society posed by particular subcultural behaviour as seen at the time. Generational anxieties may have underpinned these moral panics but the threat was in most cases specific. What was apparent in the focus groups and interviews was a lack of focus on specific subcultures. Adult derision targeted the whole Millennial generation. Generalised adult perceptions of the failings of the entire youth generation have taken on the mantle of received knowledge, involving 'inseparably cognitive and evaluative presuppositions' (Bourdieu, 2000: 100). These 'long-lasting dispositions of the mind and body' (Bourdieu, 1986: 83) have become the accepted *doxa* of adult understandings of Millennials as commitment-shy, self-centred, disrespectful, phone-obsessed and spendthrift. The Millennial Shorthand Portrait plays directly to the existing predetermined doxa of adult understandings of Millennials. And as with all good conspiracy theories, those inside the conspiracy require no further proof than the widely held belief that underpins the conspiracy. The Millennial Shorthand Portrait justifies that belief.

How has this come about? Why is there a uniformity of stereotyping of the entirety of a single generation? Davis (1997, 2017) has outlined how Baby Boomers injected themselves into the forefront of media and other means of communication. It was the cultural capital acquired by Baby Boomers as the first truly 'youth generation' that allowed them to convert that capital into economic power as leaders. That position as media mainstream leaders in particular has allowed them to consolidate their authority within the field of the media so it reflects their own generational values. Millennials mainly operate outside this field, in online media. Mainstream media across the western world is the domain of older people and reflects their values.

In Australia, Salt in particular has been in the forefront of this discourse. His 'smashed avocado' article is illustrative of his modus operandi. He constructs a paradigm of mock conspiracy (Cabalism) to place himself and his target audience as victims of a generational conspiracy. Salt and his generation have achieved financial security and created a position of superiority provided by that financial security. This sense of superiority is then transformed into mock victimhood, the idea that older people have been marginalised by the politically correct antics of the following generation. In this victimhood discourse, Salt even resorts to the signage and symbols of the toilets in restaurants frequented by Millennials in an echo of the gender culture wars. The subtext of his claim is that the ill-defined labelling of the toilets is somehow another 'hipster' Millennial conspiracy:

> Is that an M or is that a W? Is that a top hat or is that a ladies' bonnet? This is a hipster cafe: … Why can't we have some light? … Why can't we have a sign saying men and women?
>
> (Salt, 2016b)

Implicit in this sense of victimhood is Brabazon's sense of loss. Salt's ironic victimhood amplifies the sense of loss and resentment towards Millennials. Davis (1997) maintains that Baby Boomers, having acquired the cultural capital of being societal leaders, are loathe to share that capital with ensuing generations. The symbol of the Millennial hipster café represents a challenge to Salt's status because Millennials in the main function outside the field of mainstream media favoured by older people, especially Baby Boomers. There was a time when Salt and others were at the vanguard of a youth generation, but the field has moved on. He too is now tilting at windmills. This sense of loss (and quite possibly envy) manifests itself in resentment and denigration: the symbolic violence of the infamous 'smashed avocado' indulgence:

> I have seen young people order smashed avocado with crumbled feta on five-grain toasted bread at $22 a pop and more. Twenty-two dollars several times a week could go towards a deposit on a house.
>
> (Salt, 2016b)

166 Feeding the Moral Panic

The ludicrous nature of this argument has been deconstructed by Caitlin Fitzsimmons (2016). She calculated that if Gen Y were to apply Salt's strategy to their savings regime, it would take over ten years in Sydney or Melbourne to achieve a 10% deposit. Horton (2017) estimates that in London it would take 40 years.

Salt, Sinek and McCrindle and their implied co-members of the Baby Boomer cabal share a sense of being deprived because their values and their shared perspective on the world have been marginalised and superseded by the 'hipness' of Millennials. Their Cabalism reflects the fact that they all saved and 'raised their family' (Salt, 2016b). They all 'sacrificed' their youth to discipline and hard work[17] whereas Millennials have the 'freedom' to eat expensive smashed avocados 'several times a week'. Salt and the Baby Boomers have earned their middle-age affluence while Gen Y flaunt their $22 smashed avocado in their faces on an almost daily basis. This 'nostalgia' for a pre-hipster past where people knew their place and were responsible is similar to the sense of loss that Gilroy identifies as 'post-colonial melancholia' (2000: 12). In the same way that Gilroy identifies English culture as being in 'remorseless decline' (13), so the 'shrinking culture' (13) of the Baby Boomers is constructed as being under threat by the spendthrift behaviour of the '$22 a pop hipness of Gen Y'. Salt leads an imaginary Baby Boomer cabal on a quest to preserve their 'shrinking culture', a return to cafés with proper lighting and proper signs on the toilets. This strident 'conservatism' (13) fuels the generational denigration encapsulated in the 'smashed avocado' misrecognition and Sinek's 'entitled narcissism'.

Consensus and Hostility

Cohen's notion of a cabal resonates with Goode and Ben-Yehuda's concept of *consensus* (2006: 34). In order for misrecognition of a group of people to occur, there has to be wide agreement that the:

> Threat is real, serious, and caused by the wrongdoing group members and their behaviour ... and should be dealt with.
>
> (2006: 34)

The futurists rely upon the implicit assumption of broad adult agreement with their position to present their negative generational analysis as fact. That certainty is essential to their business model which relies upon conveying their 'knowledge' on the future and (in these cases) the predilections of Millennials, not only to an audience but to potential clients. In David Gosse's interview with Simon Sinek, the discourse of moral panic consensus outlined by Goode and Ben-Yehuda (2006) is revealed. His affected scientific disinterest ('apparently') establishes his credentials. He then proceeds in the rest of the interview to speak with absolute certainty on the failings of Millennials and, with the same certainty, on the reasons for those failings:

Feeding the Moral Panic   167

> The trauma for young kids to be unfriended is too much to handle... Too many kids don't know how to form deep, meaningful relationships.
>
> (Gosse, 2017)

Sinek is able to make prejudicial generalisations about youth, comfortable in the knowledge of consensus among his adult audience. He plays directly to their accepted doxa.

Sinek is inclusive in his analysis: 'When we are out with friends, as we are leaving for dinner together, we leave our cell phones at home' (Gosse, 2017). Although Sinek applies the inclusive 'we' to his understandings of what is required to correct these problems, what he actually means is 'them' (when addressing Millennials) and 'us' (when addressing his wider adult audience). When he states 'None of us should charge our phones by our beds' (Gosse, 2017) what Sinek actually means is none of *them* should charge their phones by their beds. The sense of consensus applies even when Sinek concedes the underlying adult responsibility for demonstrated failings of Millennials: 'our' responsibility is acknowledged, accepted and understood. *We* may have created the vacuum which led to these failings, but the failings are nevertheless *theirs*. Sinek's use of collective terms such as 'our' and 'we' demonstrates the implicit understandings of the generational doxa he shares with his audience.

Sinek's role as social analyst relies upon him being able to identify trends present and operating within society. His capacity to identify *concerns* (Goode and Ben-Yehuda, 2006: 33) functions at a number of contradictory levels of discourse. First, parental indulgence of Millennials has created an environment in which they have grown up feeling special:

> Some of them got into honors classes ... because their parents complained... got A's ... because the teachers didn't want to deal with ... parents.
>
> (Gosse, 2017)

However, this 'specialness' not only conveys a sense of entitlement, it actually sows the seeds for a second cause for concern – that feeling special simultaneously makes Millennials vulnerable to feelings of lower self-esteem. They:

> Find out they are not special, their mom's (sic) can't get them a promotion... we have an entire generation that is growing up with lower self-esteem than previous generations.
>
> (Gosse, 2017)

A further discourse in Sinek's commentary is one extensively identified by other commentators: that of social media.[18] The outcome of 'growing up in a Facebook/Instagram world' is that social media filters out the bad things:

> We're good at showing people that life is amazing even though ... depressed.
>
> (Gosse, 2017)

Sinek's discourse then invokes a Harvard research finding (unsourced) linking extensive reliance on social media with an uncontrollable dopamine fix:[19]

> Engagement with social media and our cell phones releases a chemical called dopamine... Harvard research scientists reported that talking about oneself through social media activates a pleasure sensation in the brain. ... . It's why we count the likes.
>
> (Gosse, 2017)

Sinek implies that naturally occurring dopamine, generated by social media and phone use, is analogous to illegal (for minors) drugs such as alcohol. Alcohol use by minors is restricted. But young people are allowed unfettered access to social media and mobile phones resulting in a 'hard-wiring' addiction to dopamine, paralleling a reliance on alcohol, causing lifelong dependence and inability to relate personally to other people:

> Social stress, financial stress, career stress, that's pretty much the primary reasons why an alcoholic drinks. [With] unfettered access to these devices and media, ... kids don't know how to form deep, meaningful relationships.
>
> (Gosse, 2017)

We must remember that Sinek is making this analysis based on a shared adult consensus that this is how all Millennials routinely behave. His acceptance of the world that Millennials apparently inhabit reflects a doxa that is the 'ultimate form of conformism' (Bourdieu and Wacquant, 1992: 74). The paradigm that Sinek operates within cannot countenance analysis at odds with his already-arrived at conclusions. The cultural capital acquired and embodied by him as (in his words) 'an unshakable optimist who believes in a bright future and our ability to build it together', along with an international reputation and nearly a million twitter followers, ensures the certainty of his analysis. This certainty that comes with his status as a celebrity social analyst ensures that not only will his warnings be taken seriously by fellow adults but that his apparent concern for the youth generation will also be taken seriously.

In fact, Sinek's air of concern masks his *hostility* (Goode and Ben-Yehuda, 2006: 33) despite expressing his admiration for 'this amazing, idealistic, fantastic generation' (Gosse, 2017). Millennials are victims of parental and other adult neglect. But they are still at fault. Sinek's apparent empathy masks the symbolic violence contained in the passive/aggressive subtext:

You[20] are sitting at dinner with your friends, and ... texting somebody who is not there ... that sends a subconscious message to the room 'you're just not that important' ... You can't put the phone away ... because you are addicted.

(Gosse, 2017)

Sinek's certainty of adult consensus allows him to apply his analysis to all members of the Millennial generation.[21] Terms like 'low self-esteem', 'trauma', 'addictive, numbing', 'never find[ing] deep fulfillment' (Gosse, 2017) are descriptors applied universally to all Millennials.

There is no sense in the Gosse interview of Sinek's analysis being applied to demographic sectors of the Millennial generation. All Millennials fail to create and foster meaningful relationships. The dearth of innovation and ideas applies to all of them, not just some. Certainty of deviance, when applied to the generation as a whole, confers the need to respond *disproportionally* (Goode and Ben-Yehuda, 2006: 36). Generation-wide problems demand generation-wide solutions. Thus, in Sinek's discourse, contextual banning of cell-phones must be applied to all Millennials, not just some. The mobile phone represents the deviance of all Millennials. Sinek and the other futurists' *amplification* of its seemingly ubiquitous use by Millennials acts as a kind of rallying call to Boomers and other older generations. The result is an *organised reaction* (89) whereby adult observation of the 'Millennial obsession' with technology is played to by the futurists in their media appearances. This 'received knowledge' about Millennials acts to reinforce already existing prejudices creating yet another feedback loop of *deviance amplification* (17).

Moral panics 'by their very nature... are volatile' but as Goode and Ben-Yehuda have pointed out they can often become *routinised* or *institutionalised*, and ongoing. In the case of Millennials, the moral panic exists as a kind of background unease and resentment, a constant, operating beneath the surface but nevertheless within the awareness of most adults. It takes the form of *informal interpersonal norms* (39) – generic understandings held, understood and mutually acknowledged by adults. So when the subject of Millennials comes up in conversation or in the media, that hostile consensus only requires a trigger association for the moral panic to generate a volatile reaction. When Sinek states that Millennials are 'narcissistic, self-interested, unfocused and lazy – but entitled is the big one' (Gosse, 2017), that operates as a trigger for consensus. In fact, the mere mention of a mobile phone or 'selfie' may be enough to trigger the required volatility of the pervasive moral panic. Any moral panic relies upon an appeal to general understandings held by the community at large. Sinek can only make his alcohol/mobile phone parallel work because his audience already have their concerns about young people and mobile phones. Any kind of detailed scrutiny would see its underlying premise unravel. The explanation of Millennial behaviour is accepted without analysis, without question.

Goode and Ben-Yehuda examined how mass hysteria and widely held beliefs generate and maintain moral panics through consensus that amplifies hostility. We have seen how futurists create a kind of symbiotic relationship between existing adult concerns, anxieties and hostility towards Millennials and their own professed expertise in amplifying and articulating their own futurist analysis of the basis for those concerns. This leads to a mutual dependence based upon the resultant aggregated 'understandings'. The futurists play to anti-Millennial consensus to create and entrench a collective misrecognition. Sinek, McCrindle and Salt only need to state that Millennials are 'entitled and narcissistic, self-interested, unfocused and lazy' to activate existing prejudices. The futurists lend a kind of academic authenticity to those prejudices.

The consensus position of these three futurists (and indeed FitzSimons' commentary on sports stars) needs to be seen within the prism of the positions they occupy within the mainstream media which provides the conduit for them to articulate their positions. Media ideological processes exist and function unconsciously so that ideology becomes truth. And the media are the authoritative authors of that truth. The futurists are not only playing to their audience's prejudice, they do so from a platform which authenticates more strongly their 'expert' opinion.

Moral panics associated with young people today exist as both generic misrecognition of the generation as a whole, and as response to concerns raised about specific behaviours within that generation. Members of the Millennial generation have grown up being stereotyped as the first generation of 'digital natives'. Their seamless adoption of, and interaction with, technology and social media marks them out as different to previous youth generations. The notion of 'digital native' signals a demarcation line between themselves and youth in the past. In academic terms, it is the confluence of Millennial status as digital natives and their subsequent identification as the first generation with the capacity to enjoy a 'choice biography' that sets them apart from previous youth generations. This has become incorporated into the collective habitus of adults as the accepted doxa of Millennials: selfish, technology-obsessed pursuers of privileged 'choice biographies'.

An added complexity is the symbiotic relationship between the Millennial generation and the futurists. Moral entrepreneurs' existence relies upon their capacity to 'explain' Millennials to adults – the Millennial Shorthand Portrait. Their contribution feeds the consensus that drives the stereotype. Moral panic and misrecognition ensues.

Notes

1 FitzSimons, P. (2013, October 17). Why Oh Why Does Gen Y Not Get It? *Sydney Morning Herald*. Retrieved from www.smh.com.au/sport/why-oh-why-does-gen-y-not-get-it-20131016-2vn4u.html

2 Because Fitzsimons has referred to the generations as Gen Y, I will in the interests of consistency refer in this section to Millennials as Gen Y.
3 The baggy green cap is only worn by members of the Australian cricket team and is used as a kind of generic emblem for Australian representation.
4 The colloquial Australian phrase is 'strong enough to kill a brown dog'. In outback mythology, a brown dog was imagined to be the hardiest of all working dogs for mustering animals and so could only be killed by the most potent poison bait.
5 Interestingly Philippoussis is actually a member of Gen X, and Robbins is on the cusp of Gen Y/Gen X.
6 See Cohen's reference to 'cherished values' (2002: 47).
7 The Socceroos afterwards went on to win the Asian Cup and qualify for both 2014 and 2018 and 2022 Soccer World Cups.
8 A four-page list of futurist speakers managed by Celebrity Speakers can be found at www.celebrityspeakers.com.au/speakers/futurist/
9 Let us not forget Sinek is putting himself forward here as an expert on Millennials. Sinek is feigning ignorance here on a subject that he supposedly has enough expertise in to be able to advise organisations about. Sinek's business model is built around being able to advise on Millennials based upon social research – upon his expertise in being able to advise on how to manage change.
10 For the future viability of the organisation being targeted.
11 This was a major media story for about a week and elicited a vociferous social media response. The Satirical website THE SHOVEL responded with this caustic response. www.theshovel.com.au/2017/05/18/this-millenial-turned-an-avocado-into-a-one-bedroom-apartment/
12 https://mccrindle.com.au/app/uploads/2016/12/McCrindle-Research_ABC-03_The-Generation-Map_Mark-McCrindle.pdf
13 Available from www.academia.edu/40079978/New_Generations_at_Work_Whitepaper_Mark_McCrindle
14 Report available from www.academia.edu/40079978/New_Generations_at_Work_Whitepaper_Mark_McCrindle
15 In the interests of full disclosure, it should be pointed out that one of the 'futurists' listed is former Australian conservative Prime Minister John Howard, born 1939.
16 It should be noted that massively high house prices are a world-wide phenomenon.
17 The claim to success based purely upon that generation's discipline and hard work would require further analysis for a generation that had the good fortune to be born and raised within the narrow window of the greatest period of western prosperity in the history of the world, by parents who sought to ensure their children's lives were materially better than theirs (having experienced the Depression and World War II). See Owram, D. (1997). *Born at the Right Time*. Toronto: University of Toronto Press.
18 Ironically, Sinek (998,000 Twitter followers), Salt (33,400), McCrindle (8500) all have a significant presence on social media.
19 There are any number of critiques of this link between social media and addiction including Thompson and Thompson (2017), Madsen (2022) and Osman (2018).
20 The implication is not you, the adult, but they, the Millennials.
21 His response to Millennials in this instance reflects a constant adult response: young people are always rude to 'middle-aged white males'.

Bibliography

Becker, H. (1963). *Outsiders: Studies in the Sociology of Deviance*. New York: Free Press.

Bell, W. (1997). *The Foundations of Futures Studies*. New Brunswick: Transaction Publishers.

Bennett, A. (2013). *Music, Style, and Aging: Growing Old Disgracefully?* Philadelphia, PA: Temple University Press.

Boston, J., Wanna, J., Lipski, V., and Pritchard, J. (Eds.). (2014). *Managing Risks, Responding to Crises and Building Resilience*. Canberra: ANU Press.

Bourdieu, P. (1986). The Forms of Capital, in J. Richardson (Ed.), *Handbook of Theory and Research for the Sociology of Education*, pp. 241–258. New York: Greenwood.

Bourdieu, P. (2000). *Pascalian Meditations*. Stanford: Stanford University Press.

Bourdieu, P. (2001). Television. *European Review*, 9(3), 245–256.

Bourdieu, P., and Wacquant, L. (1992). *An Invitation to Reflexive Sociology*. Chicago, IL: University of Chicago.

Brabazon, T. (2005). *From Revolution to Revelation: Generation X, Popular Memory and Cultural Studies*. Aldershot: Ashgate.

Cann, D. J., and Mohr, P. B. (2001). Journalist and Source Gender in Australian Television News. *Journal of Broadcasting & Electronic Media*, 45, 162–174.

Celebrity Speakers Bureau. (2019). *Celebrity Speakers About Us*. Retrieved from www.celebrityspeakers.com.au/about-us/

Cheung, E. (2007). *Baby Boomers, Generation X and Social Cycles*. London: Longwave Press.

Cohen, S. (2002). *Folk Devils and Moral Panics: The Creation of the Mods and Rockers* (New ed.). London, New York: Routledge.

Coley, D., Kershaw, T., and Eames, M. (2012). A Comparison of Structural and Behavioral Adaptations to Future Proofing Buildings against Higher Temperatures. *Building and Environment*, 55, 159–166.

Collier, G. (2017, April 29). Housing Affordability Crisis a Moan by Privileged Millennials. *The Australian*. Retrieved from www.theaustralian.com.au/opinion/columnists/housing-affordability-crisis-a-moan-by-privileged-millennials/news-story/68b289e9127fdecfe185e45a6de4c768

Creeber, G., and Martin, R. (2009). *Digital Cultures*. Maidenhead: Open University Press.

Cricinfo. (1999). *Australian Cricket Nurses New Black Eye after Ponting's Brawl*. January 21, 1999. Accessed 22 June, 2017. Retrieved from www.espncricinfo.com/australia/content/story/80026.html

Dator, J. (2002). *Advancing Futures*. Westport, CT: Praeger.

Davis, M. (1997). *Gangland: Cultural Elites and the New Generationalism*. St Leonards: Allen & Unwin.

Davis, M. (2010). *Gangland: Cultural Elites and the New Generationalism* (3rd ed.). Melbourne: MUP.

Davis, M. (2017, March 17). Two Decades after Gangland, the Precariat is Ageing and Cultural Scapegoating Thrives. *The Conversation*. Retrieved from https://theconversation.com/two-decades-after-gangland-the-precariat-is-ageing-and-cultural-scapegoating-thrives-74158

Domingo, D., Quandt, T., Heinonen, A., Paulussen, S., Singer, J., and Vujnovic, J. (2008). Participatory Journalism Practices in the Media and Beyond. *Journalism Practice*, 2(3), 326–342.

Dudo, A., Brossard, D., Shanahan, J., Scheufele, D. A., Morgan, M., and Signorielli, N. (2011). Science on Television in the 21st Century: Recent Trends in Portrayals and Their Contributions to Public Attitudes toward Science. *Communication Research*, 48, 754–777.

Everett A., and Caldwell J. T. (2003). *New Media: Theories and Practices of Digitextuality*. New York: Routledge.

Faruqi, O. (2016, April 4). Choke on My Soy Flat White, Buddy. *Medium*. Retrieved from https://medium.com/@oz_f/choke-on-my-soy-flat-white-buddy-1bbd23befe94

Fitzsimmons, C. (2016, October 23). Avocado Economics for First-Home Buyers. *Sydney Morning Herald*. Retrieved from www.smh.com.au/money/saving/avocado-economics-for-firsthome-buyers-20161021-gs7ti7.html

FitzSimons, P. (2013, October 17). Why Oh Why Does Gen Y Not Get It? *Sydney Morning Herald*. Retrieved from www.smh.com.au/sport/why-oh-why-does-gen-y-not-get-it-20131016-2vn4u.html

Gilroy, P. (2001). Joined-Up Politics and Postcolonial Melancholia. *Theory, Culture & Society*, 18(2–3), 151–167.

Goode, E., and Ben-Yehuda, N. (2006). *Moral Panics: The Social Construction of Deviance*. Cambridge, MA: Blackwell.

Gosse, D. (2017, January 4). Transcript of Simon Sinek Millennials in the Workplace Interview. *Ochen*. Retrieved from https://ochen.com/transcript-of-simon-sineks-millennials-in-the-workplace-interview

Horton, H. (2017, May 16). Millionaire Tells Millennials to Stop Buying Avocado on Toast If They Want to Afford a House. *The Telegraph UK*. Retrieved from www.telegraph.co.uk/news/2017/05/16/millionaire-tells-millennials-stop-buying-avocado-toast-want/

Kahn, H., and Wiener, A. (1967). *The Year 2000: A Framework for Speculation on the Next Thirty-three Years*. New York: MacMillan.

Kerr, J. (2010). *Future-Proof Design: Must All Good Things Come to an End?* (Masters Thesis). University of Calgary, Canada. Retrieved from www.joekerr.ca/site/files/joe-kerr---fpdesign-2011.pdf

Koukoulis, S. (2016, April 4). Millennials should Stop Moaning. They've got More Degrees and Low Rates. *The Guardian Australia*. Retrieved from www.theguardian.com/commentisfree/2016/apr/04/millennials-should-stop-moaning-theyve-got-more-degrees-and-low-rates

Lawson, B. (1997). Future Proof: The MAFF Laboratories at York. *Architecture Today*, 82, 26–32

Lumby, C. (1994). Feminism and the Media: The Biggest Fantasy of All. *Media Information Australia*, 72, 49–54.

Madsen, L. (2022). Media Panic, Medical Discourse and the Smartphone. *International Journal of the Sociology of Language*, vol. 2022, 27, 111–128.

Masini, E. (1993). *Why Futures Studies?* London: Grey Seal Books.

McCrindle, M. (2006). *Generations at Work: Attracting, Recruiting, Retraining & Training Generation Y*. Retrieved from https://2qean3b1jjd1s87812ool5ji-wpengine.netdna-ssl.com/wp-content/uploads/2018/04/McCrindle-Research_New-Generations-At-Work-attracting-recruiting-retaining-training-generation-y.pdf

McCrindle, M. (2016, December 20). *The ABC of XYZ: The Generation Map*. Retrieved from www.academia.edu/40079978/New_Generations_at_Work_Whitepaper_Mark_McCrindle

McCrindle, M. (2019). *McCrindle About*. Retrieved from http://mccrindle.com.au/about-Australias-social-researchers

McRobbie, A., and Thornton, S. (1995). Rethinking 'Moral Panic' for Multi Mediated Social Worlds. *The British Journal of Sociology*, 46 (4), 559–574.

Meng, L. (2009). Megatrends Driving Planning Education: How Do We Future-Proof Planners? *Australian Planner*, 46(1), 48–50.

Newman, N. (2011). *The Mainstream Media and the Distribution of News in the Age of Social Media*. (RISJ Reports). Reuters Institute for the Study of Journalism, Department of Politics and International Relations, University of Oxford.

Osman, M. (2018). An Understanding of Social Media Addiction through a Sociological Approach, *Proceedings of International Academic Conferences 6409169, International Institute of Social and Economic Sciences*.

Owram, D. (1997). *Born at the Right Time*. Toronto: University of Toronto Press.

Rich, B. (2014). The Principles of Future-Proofing: A Broader Understanding of Resiliency in the Historic Built Environment. *Journal of Preservation Education and Research*, 7, 31–49.

Rogers, E. M. (1995). *Diffusions of Innovations* (4th ed.). New York: Free Press.

Salt, B. (n.d.). *Bernard Salt Profile*. Retrieved from www.bernard-salt.com.au/profile

Salt, B. (2016a, October 15–16). Moralisers, We Need You. *The Weekend Australian Magazine*. Retrieved from www.theaustralian.com.au/life/weekend-australian-magazine/moralisers-we-need-you/news-story/6bdb24f77572be68330bd306c14ee8a3

Salt, B. (2016b, November 5–6). What's More Important, Living Within your Means or Taking Selfies from a Bali Swimming Pool? *The Weekend Australian Magazine*. Retrieved from www.theaustralian.com.au/life/weekend-australian-magazine/money-mortals-and-money-magicians/news-story/98775cfad5f6819d9d7b11363abf2679?utm_source=The%20Australian&utm_medium=email&utm_campaign=editorial

Slaughter, R. (1996). *The Knowledge Base of Futures Studies*. Hawthorn: DDM Media Group.

Stöber, R. (2004). What Media Evolution Is: A Theoretical Approach to the History of New Media. *European Journal of Communication*, 19(4), 483–505. https://doi.org/10.1177/0267323104049461

Thompson, W., and Thompson, M. (2017). Smartphones: Addiction, or Way of Life?, *Journal of Ideology*, 38(1), Article 3.

Toffler, A. (1970). *Future Shock*. New York: Random House.

Van Dijck, J. (2013). *The Culture of Connectivity: A Critical History of Social Media*. New York: Oxford University Press.

Vincent, M. (Reporter). (2001, June 18). Leyton Hewitt's On-court Behaviour. *ABC PM*. Sydney: ABC Radio. Retrieved from: www.abc.net.au/pm/stories/s314777.htm

Weibel, D., Wissmath, B., and Groner, R. (2008). How Gender and Age Affect Newscasters' Credibility An Investigation in Switzerland. *Journal of Broadcasting & Electronic Media*, 52(3), 466–484.

9 Conclusion

Youth is just a word.

(Pierre Bourdieu)[1]

Bourdieu's truism reflects the inherent tension in the way young people are perceived. Young people represent an age demographic loosely defined as the transition period between childhood and adulthood, reflecting their in-between status – no longer child, not yet adult. But the inherent irony in the statement underpins the complexity of the position:

> Youth and age are not self-evident data but are socially constructed in the struggle between young and old.
>
> (Bourdieu, 1993: 95)

It is the struggle between young and old that is at the heart of this research. That struggle reflects the complexity of the transformations experienced by young people as they negotiate and accommodate their changing physical, emotional and intellectual metamorphosis to adulthood. It also reflects the struggle that parents and adults have to endure in order to 'manage' that transformation. These struggles and these transformations take place in real time without access to a script or a handbook. Each individual struggle between young person and adult is a learning experience. Each confrontation becomes a marker, a baseline that is a reference point for future confrontations. Conflicts and resentments are incorporated and remembered, and inform future encounters. Patterns of behaviour are learned and embodied. Attitudes and values are accommodated within each individual young person's and each adult's habitus. It is those remembered encounters which inform behaviours upon the transformation to adulthood.

Notions of 'becoming' inform the transition from childhood to adulthood. This research has centred on young people but the concept of a 'young person' rests on the perspective of its liminal position between childhood and adult. I have spent my adult lifetime working with and for young people. Forty

DOI: 10.4324/9781003427476-9

years ago, when I began this journey, it always struck me that the 'becoming' status of young people not only defined them, it effectively stigmatised them. From the perspective of adults, young people are not fully whole – unfinished, not complete. This is an incompleteness that young people cannot jettison until they are consecrated as adults: what are you going to be when you grow up? Their incompleteness defines them.

Young people see the world from the perspective of the totality of their existence. Youth is a time of rapid becoming as reins are loosened and independence leads to new experiences, new adventures, new temptations. But that becoming is lived in real time. The adventure may be new. Their adolescence may herald new encounters, new opportunities. But it is experienced in the present. Imaginations about future possibilities may be triggered but those imaginings are also experienced in the present. For young people 'now' is the core of their existence. Imagining their future as adults may involve future projections, but that engagement is undertaken from the perspective of the present. For all intents and purposes, from their perspective, a 16-year-old's persona exists in the present as a complete human being. Becoming is in the future. They live in the present. But that 16-year-old, as we saw with Iris, Elaine and Gina, is very conscious that adults don't perceive them in that way. It is adults who see the 'becoming' as transition, who see the present through the lens of the future. From the perspective of adults, each young person is. But they exist simultaneously as their potential as an adult. It is only when they reach adulthood that their potential will be fulfilled. They will cease becoming and will simply be fully formed, complete.

There can be no intergenerational conflict without generations. Each cohort of young people that enters into the process of becoming does so at a similar time. Each shares a set of common experiences. Each shares the common understandings and encounters of the zeitgeist of their era. These generational understandings emerge from those shared experiences – of music, of film and TV and other youth cultural products. Each cohort can be seen, and indeed sees itself, as a distinct generation. Their generational camaraderie is built upon those same generational experiences, representing the zeitgeist of their generation. It is these generational shared understandings which serve to reinforce generational solidarity and which then contribute to misrecognition of ensuing generations. Informants for this research were very aware of the place of generations and how generational awareness very much helped to determine adult attitudes towards young people. For adults, generational awareness was linked very much to their identity. Frequent references to 'we' and 'you' (the collective us) by adult participants reflected this generational solidarity. Generational solidarity in turn served to buttress and fortify the generational authenticity of their youth experience. This was very apparent in the shared generational memory responses across the experience of research informants.

For the young people involved in this research, misrecognition of them as a generation was very evident in their responses. As we saw with Iris and Eliza and Gina, and Joe and Elaine and Sharon, misrecognition of them by adults was a central element of their understanding of what it means to be a young person. But that misrecognition was based upon their status as young people and it applied to them collectively as members of their Millennial and tail-end-Millennial generation. In the field of power their cultural capital, their status, cannot match that of the adults they encounter. Their status is less, because as human beings their capacity to contribute as fully fledged citizens is less. They are not yet fully formed. The walled garden and helicoptering are symbolic manifestations of this incompleteness. And above all, their vulnerabilities put them at risk. It is this risk which drives the lack of trust in young people. It is these vulnerabilities which determine that they cannot be fully trusted to carry out their role and responsibilities as citizen. The 16- and 20-year-old informants' major complaint about adult misrecognition centred on adult mistrust of them. They couldn't be trusted to do what was expected of them. Truth be told, they couldn't be trusted to behave like adults. As 'not fully formed', they do not have the requisite skills and knowledge and, importantly, experience. In the field of power that they played in with adults, notions of their still 'becoming' were all too apparent in both their comparative status and their treatment by adults.

Young people are at the core of this research. But it is the transitioning to adulthood which is key to the misrecognising of ensuing generations. The onset of puberty and the associated emotional and intellectual changes ensures that the significance of the youthful engagement with cultural products is embodied as (from the perspective of the young person) unique. From birth, the habitus evolves as it accommodates new learnings, new experiences, new relationships. It is the pace and quantum of that embodiment which informs the development of our identity. Young people upon entering their youth stage sip, gulp, guzzle, inhale the experiences which add to, and shape their aesthetic solera, an integral component of their habitus. The grounded aesthetics, those makers of meanings, undertake their continuous alchemy of consecration to transform the habitus permitting young people to gain insights and understandings. And the habitus evolves with each new experience unconsciously, or at best barely consciously, becoming more complex, more experienced, more mature. Young people are becoming, but it happens around them. It is both integral to them and separate from them. They are so busy living the experience that they aren't necessarily aware of the changes as they are occurring, or if they are it's part of the collective magic of growing up. It is only with the onset of adulthood that they gain the necessary insight and awareness to be able to *voir* and *savoir*. As George lamented: 'And as teenagers you're going to have a certain world viewpoint. And you're gonna be skewed towards that'. This is the young person 'being' – living in the present. George, with the distance of his early 30s and with the insight provided by the double language of generational disinterest, can perceptively observe of his teenagehood: 'What the fuck was I thinking?'. George's self-reflection has permitted him to see his (and others') teenagehood from the perspective of ten years removed. The capacity to look back and reflect on the George he once was is undertaken from the perspective of adulthood. His disinterested assessment is authorised by his status as an adult – the Adult Voice. But his disinterest falls short when it comes to his wider misrecognition of young people.

It is the uniqueness of the young person's experience during that short ten years or so of their youth, particularly with music but across the range of their experience of grounded aesthetics, which plays to and emblematises that experience. Embodied, ingrained, seared into their habitus those experiences and the memory of those experiences confer the mantle of authenticity, an authenticity which, because of the power to produce 'sacred social divides' (Bourdieu and Wacquant, 1992: 201,) is unquestioned. George can look back with complete objectivity and assess his own behaviour as a young person. 'What the fuck was I thinking?' reflects what many of us would see as the mistakes and the embarrassments and the peccadilloes of our own youth succinctly summarised. This is the kind of analysis, the kind of self-reflection we all undertake as adults reflecting upon our own youth experience. But George doesn't take the next step in his analysis. If we can look back and see our failings as young people with the objectivity of temporal distance, from the perspective of an adult; if we can view our own youth experiences with detachment; if our self-reflection is perceptive enough to dispassionately call our younger versions of ourselves out for our naivete and our inexperience, then it remains to be understood why do we not apply that same objectivity when it comes to misrecognising succeeding youth generations.

The answer, as we have seen, lies in the manner in which we encounter and embody grounded aesthetics. The authenticity of that process privileges the experience to the exclusion of all others. Upon ascending to adulthood, those privileged experiences, their authenticity conferred by the alchemy of consecration, take their place in the now adult's habitus as the authentic youth experiences. The same objectivity that they bring to their self-reflection on their own teenagehood permits them to objectively analyse the authenticity of their own youth experiences. This same objectivity allows them to 'dispassionately' assess the youth experiences of generations that follow. And that assessment ensures that the experiences of ensuing generations cannot measure up. The authenticity of their own youth experiences ensures that ensuing youth generations are victims of the 'sacred social divides'. These divides are derived without the need for analysis. They are natural – common sense. The alchemy of consecration has bestowed upon their youth experiences not only the mantle of authenticity, but they now equally have the authority to classify – to distinguish according to those unwritten, unspoken sacred social divides. Their 'taste' is now without question, incapable of being critiqued. The double language of generational disinterest confirms their assessment. No further validation is required.

Yet young people, having themselves been the object of adult misrecognition when they themselves were young people, upon transitioning to adulthood, then proceed to misrecognise young people from following generations. Throughout the focus groups, across all adult age groups, participants reiterated again and again their empathy with the plight of young people traversing their youth stage. Pauline's understanding of the socio-economic circumstances of many of her students placed her firmly within the ambit of an empathic understanding of the wider social and economic forces at work. Fred demonstrated similar understandings, as did George and Neil at various times. Indeed, virtually all the adult informants expressed their empathy with, and understanding of, the difficulties faced by young people in their transitioning to adults. Clearly their emotional capital enabled them, at an intellectual level at least, to view the world from the young person's perspective. Evidence of embodied emotional capital suggests that their natural empathy would reside with the young people who follow them. But as Joseph Heller (1974) has observed: 'Something happened'. Despite their stated empathy, despite their emotional engagement with the circumstances attaining to the lived experiences of young people, they then proceed to denigrate young people from ensuing generations.

As Brabazon pointed out, adults engaging with memories of their past do so via their 'imagined past', a past linked by memory, and underpinned by nostalgia. It is this imagined past fuelled by nostalgia which drives their misrecognition. Christine's nostalgia for a past where parents knew how to discipline their children illustrates this. Her full contribution is worth re-stating here:

> You're not allowed to smack your children these days. You have to talk to them like an adult. So, I think kids have then learned to ... They don't understand the consequences of something. They'll just keep fighting back or keep yelling until you put an iPad in their hand, and that's exactly what they wanted in the first place. Yeah, so I think kids can be a lot more manipulative these days.
>
> (Christine, 35)

The subtext of Christine's analysis is that 'it didn't harm us'. We were smacked. We knew the consequences. Kids these days 'just keep fighting back or keep yelling back until...'. Similarly, Pauline's nostalgia for a past built upon respect; and George's created character of Jess who laments: 'why isn't my life like that?' (George 30); and Neil's 'I think I've seen a few of the young people who are present on Facebook and actually crowd-source emotional support' (Neil, 35) represent both their denigration of present-day young people and their conviction that theirs was a youth defined by its austerity, by their capacity to learn the consequences. And in its own way, it is Fred's misremembering of the complete absence of drugs within his entire youth experience.

Each of these is a lamentation at the decline in standards and/or a yearning for a halcyon past where they and their generation could cope with whatever was thrown at them. It represents a yearning for a time in the past when things were not only simpler but better and a lament for the fact that 'the virtual agency of the no longer' is all around them. This is nostalgia for a past where they, as central characters in the play, had to deal with adversity and came through – unlike young people today. This *rosy retrospection*, this 'memorialisation' of their past, serves not only to make their youth cultural experience more authentic, it makes their 'toughness' more authentic. It was a time when you could shake off the slings and arrows of misfortune and, in George's words, of a created '1983 Jess', you:

> might have ... been crying that morning, but put on a cake of makeup, put on a bit more of a sassy attitude, put a scrunchy in her hair and gone 'Fuck you'.

For Neil and George and Christine and Pauline and Matthew and Nicole, this is their imagined youth. This is their:

> I think we had it *harder* ... I was the eldest of five ... so I was left to fend for myself. I used to *walk* ... 20 minutes to the railway station to catch the train to school and walk ten minutes to high school... I still drop Alex off every morning, pick him up ... most days. I was in Year 7 catching the train into the city ... to see Jesus Christ Superstar... I just wouldn't have let my 13-year-old catch the train into Sydney city (Emphasis added).
> (Nicole, 55)

Their youth was tough. It took tough young people to get through it. And they did. Unlike young people today where 'something is missing in the current generation' (FitzSimons); 'where the trauma for young kids to be unfriended is too much to handle...[where] too many kids don't know how to form deep, meaningful relationships' (Sinek), Christine and George and Neil and Pauline and Matthew coped. Peter FitzSimons, Simon Sinek, Bernard Salt and Mark McCrindle coped. They forwent their smashed avocado breakfasts. They used conveniences with proper signs. And if only young people today could cope like them, then the world would be a much better place and everyone could afford a deposit for a house.

This publication has probed a pattern of denigration of young people by adults which appears to be repeated across generations. Each individual passes through a youth stage in their transition to adulthood and beyond. Each individual passing through their youth stage negotiates a myriad of individual and societal learning experiences, including a series of formal and informal rites of passage. Becoming an adult human being is the destination, but the significance of the youth stage in terms of getting there reflects its hallmark role.

In the same way that young people are perceived to be 'becoming' – not quite 'finished', so this publication has been 'becoming' for most of my adult life. It began as a sequence of unrelated, unconnected, random episodes; observations, overheard conversations, anecdotes relayed by young people and adults; and my own observed interactions between young people and adults, and offhand comments made by adult friends about young people. These origins were complemented by my own journey to adulthood, my own engagement with the idealism of the late '60s and early '70s, and, despite my own predilection for misrecognising young people, my commitment to try and put into practice the ethos underpinning that idealism in my relations with young people. This publication is the culmination of that journey.

Undertaking this research project has provided a number of epiphanies for me as researcher. Many of these epiphanies involved gaining insights into how young people transform from young person to adult, and how that transformation inextricably links the youth experience to adult understandings. The most significant (and surprising) of the data collection process was during a focus group of 16-year-olds; indeed the experience had me totally nonplussed. Discussion in the focus group had moved tangentially to a discussion of four- and five-year-olds and the freeform nature of the discussion turned to how four- and five-year-olds were now being given access to I-Pads. Xanthe, who raised the issue initially, commented that four- and five-year-olds were using them constantly. Then, as if channelling Fred or Pauline or any of the older participants, she expressed her outrage at their access to I-Pads: 'I had books as a kid, and dolls and all that kind of stuff!' (Xanthe, 16). This was a totally spontaneous response which elicited vociferous agreement from the other members of the focus group. They had spent the previous 45 minutes recounting their own experience of being misrecognised by adults for their lack of trustworthiness and the confines of the walled garden, and adult concerns with their obsession with mobile phones and digital technology. And yet here they were lapsing into the same misrecognition they themselves were victims of – and applying the generational double language of disinterest. It was a response I had in no way anticipated. The pattern of repetition of misrecognition by older participants was being repeated by the youngest of the informants. Clearly, it would appear that misrecognition is a circular, culturally embodied phenomenon destined to repeat across the march of the generations.

Clearly, Xanthe and her focus group's misrecognition of four- and five-year-olds repeats the misrecognition they themselves received from adult generations. At 16 years of age, they have already acquired elements of the double language of generational disinterest. The sacred social divides have already gained a tentative hold on, and within, their habitus. Meanwhile, the confines of the walled garden await to be swept aside as the rapid onrush of adulthood beckons, then welcomes and embraces them. The Adult Voice awaiting them is already in rehearsal.

Note

1 Bourdieu, P. (1993). *Sociology in Question*. London; Thousand Oaks, CA: Sage.

Bibliography

Bourdieu, P. (1993). *Sociology in Question*. London; Thousand Oaks, CA: Sage.
Bourdieu, P., and Wacquant, L. (1992). *An Invitation to Reflexive Sociology*. Chicago, IL: University of Chicago.
Heller, J. (1974). *Something Happened*. Alfred A Knopf: New York.
Mitchell, T., and Thompson, L. (1994). A Theory of Temporal Adjustments of the Evaluation of Events: Rosy Prospection & Rosy Retrospection, in C. Stubbart, J. Porac and J. Meindl (Eds.), *Advances in Managerial Cognition and Organizational Information-Processing*, pp. 85–114. Greenwich, CT: JAI Press.

Index

Note: Endnotes are indicated by the page number followed by 'n' and the endnote number e.g., 20n1 refers to endnote 1 on page 20.

Adult Voice 41–2, 54, 60, 68, 90, 104, 108–9, 112–13, 150, 154, 178, 181
Aesthetic Solera 11–12, 94, 110, 134, 142, 177
alchemy of consecration 10, 20, 31, 39–40, 57, 129, 150, 177–8
authenticity 1, 93, 102, 113–14, 117, 125, 129, 136–7, 139, 170, 176, 178; adulthood 20–2, 29, 31; trolling 141–6, 150–1; embodiment at youth 8–12; generational distinction 39–41, 45, 54; self-affirming aspects 59, 68, 74, 83–4
authority 2, 5, 9, 11; and Adult Voice 41, 55–6, 61, 82, 100, 114, 118; aficionados 24–5, 28, 31, 32n2, 39; to classify 178; double language of disinterest 126, 140, 142, 150, 158, 165; symbolic capital 19–20; young people's technological mastery 22

Brabazon, T.: and loss 114, 137, 142, 164, 179; memory is not safe 44; popular memory 39–40, 43–4; rock criticism 45–7, 137
Bourdieu, P. 9–12, 45, 70, 81–3, 107, 125–6, 136, 175, 182n1; alchemy of consecration 17–27; Don Quixote effect 30–1; double language of disinterest 41; embodied capital 114, 153; emotional capital 65–7; force of custom 39 media 86–8, 157; predisposition 110, 164; theory of habitus 1, 4, 92, 105, 128; taste 116, 168, 178

Bourdieu, P.: internal rationale 83, 107; sacred social divides 178; socialised subjectivity 17; and Wacquant, L. doxa as the ultimate form of conformism 168

certainty 8–10, 21–2, 28, 31, 74; at risk 83–5, 93, 113–14, 137, 150, 166, 168–9
code learning the 40–1, 93, 105, 107–9, 157
Cohen, S. 1; deviancy 6, 10, 12; dislocation of social structure 152; elements central to a moral panic 155; folk devils 27–8; media 86, 90; movement advocates 157–8, 163, 164, 166, 171n6; sensitization 154; threat to societal values 156
cultural capital 54–5, 66–7, 137, 177; adults 30; collective magic and technology and personal style 21–7; embodied 4, 11–12, 18–19; futurists 156–8, 165, 168; incorporation 39–41, 60, 103–7

De Nora 8, 12; corporeal ordering 134, 136; embodied awareness 12, 42, 130–4; latching 24; music 131; self-programming 46, 130
deference 9, 20, 39, 54–6, 85, 106–8
Don Quixote Effect 30–1, 53, 60
double language of disinterest 11, 41, 53, 65–6, 112–14, 126, 150, 181
doxa 10, 81, 100–1; adulthood 61–3, 68–70, 73, 125–6, 140, 142; authenticity 57; futurists 158, 164,

167, 170; misrecognition and popular culture 31, 45, 52–4; social world and field 20–3; stereotyping 154; young people 88–9, 93; young people's interaction with adults 106–9, 113–14, 117, 119–20

emotional capital 65–7, 117, 125, 179
embodiment 8–12, 27, 46–7, 82–3, 93, 129, 138, 177

Faulkner walled garden 5–6, 11, 40–1, 61, 71, 73, 85, 100–5, 119–20, 177, 181
field 10–11, 65, 70, 81–2, 126, 137; learning the code 40–1; media 87, 90–1, 165; popular music 47, 143; respect 54–5; social world and doxa 18–22, 30–1; status 114, 177; young people in adult fields 106–8, 117

generation 1–4, 8–12, 21–31, 39–48, 48n2, 52–3, 57–63, 66–8, 71–4, 171n17, 176–80; generational folk devils 27–9; media 91–3; millennials 116–18, 151–6, 161–70; misrecognition 78; music 126–8; shared generational experience 80–4, 131–46; walled garden/helicoptering 101–2, 109–16
Goode and Ben-Yehuda 6, 29, 86, 167; consensus 166; crucial elements to a moral panic 28; disproportionality 169; hostility 168; mass hysteria 170; routinised or institutionalised moral panic 28, 169

habitus 1, 4–5, 10–11, 73–4, 83–4, 120, 177–8; bounded agency 89, 92–3; Don Quixote effect 30–1; embodiment 41, 43, 46, 52–3, 69–70, 150, 154, 181; evolution of 98–100, 105–6, 108–17; millennials 170, 175; misrecognition 21, 23, 26–7; music 128–34, 140, 144; reflexive modalities 79–80; social world field and doxa 17–18; symbolic capital, social and temporal distance 61–3
helicoptering 11, 60, 101, 177

identity 2–5, 11, 23, 28, 42, 46, 53, 79, 81, 90–2, 110, 119, 130–1, 135, 176–7

intergenerational conflict 1, 4, 18, 40, 176
introjection 8, 40, 42, 45–7, 65–6, 92, 131, 134, 140, 142, 146
investment and parental investment 5; *libido sciendi* 11, 24, 83 personal style 27; respect 93

media 1, 6, 27, 42, 70, 78, 80, 108, 115, 126, 137, 140; agents of moral indignation 85–93, 94n4; fields 19, 41; futurists 151–2, 156–61, 169–70, 171n11; millennials 68, 112; Miley Cyrus 101–3; moral entrepreneurs 29; moral panics 6–8, 156, 164; stereotyping 64, 165
Miley Cyrus 11, 40–1, psychologising of 100–4; as role model 108–9
Millennial 1, 6, 9, 59–62, 65, 81, 101, 111–13, 141, 146, 150, 177; deviance 12, 29–30; futurists 151–70, 171n9, 20; profligacy 113–20; shorthand portrait 150, 154–5, 157–8, 163, 164, 170; stereotyping 68–72, 81, 84–5, 92–3
misrecognition 36, 39–40; fear 25, 28–31; forgetting 125–7; generational misrecognition 39, 127; generations 51–2, 56, 78, 81–3, 86, 88–9, 93, 112, 114–19, 130, 139–40, 144–6, 150, 176–9, 181; becoming institutionalised 150–2, 166, 170; Millennials 66–74; Miley Cyrus 41–2; social and temporal distance 60–1, 64; symbolic violence 9–12, 21–3
moral entrepreneurs 10, 12, 27, 29, 52, 151, 155–7, 170
moral panic 45, 103, 105, 113, 118–20; futurists 150–70; media 86–7, 90–1, 93; moral entrepreneurs and young people 27–8, 36; music 128, 131; shared experience 25, threat to society 6–7, 17

neo-tribe 24, 28, 119

predisposition 4–6, 11, 110

social space 19, 26, 30–1, 51–4, 60, 67, 70, 106, 116, 126
social world 7, 10–11, 18–19, 21, 26, 28, 40, 53–4, 67, 70, 81, 89, 101–8, 115, 126, 128

status 6–7, 153, 165, 168, 170, 175–8; adult 19–21, 57, 79, 81–3, 85, 114–19, 125–6, 137, 139, 142, 146; authority 24–5, 28, 31; celebrity 105–11; in-betweenness 36–7, 39–42, 53–4; media 87, 89–90, 98–101; social and temporal distance 61–3, 67, 74; young people 9–10
stereotype 62, 64, 68–74, 83, 93, 113, 118, 151, 155–6, 170; folk devil 28; in-groups 81
symbolic capital 18–21, 39, 41, 56–7, 63, 65, 74, 100, 114, 116

taste 11, 23–6, 41–2, 47, 92, 116–20, 130, 133–6, 138, 140–1, 146, 178
temporal distance 61–4, 74, 178

walled garden 5, 11, 40–1, 61, 71, 73, 85, 100–5, 119–20, 177, 181
Willis 18, 42, 46, 62, 116; grounded aesthetics 6–8, 11, 24, 28, 38, 42, 80, 83–4, 92, 129, 134, 146, 177–8

zeitgeist 8, 10–11, 27, 38–42, 57, 80–3, 131, 176

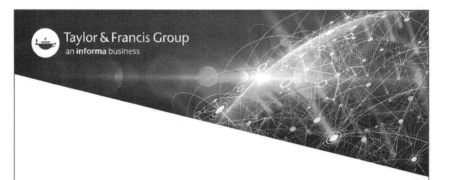

Printed in the United States
by Baker & Taylor Publisher Services